Saying Yes to Japanese Investment

Simon Partner

PRENTICE HALL
Englewood Cliffs, New Jersey 07632

Prentice-Hall International (UK) Limited, *London*
Prentice-Hall of Australia Pty. Limited, *Sidney*
Prentice-Hall Canada, Inc., *Toronto*
Prentice-Hall Hispanoamericana, S.A., *Mexico*
Prentice-Hall of India Private Limited, *New Delhi*
Prentice-Hall of Japan, Inc., *Tokyo*
Simon & Schuster Asia Pte. Ltd., *Singapore*
Editora Prentice-Hall do Brasil, Ltda., *Rio de Janeiro*

© 1992 by
Prentice-Hall, Inc.
Englewood Cliffs, NJ

All rights reserved. No part of this
book may be reproduced in any form or
by any means, without permission in
writing from the publisher.

10 9 8 7 6 5 4 3 2 1

Library of Congress Cataloging-in-Publication Data

Partner, Simon.
  Saying yes to Japanese investment: how you can benefit by doing business with the Japanese/Simon Partner.
    p.   cm.
  Includes index.
  ISBN 0-13-785049-2
  1. Investments, Japanese—United States. 2. Corporations, Japanese—United States. 3. Corporations—United States—Finance. 4. United States—Foreign economic relations—Japan. 5. Japan—Foreign economic relations—United States. I. Title.
HG4910.P37 1992   92-16865
332.6′7352073—dc20   CIP

ISBN 0-13-785049-2

PRENTICE HALL
Professional Publishing
Englewood Cliffs, NJ 07632
Simon & Schuster. A Paramount Communications Company

Printed in the United States of America

To
John and Tina Patterson

CONTENTS

Preface *vii*

Introduction *ix*

Chapter 1. Samurai on Main Street *1*

Chapter 2. "Over Here": Fears and Phobias *15*

Chapter 3. The Best of Both Worlds *63*

Chapter 4. Why Here? *85*

Chapter 5. Talking Turkey, Talking Sushi *111*

Chapter 6. Capital Concepts *141*

Chapter 7. Working for Japan Inc. *173*

Chapter 8. Selling to the Japanese *193*

Chapter 9. Menus and Sources *215*

Index *265*

PREFACE

As a practicing consultant and writer specializing in the Japanese economy and business, I am confronted almost daily with the immense divide that still separates the two sides in the world's most important economic and political alliance. The Americans and the Japanese have an enormous amount in common—a commitment to democracy and free enterprise, a thriving business environment producing unprecedented innovation and wealth creation, a defensive alliance that has lasted 45 years, and one of the world's largest, most vibrant trading relationships. Yet in spite of all these ties, the relationship between the United States and Japan is characterized by recrimination, hostility, and fear.

Yes, there are valid reasons for the United States to criticize Japan, and vice versa. That's always true of any important relationship. But I sincerely believe that fully half of the problems between the United States and Japan are caused not by genuine grievances, but by a profound failure to communicate. When President Bush was preparing his visit to Japan in January 1992, it was remarked in the press that there was not a single staff member in the White House who spoke Japanese! No wonder the visit was widely perceived in Japan as a public relations disaster.

Ask an American and a Japanese business executive what each sees as the major problems between the two countries, and you will be amazed at the difference in their responses. Americans see Japan as recalcitrant, opportunistic, and threatening, while the Japanese see themselves as put upon, made scapegoats for America's own decline, and victims of racial discrimination. What they have in common is a failure to understand one another, or to get their message across effectively.

I have worked for several years as a consultant promoting business ties between Japanese and U.S. companies. I also write about Japan for various business publications and, as a fellow at Columbia University, research academic issues relating to the Japanese economy. At the heart of all these activities, I see a single, coherent professional mission: Communicating Japan. This book is intended as a step in redressing the communications gap between the two countries. It focuses on the very real benefits that both sides can reap from this vibrant relationship.

The book was compiled using published news and analysis, my own personal experiences as a consultant, and extensive interviews with both Japanese and American business executives. Except where otherwise noted, the quotes I use in the book are from personal interviews. In some cases, names of interviewees have been altered to protect confidentiality.

Many people have assisted me in writing this book with their valuable time and experience. In particular I would like to thank Daniel Schwartz, president, Ulmer Brothers, Inc., both for his comments and for permission to publish proprietary research material; Paul K. Kelly, president, Knox & Co.; Ryuji Kitamura, president, Enprotech Corp.; Masakatsu Sakamoto, executive vice president, The Nikko Securities Co. International, Inc.; Taketo Furuhata, president and chief executive officer, C. Itoh & Co. (America), Inc.; Fred Broda; Toshiyuki Hatakama; Sheldon Weinig, chairman, Materials Research Corporation; Gordon Eng; Shima Enomoto; Ronald Cohen, Philip Ruppel, Sheck Cho, and Drew Dreeland, all of Simon & Schuster; and, for his invaluable erudition on all matters relating to the Japanese economy, Professor Hugh Patrick, director, The Center on Japanese Economy and Business, Columbia University.

INTRODUCTION

Japanese investment in the United States went through an unprecedented growth phase during the 1980s. In the process, Japanese money has become one of the most controversial topics of our day.

Some recent polls have indicated a strong—and growing—anti-Japanese sentiment in the United States. It seems that the larger the issues get, the more polarized the sides become: on the one hand, an irate American public that feels Japan has gone a step too far, yet wishes America could catch up with Japan's achievements; on the other, a Japanese public who feel they have been unfairly singled out and blamed for America's own weaknesses. Some influential Japanese have responded with tough rhetoric aimed at "standing up" to the Americans. An example is the recent hard-hitting best-seller, *The Japan That Can Say No.*[1]

But the confrontational debate has obscured the enormous opportunities for constructive collaboration that exist between the two most technologically advanced nations on earth. Practical Americans should seriously think about the following points:

- *We are not at war with Japan.* U.S. Ambassador to Japan Michael Armacost has said: "It would be stupid to forfeit our relationship by treating Japan as anything other than what it is: a friendly nation."

- *Japan and its Asian trading partners are the fastest-growing markets of the 1990s.* Any U.S. company that fails to exploit this growth will be missing the boat in the foreseeable future. The Japanese have the greatest influence and contacts in these explosive markets. The opportunities for constructive collaboration and joint ventures are enormous.

- *America needs Japanese money.* We may not like it, but our government's deficits have to be funded. We should not forget, though, that the dependence is mutual: the Japanese need a strong U.S. economy, and they are ready to pay a high price for access to U.S. markets.

- *Dealing with the Japanese does not mean selling out.* In a good deal, both sides win. In many recent deals, the American side has won mightily.

As the controversy has grown over Japanese investment and trading practices, a series of thoughtful books have emerged, analyzing various aspects of the debate. Most of these books focus on why Japan has been so successful, and whether Japan's success is good or bad for America. On the whole, though, they deal with questions of macroeconomics and government policy—important issues for policy-makers and economists, but frustratingly immaterial for ordinary readers.

Important as these books are, they do not address the enormous opportunities arising from Japanese investment, or the practical concerns of many Americans:

- How might I benefit from the Japanese investment spree? When is it and when is it not irresponsible to accept Japanese money?

- Would the Japanese be interested in buying my company?

- What are the negotiating strengths of the Japanese? And what are their weaknesses?

- How do I make sure I'm getting the best possible deal?

INTRODUCTION

- Will a joint venture in the United States provide me with greater access to the Japanese marketplace?
- Should I be thinking about working for a Japanese company?

These are the questions that are addressed by this book. They are questions that are becoming increasingly important for a wide spectrum of the American population.

This book provides the reader with a guide to some of the difficult economic and ethical issues arising from the influx of Japanese money. But it also points out—in a constructive and responsible way—the abundance of opportunities that Japan's wealth is creating for Americans.

The book illustrates the extent of the Japanese presence today and provides a realistic assessment of the prospects for the 1990s. It demonstrates—through examples—the astonishing breadth of endeavors in which Japanese investors have already become involved, and the increasing adventurousness with which they are ready to commit their resources.

It discusses the present wave of anti-Japanese sentiment, and shows how many of our common fears about the Japanese are completely unfounded.

It puts our present problems with Japan in their historical perspective. Americans' anti-Japanese bias has led to needless aggression and suffering in the past.

It analyzes some of the writing on both sides of the debate, discussing, for example, *The Japan That Can Say No*, and places them in the perspective of the vital underlying friendship and mutual dependence of the United States and Japan.

It presents some hypothetical situations to show that, under some circumstances, the threat posed by Japan's increasing presence could be very real.

The book presents case studies to demonstrate that a constructive approach to Japanese investment (both by government and individual businesses) can head off the potential threat and result—as successful deals should—in great benefits to both sides.

The book examines in detail the underlying motivations for the increasing Japanese investment presence in America. Many analysts overlook the fact that individual Japanese companies choose to invest in the United States for many different reasons. Each of these motivating factors implies a range of opportunities for American businessmen, and these implications are developed in a detailed review of appropriate strategies for maximizing the benefits to both parties.

The book examines and itemizes practical steps that American companies can take to develop beneficial links with Japanese sources of capital. It identifies the major Japanese players and the companies that are investing in the United States, and explains their investment priorities and how they should be contacted. It provides pointers of negotiating tactics to build on American strengths and exploit Japanese weaknesses when discussing deals. And it outlines various alternative structures for accessing Japanese investment capital.

Finally, the book addresses the personal opportunities for individuals that are being created for Americans in various walks of life by the growing Japanese involvement in our society. For example, it highlights the benefits and drawbacks of working for a Japanese company, it reviews the types of services that Japanese communities in the United States might buy from American providers, and it offers guidelines on winning Japanese business.

Endnote

[1] Shintaro Ishihara, *The Japan That Can Say No* (New York: Simon & Schuster, 1991).

1 SAMURAI ON MAIN STREET

We've all heard that "The Japanese are coming." Newspapers regularly report the latest megadeal involving a Japanese buyer. In America's major cities, the most expensive shops seem to be catering mainly to Japanese customers. Hotels on the west and east coasts are teeming with Japanese tourists and businesspeople. Communities are growing up where the majority of the population seems to be Japanese.

The Japanese communities in the New York and Los Angeles area now number in the tens of thousands. In some smaller cities, such as Atlanta, Georgia, the size of the Japanese population is estimated to be doubling every two years.

Official statistics indicate that there has indeed been a substantial growth in the Japanese presence. Nonimmigrant admissions of Japanese citizens far outnumber those of any other country: in 1984, 1,442,000 Japanese were admitted. By 1987, the number had swelled to 2,124,000. That's a 14% compound growth rate. (The nearest rival, Britain, had 1,392,000 admissions in 1987.) The total Japanese-born population resident in the United States was 222,000 in 1980—of whom 43% were U.S. citizens.

Trade

Japan has been a major trading partner of the United States for decades. And for many years the United States has sustained a trade deficit with the Japanese. In recent years, however, both trade and the deficit have grown enormously (see Table 1.1).

TABLE 1.1: U.S. TRADE DEFICIT WITH JAPAN 1980 TO 1990

Year	Imports from Japan ($ million)	Exports to Japan ($ million)	Deficit ($ million)
1980	$30,714	$20,790	$ 9,924
1984	57,135	23,575	33,560
1985	68,783	22,631	46,152
1986	81,911	26,882	55,029
1987	84,575	28,249	56,326
1989	93,455	43,673	49,782
1990	89,677	47,857	41,820
% Annual growth 1980–1990	11.3%	8.7%	

Source: U.S. Department of Commerce, Survey of Current Business

The trade deficit with Japan in 1990, at $41,820 million, was 38.5% of the total U.S. deficit. Although in dollar terms that's below the 1987 peak of $56,326 million, it's hardly surprising that voices are being raised in Washington.

Investment

Investments in the United States by foreign nationals are generally divided into two categories: direct and indirect.

Indirect investments include purchases of stocks and bonds, including U.S. Treasury securities. The Japanese have been major investors in these securities in recent years, effectively underwriting the U.S. budget deficit.

Net purchases of U.S. securities by the Japanese totaled $17.4 billion in 1990, but the volume of investment is much greater still. During the 1980s, the U.S. government has come to rely on Japanese investors to purchase a third of all newly issued United States debt.

Net indirect assets of the Japanese actually far exceed direct investments. But it is the direct investments that have caused the most furor. These are often highly visible investments such as the acquisition of Rockefeller Center in New York City or Columbia Pictures. It is about these investments that critics claim we are "selling out" to Japan or that America is losing her sovereignty.

Japanese direct investments have indeed grown rapidly in recent years. According to the Commerce Department, in 1980 net investments totaled a mere $4.7 billion, or 5.7% of total foreign direct investment. By 1990, that number had grown to $83.5 billion, or 20.8% of the total. The compound annual growth rate was 33.3%.

Nor, in spite of a slow-down in 1991, does the trend show any sign of declining. The relatively strong yen, combined with the massive cash surpluses generated by Japan's export success, have put Japanese companies in an overwhelmingly strong financial position.

Employment

Japanese companies have become significant contributors to the United States economy. According to the Department of Commerce, Japanese companies in the United States (excluding banks) employed 504,000 people in 1990. See Table 1.2 for the break out by business area.

TABLE 1.2: EMPLOYMENT BY JAPANESE COMPANIES, 1990

Manufacturing	242,000
Wholesale trade	82,000
Retail trade	35,000
Finance (except banking)	55,000
Real estate	3,000
Services	49,000
Other	38,000
Total	504,000

Total assets of these companies were $278 billion.

Japan's Ministry of International Trade and Industry (MITI) has estimated that Japanese investment will have created 840,000 U.S. jobs by the end of the century.

Acquisitions

In the last few years, there has been an accelerating trend of major acquisitions by Japanese companies—acquisitions of companies and properties that were leaders in their industry, and in many cases household names in the United States. This trend, perhaps more than any other factor, has led to a growing perception by the American public that America is "selling out" to the Japanese.

Most of these "premium" acquisitions have taken place in the past five years. But the trend can be seen building up through the latter half of the 1980s.

In 1986, Sumitomo Bank Ltd. of Japan, one of Japan's largest banks, made a $500 million investment in New York's most prestigious investment bank, Goldman Sachs & Co. Goldman, which is a partnership, had been becoming increasingly concerned about securing access to the large amounts of capital required to do big deals in the merger-happy 1980s. In particular, Goldman was leading a trend toward the increasing use of its own capital by investment banks seeking a higher return than that traditionally provided by their intermediary role in Merger and Acquistion (M&A) deals. Sumitomo, meanwhile, was seeking a larger role in the worldwide investment banking arena. Japanese banks in the 1980s have tended to be the world's biggest investors, but they have had to catch up on the innovations and technologies that have made New York and London the world's investment banking centers. Perhaps Sumitomo hoped to gain access to some of Goldman's expertise through the affiliation. However, after the acquisition, the United States banking authorities refused to allow any collaboration between the two companies. Sumitomo is a commercial bank and is, therefore, prohibited by U.S. law from engaging in many securities-related transactions. Some analysts said that the restrictions imposed were unexpectedly harsh, and a disappointment to Sumitomo, which had reportedly been hoping to send trainees to Goldman to learn investment banking skills.

However, the Sumitomo/Goldman deal was dwarfed

both in size and publicity by a series of mammoth transactions in the banner year of 1988.

In January, Sony Corporation completed its $2 billion acquisition of CBS Records Group. From Sony's point of view, the acquisition was a vital step in its global strategy to become an integrated entertainment company, providing hardware in the form of audio and video equipment, and software in the form of recordings. The acquisition was by far the largest to date by a Japanese company, and the status of CBS as a household brand name shocked many Americans into a new realization of Japan's strength.

But this deal was topped shortly after by the $2.7 billion acquisition of another household name—the Firestone Tire and Rubber Co. was acquired by Bridgestone Corporation in May 1988. Firestone had been undergoing a long and agonizing decline throughout the decade, cutting back its capacity by close to 50%, and enduring losses, harrowing quality problems, and bitter strikes. At the root of Firestone's difficulties was increasing competition from aggressive foreign tire companies, including Bridgestone. Bridgestone, which was not related to Firestone in spite of the similarity of the names, had been growing rapidly through the 1980s due to the combined influences of a fast-growing domestic market, aggressive marketing and pricing strategies, and highly efficient manufacturing processes (Bridgestone was the winner of the coveted Deming Prize for manufacturing management in 1968). Bridgestone, which saw the American market as an essential platform for its global growth ambitions, bought a plant from Firestone as early as 1985, turning its performance dramatically around (See the first case, New Faith in Manufacturing, Chapter 3). Perhaps Bridgestone was looking to achieve a similar effect with the entire company. Certainly the Firestone shareholders benefited from a price that approached 20 times 1987 earnings of $145 million. In the meantime, integration of the Firestone operation has been a vast undertaking for Bridgestone, with limited success as yet.

Meanwhile in the banking arena, the Bank of Tokyo Ltd. negotiated the purchase for $750 million of Union

Bank of Los Angeles, completing the deal in October. Union Bank was in fact already under foreign ownership: It was one of the last holdouts of Britain's mainly disastrous foray into United States commercial banking. Its parent was Britain's Standard Chartered PLC. For Bank of Tokyo, the acquisition provided coveted access to the "middle-market" business customer, a level below the *Fortune* 500 corporations that Japanese banks had traditionally serviced. The California location provided a second foothold (Bank of Tokyo had already bought California First Bank in 1981 for $30 million) in one of America's fastest growing banking markets, and one with a strong and growing Asian community. The acquisition also made Bank of Tokyo into the largest foreign bank in America. At the time of the acquisition, Union Bank had assets of about $9 billion.

In November 1988, the Nippon Mining Co. Ltd. bought Illinois-based Gould, Inc., for slightly over $1 billion in cash. Gould, a maker of electronic components and computers, had sustained a huge loss of $96 million in 1987, on sales of $933 million. For Nippon Mining, the Gould acquisition represented an opportunity to diversify into high-technology manufacturing, out of the company's traditional base in metal smelting.

To round out the year, in December 1988 the Intercontinental Hotel Corporation, located in Montvale, New Jersey, was acquired by the Seibu/Saison Group of Japan. Although Intercontinental Hotels are another high-profile brand name, this acquisition was arguably a global rather than a U.S. acquisition. The owner of Intercontinental was another foreign company, Britain's Grand Metropolitan PLC. Of the 100 hotels in the chain, the majority are overseas, including the Grand and the Intercontinental in London. In the United States, the chain ran the Barclay in New York, and the Mark Hopkins in San Francisco. The purchase price was $2.2 billion.

Sony set another record in 1989. Pursuing its strategy of acquiring entertainment "software," the Sony Corporation paid $3.5 billion for filmmaker Columbia Pictures Entertainment, Inc., as well as an additional $273 million to acquire Guber-Peters Entertainment to manage Columbia. These acquisitions sparked one of the most serious furors of all the Japanese takeovers to date. Although Columbia Pictures was clearly not in a sensitive industry from the point of view of defense or essential technologies, it was regarded by many as a vital cultural property, a piece of the fabric of American life. Questions were raised about the use by the Japanese owner of Columbia's creative resources to make propaganda for Japan or about possible censorship by Sony of creative material that might reflect badly on Japan.

Perhaps the most controversial of Japanese takeovers was, paradoxically, among the least threatening: the 1990 acquisition by the Mitsubishi Estate Company of a 51% stake in the Rockefeller Group for $846 million. The Mitsubishi Estate Company is one of Japan's wealthiest landlords. Since before the turn of the century, it has owned the stretch of land known as Marunouchi that adjoins the Imperial Palace in Tokyo. For years, much of the land in Marunouchi was undeveloped, known locally as the "Gambler's Meadow." An early writer described it as an "abode of foxes and badgers." But as Mitsubishi gradually developed the land, it became the most prestigious address in Tokyo—aided by its close proximity to Tokyo Station. It is now among the most valuable real estate holdings in the world. As a result, Mitsubishi Estate, a relation of the vast Mitsubishi industrial empire, has access to enormous capital resources. Perhaps because it is hard to find properties of comparable quality to Marunouchi, Mitsubishi Estate has made few overseas acquisitions. But the Rockefeller Group, with its ownership of New York's landmark Rockefeller Center, is clearly an appropriate candidate. However, the fact has been largely overlooked by an indignant public that Rockefeller Group actually owns only a minority of the Rockefeller Center: 71% was spun off to the public in the form of a real estate investment trust. The investment therefore gave Mitsubishi Estate only a 15% stake in the Center.

Another acquisition of note in 1990 was the purchase by General Coast Enterprises of the Pebble Beach Company, owner of the Pebble Beach golf course resort in California. One of the most famous courses in the nation, Pebble Beach is known among other things for the single, wind-swept cypress tree that has been used as a setting for numerous films. General Coast, controlled by a noted Japanese investor in sports properties, bought the Pebble Beach Company for $800 million.

Finally, 1990 was rounded out by the largest Japanese acquisition to date: the colossal $6.1 billion buyout of MCA, the entertainment giant, by Japan's Matsushita Electric Industrial Company. This acquisition clearly followed Sony's path of diversification by electronics firms into entertainment "software."

In 1991, the pace of Japanese mergers slowed dramatically—by over 60% in dollar terms—as a result of tightening liquidity in Japan, and the recession in the United States. Moreover, although the size and number of Japanese acquisitions in the United States had grown dramatically in previous years, it was often overlooked—much to the dismay of the Japanese—that the Japanese were by no means the largest investors in the American economy.

According to Commerce Department statistics, Japan in 1990 ranked second in total direct investments in the United States, behind Britain. Canada, Germany, and the Netherlands also had strong investment positions, as illustrated in Table 1.3.

TABLE 1.3: FOREIGN DIRECT INVESTMENT POSITION IN THE UNITED STATES, 1990

Country	Investment Position ($ Millions)
United Kingdom	$108,055
Japan	83,498
Netherlands	64,333
Germany	27,770
Canada	27,733
Other	92,346
Total	403,735

U.K. investments grew at a compound rate of 23.8% annually between 1980 and 1990. Dutch investments grew at a 12% compound rate. German investments grew by 14% annually.

According to *Mergers and Acquisitions* magazine, only 5 of the largest 25 foreign acquisitions of United States interests in 1990 were Japanese—and the largest Japanese investment ranked tenth overall. (In 1989, only 3 of the largest 25 foreign acquisitions involved Japanese buyers.) And of the largest 100 transactions of all kinds in 1990, only 6 involved Japanese buyers. (In 1989, only 3 involved Japanese buyers). *Mergers and Acquisitions* also prepared a summary of the 100 largest deals of the decade (January 1, 1980 to December 31, 1989). Only 4 involved Japanese buyers—the largest being number 37 on the list. Of the 50 largest foreign acquisitions of the decade, only 7 were Japanese.

Although the pace of major Japanese investments has indeed increased in recent years, it is perhaps not these landmark purchases that should be attracting the attention of a concerned public. According to Ulmer Brothers Inc., in 1990 53% of Japanese investments in the United States (by number of deals) were under $10 million. Although the average deal value in 1989 was $170 million, the median was only $18 million.

These smaller deals represent the real underlying trend in Japanese investment. A review of the scope of these deals indicates the great variety of enterprises and industries in which Japanese companies are becoming involved through acquisition or investment. The variety of businesses acquired by Japanese firms should caution us against excessive generalization. The only clear conclusion is that the variety is huge and still growing. Let's have a closer look at some of the smaller acquisitions made by Japanese companies in recent years.

Hotels and Resorts

In 1989, The Victoria Company of Tokyo acquired the

Stratton Corporation of South Londonerry, Vermont. Stratton, formerly a subsidiary of Moore and Munger, Inc., operates a ski resort at Stratton Mountain in Vermont, as well as retailing sports goods. This acquisition is not a first for Victoria: It already owns the Breckenridge Ski Resort in Colorado.

In October 1990, the Kyo-ya Company Ltd. acquired Grand Cypress Resort in Orlando, Florida, for a price reportedly in excess of $200 million. Grand Cypress is a 1,500-acre resort featuring a 750-room Hyatt Regency hotel, a marina, and two and a half golf courses.

Financial Services

In 1989, the ORIX Corporation of Tokyo acquired Commercial Alliance Corporation, a subsidiary of Forst Interstate Bancorp. Commercial Alliance, based in New York, specializes in capital equipment financing and management services. ORIX is the largest leasing company in Japan. The deal was reportedly for $190 million in cash.

Engineering

In the early 1980s, UGI Corp. of Valley Forge, Pennsylvania, formed a joint venture with Nippon Sanso KK, a Japanese manufacturer of gas and industrial equipment, to build air separation plants. In 1989 the joint venture, called Ansutech, was bought out by Nippon Sanso.

This was not the only acquisition made by Nippon Sanso in 1989. In September, the company acquired the Thermos Company, a household name in the United States and Britain, known for its vacuum food and beverage containers. The Thermos Company was a unit of Household International, Inc. The price was $134 million in cash.

Aviation

In 1989, The Toyota Motor Corporation's U.S. aviation unit acquired Airflite, a California-based aircraft service and storage company. The purchase price was not disclosed.

Electronics

In 1989, the Hoya Corporation of Tokyo acquired Micro Mask, Inc., of Sunnyvale, California. Micro Mask is a high-tech company that manufactures photomasks—photographic negatives used for making integrated circuits. Hoya, which is a major Japanese optics manufacturer, made the acquisition through a friendly tender offer, for a total purchase price of $25.3 million.

In August 1989, the Kyocera Corporation of Kyoto, Japan, acquired the Elco Group of Companies of Newport Beach, California. Elco was a subsidiary of Wickes Corporation, which had itself been the target of a leveraged buyout in 1988. Elco was spun off by the new owners of Wickes, two limited partnerships controlled by investment bankers The Blackstone Group and Wasserstein, Perrella. Elco is a leading manufacturer of connectors used in the electronics industry. Kyocera, short for Kyoto Ceramics, is a ceramics manufacturer that has been highly successful in capturing the market for advanced ceramic materials. The Elco acquisition was reportedly for about $250 million.

A similar acquisition took place in July 1989. Tokuyama Soda Co. Ltd., a Japanese heavy chemicals company, acquired General Ceramics, Inc., of Haskell, New Jersey through a tender offer. General Ceramics makes specialized ceramic products for the medical, automotive, and defense industries, including components for nuclear weapons. Because of the defense connection, this acquisition was subject to review by the Committee on Foreign Investment, which permitted the acquisition only on condition that certain defense-related assets were sold to a U.S. company. The purchase price was $62 million.

Printing

In 1989, the Knight Color and Chemicals Company of Montrose, Minnesota, was acquired by Sakata Inx Corporation of Osaka, Japan. Knight was a maker of chips that are used to make printing ink. Sakata is a printing ink manufacturer. Terms of the acquisition were not disclosed.

Computers

In July 1989 the Fujitsu Corporation of Japan acquired a 46% stake in the Pocket Computer Corp. of Sunnyvale, California. Pocket Computer is a maker of pocketbook-size IBM-compatible computers. At the time of the acquisition, Fujitsu, a major Japanese computer maker, announced that it would provide Pocket Computer with computer chips and other technology.

Chemicals

In November 1990, Ishihara Sangyo Kaisha Ltd. of Osaka bought SDS Enterprises, Inc., a unit of the Fermenta chemicals concern, for a reported $300 million. SDS is a specialty chemicals manufacturer, which also conducts research and development. This acquisition reflects a widespread trend toward foreign ownership of the U.S. chemicals industry.

Semiconductors

Numerous acquisitions have taken place of American pioneers in this rapidly consolidating field.

In December 1990, the Sanken Electric Co. bought Sprague Technologies' semiconductor group for $58 million in cash.

Foods

Not all acquisitions have been in the prestige end of the business. In July 1990, Kyotaru Company Ltd. of Tokyo acquired Best Western Foods of Los Angeles for $41.5 million in cash. Best Western is a meat packing company that specializes in processed beef, supplying half the beef consumed by the nation's Arby's restaurant franchises.

Publishing

In August 1990, Japanese Independent Communication Co. Ltd. acquired a 50% interest in the New American Magazine Co., publisher of *Smart, Mother Earth News,* and *Psychology Today* magazines. Terms of the deal were not disclosed.

Pharmaceuticals

In August 1990, Ono Pharmaceutical Co. of Osaka, Japan, acquired a 6.5% stake in Telios Pharmaceuticals, Inc., of San Diego, California. Telios holds the rights to an exciting treatment for kidney disease scarring.

In April 1990, Fujisawa Pharmaceutical Company of Osaka acquired 71% LyphoMed. Inc., of Rosemont, Illinois, for $773 million. Fujisawa already owned the remaining 29% of LyphoMed. One of the nation's larger generic drug companies, LyphoMed had been sustaining losses in recent years.

Music and Entertainment

In August 1990, Clarion Company Ltd. of Japan bought McIntosh Laboratory, Inc., of Binghamton, New York, for $30 million. McIntosh is well known in the United States as a maker of top-of-the-line stereo equipment and was one of the few remaining independent U.S. audio equipment firms. Clarion is a worldwide maker of car and home audio and video equipment.

Optics

In April 1990, the Nippon Sheet Glass Co. Ltd., bought Epitaxx Inc, a small Princeton, New Jersey, high-technology start-up. Epitaxx, initially funded by U.S. venture capitalists, makes specialized products for use in fiber optic communications. Although Epitaxx's sales at the time of the acquisition were only $5 million, the purchase price was reportedly in the $12 million range.

Real Estate

Estimates by the U.S. Department of Commerce suggest that Japanese buyers accounted for 71% of all purchases of real estate by foreigners in 1990. In 1989, the percentage was 56%. Using very different data gathering methods, Kenneth Leventhal & Company estimated that Japanese purchases of U.S. real estate totaled $14.8 billion in 1989, compared to $16.5 billion in 1988. Leventhal indicated that 36% of the 1989 investment was in California, of which 40% was in the greater Los Angeles area. California, Hawaii, and New York state accounted for 81% of the total Japanese investment.

The vast range of deals involving Japanese investors in the American economy underscores the deep and complex ties binding the two nations. For American businesspeople, the opportunities for profitable collaboration are immense.

How did these profound links come about? In the next chapter, we look at some of the historical background to the Japanese presence in America.

2 "OVER HERE": FEARS AND PHOBIAS

In 1941, after Japan brought America into the war, the pubs and nightclubs of England's major cities were suddenly filled with brash, overconfident, handsome young men from across the Atlantic. To the beleaguered Britons, besieged within their confining shores, weary of shortages and the blitz, and the dreary smell of defeat, the Americans brought with them the whiff of open spaces and boundless optimism.

They were ready to give Hitler a taste of his own medicine, and they were eager to administer the dose as soon as possible. But their generals had yet to distill the prescription, and in the meantime there were new sights all around them, there was an admiring populace to do them homage, and there were opportunities for adventures to which the locals seemed to give their ready assent. The German radio propagandist "Lord HawHaw" warned the British servicemen with some justification that while they were obeying the call to arms, their cozy nests were warming the feet of a new breed of cuckoos—in size eleven Texan boots. Some Englishmen could have been forgiven for wondering aloud who was the real invader. In the boot camps and in the popular press, a caustic if affectionate appraisal of the boisterous newcomers went into circulation: They were "overpaid, oversexed, and over here!"

The Americans became a feature of the European landscape from that point on. Once the fighting was over, they extended the same geniality that had warmed the hearts of the English girls to allies and vanquished foes alike. American military bases became permanent installations, slices of the New World to remind the old of its degeneracy. American administrators stayed to oversee massive injections of aid. American businessmen flocked to set up subsidiaries in order to profit from the resurgence of prosperity. In an abject Japan, the presence of the occupying power was even more ineluctable.

Today's gray-suited, travel-stressed American corporate executive might well wonder what has become of his country's former dominance. As he (or she) sits in a featureless hotel room entering penny-pinching calculations into a laptop computer, the probability is that the suite next door will be occupied by a group of laughing Germans or Japanese who are here to outbid him in tomorrow's negotiations. While America is by no means a poor or a defeated nation, the undisputed leadership that she enjoyed in previous decades has passed out of her hands. Of the nations that have risen to claim their "place in the sun," Japan is foremost on people's tongues.

With wealth and influence has come presence. On America's home territory—in her great and even her small cities—the Japanese are suddenly "over here" with a vengeance.

Anyone walking the streets of midtown New York could be forgiven for occasionally wondering if this is not some new Asian capital—although the dirt and the beggars serve to remind that this could never be Tokyo. The streets of the West Coast cities are even more Asian in tone. Even on visits to the American heartland, the evidence of the Japanese presence is burgeoning. In Lincoln, Nebraska; in Dubuque, Iowa; in Fort Wayne, Indiana, the hotel bars are growing crowded with groups of itinerant Japanese, lured by eager state authorities and the promise of fallow land and avid consumers.

For many, the Japanese in America are a source of fascination and expanded horizons. For others, they are a looming threat to American sovereignty—a kind of Pearl Harbor from within. And this new presence has materialized so swiftly that many Americans find themselves caught without a viable framework to replace the preconceptions that, like the last generation of electronic goods, have become suddenly obsolete.

Thirty years ago, most people probably thought of the average Japanese as a poor, broken-spirited creature, working pathetically long hours in an ill-lit factory making shoddy products for a measly wage. Fifteen years later, he was a lemminglike tourist being herded around by the busload to snap photos of his unsmiling compatriots in front of the monuments of the world. Today, he may well be your boss, or your best customer, or the savior of your company, or your next-door neighbor.

The Japanese have become to Americans today what Americans were in postwar Europe—a palpable presence. The Japanese are in the newspapers, they are on the television screens (which, of course, they manufactured), they are on the streets of the cities, and they are in the house next door.

Is the Japanese presence in America a good thing? Why are the Japanese here? What are they trying to accomplish here? Are they abusing our tradition of openness? What are they giving us in return? Are they plotting to usurp our patrimony? Or are they creating jobs and revitalizing our economy? What opportunities do their wealth and their presence create? How is the ordinary American being affected? What can we learn from them? Are they friends or enemies? The debate over these questions, in many cases made urgent by new and highly publicized incursions into the American domain, is forcing many Americans, from decision-weary policymakers to storekeepers and restaurateurs, into a radical reevaluation of Japan and the Japanese presence in America. Behind the debate is a fascinating story of the people of a nation in the throes of a unique transition, reaching out in friendship and in rivalry to their former conquerors and benefactors.

The Extent of the "Japanese Threat"

On October 31, 1989, the Mitsubishi Estate Corporation announced that it had purchased a controlling interest in New York's Rockefeller Group. The announcement received worldwide attention, because the Group's crown jewel, Rockefeller Center, is not only one of the most desirable pieces of real estate in New York City; it is also a symbol of the legendary wealth that its founding family embodied, of the greatness and power of the city and of the nation stretching for 3,000 miles beyond, of the awesome potential for individual achievement that is latent in the American ideals of freedom and enterprise.

The world's press were not hesitant in pointing out the significance of the acquisition. It was yet another example of America's abdication of her role as the land of fabled wealth, to be replaced by yen-glutted Japan. It made a good story, and for a day the sidewalks above the famous skating rink were cluttered with journalists asking passers-by for their comments on the change in ownership. Many expressed amazement, even outrage, that this piece of the fabric of American life would be American no longer. "What," asked one, "are they going to do away with the Christmas tree? They don't even have Christmas over there, do they?"

The foofaraw over the Rockefeller Center lingered barely into the month of November, and the Christmas tree duly appeared, as gorgeously American as ever, crowned still with a star and not (so far, at least) with the Rising Sun. Americans, still undisputed masters of the craft of brand creation, should recognize that the identity and goals of the owners of an asset, and the image of that asset as presented to the public gaze, can be two very different affairs.

For all its publicity value, the Japanese acquisition of Rockefeller Center is not demonstrably against the American national interest. But other proposed transactions have excited considerably more serious political attention. In 1987, the acquisition of Fairchild Semiconductor by the

Hitachi Corporation of Japan was blocked by the American government on the grounds that the Pentagon's access to essential defense technology would be impaired. In 1989, a painfully forged compromise over the FSX, a fighter-aircraft joint venture with Japan, was almost demolished by congressional concerns over the sharing of advanced U.S. technology. And when Boeing recently announced a $4 billion joint venture with a Japanese consortium to develop a new commercial aircraft, the cry went up that America's last bastion of manufacturing preeminence will be undermined. Other critics have pointed out that the Japanese now own more than a third of the residential real estate on Hawaii and more than half of the office space in downtown Los Angeles.

How much of a threat to American national interests does the Japanese presence really represent? Common sense tells most Americans that the purchase of American assets by a foreign power cannot be a good thing. But it is harder to say exactly what the adverse effects are or will be. The truth is that America has a long history of accepting foreign investment: foreign capital may be said to have been the fuel that propelled America to economic might. Nor is Japan the biggest investor in American assets. In 1989, British investment totaled $108 billion, and Dutch $64 billion, compared to only $83 billion from Japan. Yet British and Dutch investment are relatively uncontroversial.

The view that there is something wrong with Japan buying up America is not confined to the man in the street. There is a vociferous school of highly respected academics and policymakers who believe that Japanese acquisition of American assets is dangerous. The milder of them generally content themselves with pointing out the self-evident undesirability of loss of ownership. But at the more extreme end, some members of this group argue that Japan is engaged in a long-term quest for world domination, that the expansionist fervor which led Japan into the fiasco of World War II is very much alive and well, and is now thrusting the Japanese toward ever-greater economic power. By this line of reasoning, the increasing Japanese investment in the United States is a Trojan horse that will one day be used as a powerful weapon against Americans.

How can the Japanese harm American interests simply by being here? I would like to take a few steps down the road of possible consequences to see if there really is a threat from the increasing Japanese presence to the wealth or freedom of ordinary Americans. Speculatively speaking, there are a number of avenues to follow.

First, there is the economic avenue. The Japanese have clearly demonstrated their ability—for example, in the television manufacturing industry—to put Americans out of business. Many other industries—a widening array, in fact—currently appear to be threatened. But does investing in America in itself increase the threat? The Japanese have not to this point needed to invest directly in the United States in order to compete against American producers. Liberal trade laws have permitted the Japanese to gain overwhelming market share with only a network of local distributors.

In recent years, Japanese manufacturers have recognized the growing threat of protectionist measures and located factories within the United States in order to become more integrated with the American economy. These "transplant" factories have brought such an economic benefit to the areas, usually rural, in which they have located that state governors are beating a path to Tokyo to offer incentives and "welcome packages." On the other hand, in some industries, most notably automobiles, the new factories threaten to cause severe overcapacity problems, which may turn out to be among the most disruptive economic consequences of the investment influx.

What about the threat that Japanese companies will use acquisitions as part of a strategy to gain market dominance? Market share gains have until the 1980s been largely built through competitive pricing and superior product quality. But the enormous cash surpluses created by record profits and booming markets have made it economical for Japanese companies to buy market share in industries in which they have no significant quality or cost edge, such as tires or commercial banking. Hence, the purchase of Firestone by Bridgestone, and hence the acquisition of a substantial percentage of California's banking assets within the last decade.

But gaining a dominant market position by acquiring American companies or assets is hardly in itself a threatening strategy. American shareholders have benefited from being paid top dollar in the buyout. Americans are still being employed in equal or greater numbers: usually only a few senior executives are replaced with Japanese expatriates. And American antitrust laws continue to protect consumers and competitors from any company or cartel taking too much control of a market. From an economic point of view, it seems far preferable that Japanese companies should build market share through the acquisition of American companies rather than through product or pricing strategies that put those same American companies out of business.

Then there are the technological consequences of Japanese investment. Here the threat from Japanese acquisition of American technologies is much more clear.

American and Japanese companies are now engaged in a constant race to develop and commercially exploit new technologies. Aside from their accumulated wealth, it is superior technology that is the basis for the continued economic preeminence of America and Japan over other nations. Japan has made immense strides in achieving technological competitiveness. Only 20 years ago, the Japanese were known as imitators who merely improved manufacturing efficiency in existing technologies. Today, they are at the forefront of development in a wide range of frontier technologies. A recent Pentagon study found that the United States maintains a technological lead in only 3 out of 25 designated essential technologies. But while America's lead is being eroded year by year, the United

States remains a luxuriant hothouse of new ideas. Many of the technologies that will revolutionize our lives in the twenty-first century are sprouting now in the nation's universities and research laboratories. The Japanese, indeed, have 24,000 students enrolled in American colleges and universities. Moreover, there are still industries in which the Japanese have never challenged American technological preeminence. One example is the aerospace industry, in which Japan lags so far behind that she currently offers no competition to American manufacturers.

The Japanese are ready to pay for American technology, and the pursuit of technology has been the motivating factor behind many Japanese acquisitions and joint ventures. Technology is the first essential raw material of industry. Like other raw materials, it can be used by domestic manufacturers to add value by shaping it into a finished product, or it can be exported to be manufactured elsewhere, and possibly reimported as a finished product. There are those who see a future for America as a research and development (R&D) laboratory for the world, developing technologies and selling them to foreign manufacturers who will transform them into finished products. But to accept this concept, we would have to accept a dependence on whole industries that have been nurtured overseas. As Japanese companies gain control of advanced technologies through acquisition, there is a real danger that the remaining American companies will pay a price in increased competition and eventual displacement by Japan.

Why has America's technological leadership become threatened? Numerous case studies point to a combination of the unwillingness of U.S. investors to subsidize long-term projects (long term in this case meaning more than three years) and the availability in Japan and Germany of abundant, cheap capital.

But even while acknowledging the threat to their future, the owners of American technologies point to another side to the issue that reveals it in a much more complex light.

In October 1989, a Japanese consortium agreed to underwrite a large part of the $4 billion cost of a Boeing development project in exchange for a stake in this spectacular business. Critics immediately raised an alarm. For a paltry billion dollars, the Japanese would be given access to essential technologies in the one industry they had thus far failed to penetrate. Japan's powerful Ministry of International Trade and Industry (MITI) is on public record stating it would like Japan to have a 10% share of the worldwide commercial airliner business by the end of the century. It will, say the Cassandras, be like automobiles all over again, with even graver consequences.

But the critics hardly know who to turn to with their worries. This is not a misguided government decision, or a sellout by a cynical loser. Boeing is the world's leading aircraft maker, in the midst of the greatest boom in its history. Surely the managers of this vastly powerful company are not so desperate as to sell their patrimony for a short-term cash infusion?

We must, I think, assume that Boeing's management members are intelligent people who have reached their decision for sound reasons of business strategy. We can speculate on Boeing's motives.

The most obvious of these is that $4 billion is a vast sum of money, and its investment in a single project a vast risk. It is understandable that Boeing would wish to share the cost and the risk with a joint venture partner. But for a project of this prestige in a booming industry, the American investment community would surely have little difficulty in raising the required sum. Why go to Japan?

Clearly, Boeing is looking for more than just a monetary partnership. Mitsubishi, Kawasaki, and Fuji—the chosen joint venture partners—have established expertise in component production and a long-standing supplier relationship with Boeing. One possible problem in finding an equivalent U.S. partner is that the only American companies with the requisite capabilities are already competing with Boeing—and any collaboration might be interpreted as a breach of antitrust laws.

Boeing is in a sense the victim of its own success: its facilities are already so strained by its bulging order book and awesome production schedule that it has insufficient capacity to manage in-house the colossal task of developing a new aircraft. Expansion of the company's own facilities is limited by the cyclical nature of the industry, which makes overexpansion dangerous, and by the tight labor market in Boeing's home city of Seattle. Even for its current models, the company is increasingly looking to subcontractor relationships to help keep up with its schedule. For example, two-thirds of the value of a 747 jumbo jet is currently provided by outside suppliers, including Mitsubishi, Fuji, and Kawasaki.

But perhaps much more significant than the tactical resource question is the fact that of the 6% annual growth expected in the commercial aircraft industry through the 1990s, a large proportion will be in Asian markets in which Japanese firms have established influence, and more particularly in Japan itself. Boeing arguably cannot afford to deny its powerful Japanese partners a share in its business, for fear that they react within Japan's clubby industrial clique by blocking Boeing from lucrative sales opportunities. With their cooperation, on the other hand, vital doors may be opened. Perhaps even more chilling are the incalculable consequences if MITI decided to form an industrial partnership to go it alone in the development of an all-Japanese commercial aircraft. American aviation technology is based on principles that are decades old, and a completely fresh approach could conceivably produce breakthroughs that might make the American aircraft industry obsolete. If anyone could pull off such a feat, it must surely be the Japanese.

When we examine the case of Boeing, we see that the question of the Japanese threat in acquiring American technology is much more complex than it originally appeared. Perhaps rather than analyzing the situation in terms of threat and defense, we must acknowledge that America and Japan are now in a position of mutual dependence that can, at best, be used as a basis for shared leadership in exploiting the opportunities of the twenty-first century—an approach that many Japanese have enthusiastically adopted.

The Worst Case: Japanese Neocolonialism

Finally, we must examine the political consequences of Japan's investment in America, and of all the potential threats, these are perhaps the most convincingly alarming in their implications.

Let us again take an example, this time a hypothetical one. The year is 1998. The Oregon Pacific Corporation, now known as Matsuo Pacific, signs a contract with its parent company, Matsuo of Japan, to deliver 1 million tons per year of American lumber for use in the Japanese construction industry. Approximately 50% of the lumber will be reexported to the United States as components in prefabricated housing units.

On learning of the proposed transaction, the environmental lobby is up in arms. An environmental activist group sues Matsuo Pacific in the Oregon courts, claiming that the exports would be in contravention of the company's agreement with state forestry authorities limiting exploitation of publicly owned forest land. Simultaneously, a consumer rights' group sues Matsuo's U.S. distribution arm and another Japanese company with close links to Matsuo, on the grounds of price rigging in the California residential construction industry, in which they have a combined 60% market share.

It is an election year. Not only is the governor of Oregon standing for reelection, but so also are the state judges. Two judges have to withdraw from the case on grounds of conflict of interest: Their campaigns are being financed by Matsuo. By the time that the case comes to trial before a third judge, a group of Congressmembers in the state legislature have introduced a motion granting a special exemption to Matsuo from the state's forestry code. The reason cited: the compelling economic benefit of the generous long-term contract signed by Matsuo Pacific. The contract will assure hundreds of jobs in rural areas in the forest belt. The governor himself, standing for reelection to his second term in an extremely well-financed campaign, makes a special plea to the Congress to pass the exemption motion. The environmental lobby is in an uproar at the passage of this motion, but the majority of the people of Oregon are apathetic. Matsuo Pacific has made a heavy investment in the Oregon economy, and it has taken care to foster an excellent image in the state. It is hard for most people to see the company in the role of a villain.

In California, meanwhile, the consumer rights group's antitrust case comes before the federal court. The judge in the case is guided by directives from the Justice Department in Washington, which has presently adopted a permissive attitude toward the activities of Japanese-owned companies. The companies themselves argue in separate presentations to the court that their prices are determined by their basis of costs, which for both companies includes a heavy goodwill element due to the high prices they paid to buy out local competitors, as well as shipping costs and high labor costs in Japan. The plaintiff consumer group produces compelling statistical evidence to show that the companies have acted in concert to raise prices and force remaining competitors out of the market. Although the judge rules against the Japanese-owned construction companies on some limited points of the suit, he imposes the minimum penalty and does not take effective action to break up the cartel. The defendants appeal even this judgment, and the case looks set to drag out for years in the courts.

As the tension remains high in this hypothetical drama, John Nation, columnist for the fictitious *Los Angeles Daily*—the only major daily in California not under Japanese ownership—makes the following comments to his readers:

> "For twenty years, the people of the West have been gorging themselves on the good life of food, drink, and sunshine while with every passing year they have sunk further into

a trap from which there may now be no escape. From Vancouver to San Diego, the economy has boomed, thanks to our happy position on the Pacific Rim, referred to frequently in this column as the 'golden frontier of the twenty-first century.' Now the new century is at hand, and with it will come an awakening to the great patrimony we have given away.

"I ask you, readers of the only newspaper that can still make such comments without fear of censorship, to consider the facts. Forget for the moment the legal brouhaha which seems expressly designed to confuse us all. Join me instead in looking a couple of simple, awful truths in the eye.

"The State of Oregon exports raw materials—unfinished lumber—six thousand miles across the ocean to a foreign nation. The materials are processed there and reexported—to California. The wood has made a 12,000 mile round trip to be sold at an inflated price to Oregon's next-door neighbors. Meantime, our priceless natural resources—virgin forests of centuries-old redwoods that will take generations to replace—are being turned into grinning, toothless strips of desert.

"Those of you who have studied the history of exploitation in this cruel world, I ask you to consider the case of India, which for centuries was ruthlessly robbed of its resources by hypocritical colonial overlords. Raw Indian cotton was exported to the mills of England's Lancashire, to be turned into finished cloth for sale—where? In the village bazaar not twenty yards from its origin. 'All things' said Marcus Aurelius, 'from eternity are of like forms and come round in a circle.' "

This hypothetical case is not as far-fetched as it may sound. Even today, about half of U.S. exports to Japan are of raw materials, of which lumber is a major component, while Japan's exports are almost entirely of finished goods.

The parallel between the Japanese presence in the United States and earlier colonial relationships is provocative. Relative to the population, the number of British residents in India was tiny—much smaller, probably, than the number of Japanese in the United States relative to the American population today. One of the keys to maintaining the colonial relationship was separation. Although the British were few, their physical characteristics and life-style ensured that they were always recognized as a separate, elite group. It was for this reason that such great play was made of the distinctiveness of race. The Indians were never allowed to forget their racial differences with the British. In particular, features regarded as superior—greater height, fairness of skin, and so on—were dwelt on in such a way that the superiority of the white race was eventually taken for granted by Indian and Englishman alike.

A very few conversations with almost any Japanese will reveal that the Japanese are also intensely conscious of race. The origins of this consciousness may be very different from the British example, since the Japanese themselves were long stigmatized by Westerners. Nevertheless, Japanese mythology emphasizes the uniqueness of the Japanese race, as first articulated by the divine incarnation of the line of emperors. And Japanese geography, language, and history have always, but never more than in the twentieth century, contributed to a sense of the separateness of the Japanese. Indeed, many respected Japanese analysts even today view American alarm at Japan's economic success as a form of transposed racism.

In addition to the strong racial consciousness fostered by the British, another hallmark of colonialism was the maintenance of a separate life-style by the British masters from their Indian subjects. The bungalows of the British were in enclaves separated from the "native quarters." British clubs were sacrosanct. A lowly second lieutenant could be waited on like a prince in the hallowed precinct of Calcutta's Bengal Club. A native prince, ruler of millions in his own land, could not even set foot inside.

Japanese separation is doubtless a good deal more subtle, but there are nevertheless many signs of it. Japanese expatriates have a strong tendency to lead self-contained lives mixing primarily with other Japanese. There are many factors that encourage this tendency: long working hours, a tradition of dedication to the company, differences of outlook from other nationalities, and discomfort with the English language.

One of the most notable features of Japanese separateness is the uniqueness and difficulty of the Japanese language. It is often noted that the Japanese are extraordinarily helpful and encouraging to beginning students of their language, showing praise where it is hardly deserved. But if a student masters the language to the point of real fluency—effectively impossible except by living for several years in Japan—then the encouragement may be replaced by reserve or even hostility. The foreigner has gained access to a club to which he was not invited, and the members are likely to find other ways to make him unwelcome.

Perhaps it is absurd to draw parallels with dead colonial regimes: America's national sovereignty is hardly threatened. But colonialism was about power, specifically, the power to exploit a weaker nation. Japan's accretion of power is a genuine cause of concern for Americans.

We would do well to remember that we naturally see the colonialist era from the perspective of the formal pomp of its latter days. But while India was the crowning glory of the British Empire for a hundred years, for a much longer period before that, "India" was merely a disparate and vaguely defined group of trading partners, over some of which Britain had more or less influence depending on the prevailing circumstances.

The British certainly did not develop their institutions in India with the intent of colonizing the subcontinent. Their only real interest at the outset was in making money. Colonial domination emerged more or less as a *fait accompli* after about a 150 years of maneuvering, alliances, double-dealing, and downright violence.

And it should be remembered, to continue the British example, that the status of India as a subject nation was always tenuous in the extreme, maintained as it was by a tiny corpus of British expatriates. What made India continue to accept her subject status? Arguably Britain had superior military skills, but it is inconceivable that a few thousand men could impose their will on hundreds of millions by sheer force of arms alone. Much more significant was a need for European technology and capital that could be provided only at the cost of India's sovereignty. Indians accepted British managers in their factories, British administrators in their government, and British officers over their army, because without them, there would have been no factories, no army, no administration: Without the superior technical skills and capital resources provided by the British, there would, in fact, have been no India. In this century, as native Indians gained training in the skills of a modern industrial state, the need for the British became more and more obsolete, and the British probably had no choice but to leave. Yet even to this day the unavailability of capital remains a serious handicap to Indian economic advancement.

Let me repeat: the British offered superior technical skills and abundant capital. Let me now offer an example that contains a somewhat chilling parallel. The Nissan Car Company sets up a factory in America, ostensibly in order to circumvent protectionist barriers. The factory manufactures automobiles for the American marketplace. Within five years, 70% of the components are made in America. Other than 13 Japanese managers the entire work force of 3,000 is American. The factory has healthy and profitable sales while the "Big Three" American car manufacturers suffer a continuing decline in market share and are subject to unprecedented volatility of earnings.

Japanese managers are running an American factory producing American cars for the American market. Why? Why does America need them? Why can they succeed? The answer can be only that the Japanese enjoy technical and managerial skills that are unavailable in America. Add to these an abundance of capital which has become essential to the fiscal survival of the U.S. government, and the parallel is thrown into yet sharper focus.

However, just as a bid for colonial power would certainly not have explained the motives of the first Scottish trader-adventurers as they set up their outposts far from the constraints of domestic authority on India's east coast, so the perception of a threat to American sovereignty, while it may contain a valid warning for the future of American-Japanese relations, would certainly not explain the motives of individual Japanese companies in setting up offices and subsidiaries in the United States. A more detailed look at individual companies would reveal a variety of reasons for being in America, and perhaps also a good deal of confusion about just what some companies are doing here.

Arguments and Counterarguments

The following pages summarize the major arguments both for and against deepening ties with Japan. Because the topic of Japan has become so emotionally charged in recent years, it is hard to separate arguments strictly on Japanese investment in the United States from broader issues of U.S.-Japan relations. For the sake of convenience, the arguments here are separated into "hawks" and "doves."

Hawks

1. Japan's trade practices are unfair. This criticism is, of course, more relevant as an argument in favor of protectionist trade measures than against Japanese investments. But there is a spill-over effect. We might call it the "Japan-basher" syndrome. Proponents of this way of thinking argue that since Japanese companies' gains are essentially ill gotten—that is, through unfair trade practices—they should not be allowed to use the profits to buy up their victims, the abused American companies.

There is also a more specific argument that Japan does not allow American companies access to acquisitions in Japan with the same freedom that Japanese companies have in America.

The trade debate has now been dragging on for over a decade, and in many ways it has come to symbolize the frustrations of the U.S.-Japanese relationship. The primary motivation for trade talks has been the U.S. trade deficit with Japan, which grew from a worrying $10 billion in 1980 to a truly alarming $56 billion in the peak year of 1987 (by 1990, the merchandise trade deficit with Japan had dropped to $42 billion).

The trade deficit has actually encouraged Japanese investment in the United States in a number of ways. First, it contributed to a huge buildup of cash in Japanese exporting companies. By using this cash to acquire American assets, Japanese companies are essentially recycling the dollars paid to them by American buyers, and accepting American assets in their place. When one considers how volatile the dollar has been during the 1980s—losing approximately half its value against the yen and most other currencies between 1985 and 1987—it's not surprising that Japanese companies would rather have real estate or corporate assets.

Second, the devaluation of the dollar that was initiated by the U.S. government in 1985 in order to encourage U.S. exports and thus reduce the trade deficit also had the effect of halving the price of U.S. assets for Japanese companies. Compared to the sky-high prices prevailing in Japan for virtually any investment, U.S. assets became extraordinarily cheap.

And third, Japanese companies have been investing in American factories and equipment in order to reduce the need for exporting to the United States. Japanese investment in U.S. manufacturing facilities has in fact contributed to a reduction in the trade deficit: Automobiles manufactured in the United States by Japanese transplants not only don't have to be imported; they are actually being exported to Japan.

The trade debate is in many ways inseparable from other political, economic, and social issues in Japan and the United States. Early negotiations focused on specific trade barriers that existed in Japan, for example, tariffs on imported automobiles. Japan had erected a wall of tariffs during the period of industrial reconstruction after World War II, in order to protect fledgling industries. But by the 1970s, Japan's industries could no longer claim Third World status, and the tariff system had become an anachronism. American negotiators attacked one tariff after another, and the Japanese reluctantly pulled down many tariff walls.

But in spite of the Japanese capitulation to many American demands, the deficit continued to grow. Even when tariffs were lowered to below U.S. levels, Japanese buyers continued to buy Japanese. Some said the quality of Japanese goods was simply higher. The prime minister of Japan, Yasuhiro Nakasone, even begged the Japanese people in a television address to buy more American products, but to little avail. American analysts concluded that the problem was wider than just tariff barriers. American products were uncompetitive because the yen was artificially low against the dollar—a result of Japan's protective financial policies and lack of participation in global financial markets. So the next demand by American negotiators was for liberalization of Japanese financial markets. Between 1984 and 1988, successive layers of regulation were stripped from the Japanese financial system, setting the stage for a dramatic revaluation of the yen.

The tumbling dollar did have an impact on the trade deficit, which has been falling since 1988. But the deficit with Japan remains stubbornly high, prompting negotiators to shift the emphasis of talks once again. This time, talks have focused on what American officials describe as "structural impediments" to increased American sales to Japan. In other words, even if a specific tariff barrier is removed, various peculiarities of Japanese society and the Japanese economy prevent American companies from making inroads. Included in the talks were such "structural impediments" as Japan's complex and inaccessible retail distribution system, and the system of cross-ownership of shares that effectively ties up supplier relationships and excludes outsiders from selling to major Japanese companies. In 1990, an agreement known as the "Structural Impediments Initiative" was signed which addressed many of these concerns, as well as Japanese concerns about America's low rate of saving. But although agreement was reached, many observers question whether it was more than symbolic: Is it, after all, possible to alter fundamental social and economic structures at the behest of a foreign power?

Although much progress has been made in trade negotiations with Japan, many thorny issues remain. The Japanese have been roundly attacked recently for failing to open up their protected agricultural products market—an American delegation was recently threatened with arrest for daring to display grains of American rice, a forbidden import, at a trade fair. There have also been persistent accusations that the Japanese habitually use trade negotiations as a way of dragging their feet and gaining time, only agreeing to concessions after they have achieved an insuperable position. And there is also a recurring theme of "dumping"—accusations that Japanese producers are selling their products in the United States at below cost in order to gain market share.

A fascinating analysis of America's trade problems with Japan is contained in *Trading Places,* a book by Clyde V. Prestowitz, Jr.[1] Prestowitz was Counselor for Japan Affairs at the Commerce Department, and was intimately involved in many of the trade disputes with Japan during the 1980s. In *Trading Places,* he gives a detailed account of some of the more notable negotiations, including a chapter devoted to a series of semiconductor disputes.

But what Prestowitz really sets out to do in his book is to explain why the negotiations with Japan have been for the most part futile. On the one hand, he portrays an American system that is paralyzed by internal conflicts, and supported by feeble and ineffective laws. For example, in several instances where Prestowitz and the Commerce Department team had negotiated favorable agreements with the Japanese, the agreements were effectively sabotaged by other sections of the government which had conflicting interests, most notably the Pentagon, which did not want to damage the security relationship with Japan. When individual U.S. companies attempted to gain redress in court against unfair Japanese practices such as dumping, the courts moved too slowly and their powers were too limited to provide effective relief. Moreover, other U.S. companies welcomed the lower prices and opposed the legal actions. Often, by the time any effective action was taken, it was already too late to save an American industry.

On the other hand, Prestowitz portrays a Japanese system that is highly centralized, and highly unified in its aims. He describes how the Ministry of International Trade and Industry has guided corporate goals over the decades, selecting key industries for development, providing seed money and guidance, and negotiating skillfully on industry's behalf to gain competitive advantage in international markets while protecting domestic markets from foreign incursion.

At the center of Prestowitz's argument is the belief that the American and Japanese economies are guided by fundamentally different principles. The American capitalist system, economic management, business law, and political initiatives are all guided by the principle that business exists to benefit the consumer. The business system aims to provide a competitive environment in which the consumer can choose from a range of products, and purchase at the lowest price. The law prevents companies from colluding to increase prices, as well as providing a host of other protections to the consumer.

In Japan, on the other hand, the consumer is relatively low on the list of priorities. Instead, the main beneficiary of Japanese law and policy is industry itself. The Japanese system, argues Prestowitz, targets industrial development as an essential goal of government policy and encourages protection of domestic markets, as well as the formation of cartels and other collusive practices that may well hurt the interests of the consumer. According to Prestowitz, the reason for this differing approach is that Japan views its industrial strength as an essential component of national security. Since Japan's constitution forbids it from becoming a military power, security is seen as residing in the creation of wealth and technological leadership. Thus, the role played by MITI in developing industry is similar to that of the Pentagon in developing U.S. defense. The country comes first, not the individual.

Prestowitz uses a metaphor to describe the differing philosophies of American and Japanese business and policymaking. America has become a culture of cowboys: the environment supports the individual, the entrepreneur, the inventor, the lone company struggling against entrenched competition. Japan, on the other hand, is a culture of settlers, who work together, pulling the wagons around the fire for mutual protection. Prestowitz reminds us that America was built by settlers, not cowboys, and that we would benefit from a return to this philosophy.

Prestowitz spent years living in Japan and is a self-professed lover of the Japanese. Although he is critical of the Japanese system, it is really America that in his opinion needs to change. But although Prestowitz does a brilliant job of describing the deep-rooted problems that have eroded American competitiveness, his formula for renewal is confined to a few pages in the back of the book—and it calls for such sweeping changes that parts of it sound like wishful thinking. These include reducing budget deficits, increasing savings, overhauling industrial priorities, banning lobbying by foreigners, and a host of other measures, some moderate and practical, others sweeping and perhaps beyond the power of the country's most able politicians.

The trade dispute has also spilled over directly into the arena of Japanese mergers and acquisitions. American critics have long contended that U.S. companies are far more open to Japanese buyers than are Japanese companies to Americans. There have in fact been remarkably few acquisitions of Japanese companies by U.S. buyers, and there have been no successful hostile takeovers by foreign companies.

In 1988, American investor T. Boone Pickens—well known as an aggressive corporate "raider" in the United States—acquired a 20% stake in the Japanese Koito Company, making him the largest shareholder in the company. Using his shareholding as a basis, Pickens accused the company of failing to maximize profits. According to Pickens, Koito sold its products virtually exclusively to the Toyota Company, which owned 5% of Koito, at prices that were too low to yield an acceptable profit. The interests of Toyota and of Koito managers were being placed before those of shareholders, accused Pickens. In fact, the practices described by Pickens are typical of a vast number of Japanese companies that exist within the orbit of a major conglomerate or *keiretsu*, acting as subsidiaries even though the controlling company has only a minority stake. Shareholders tend to be given a lower priority by Japanese companies than by their American counterparts. But Japanese shareholders seldom complain.

Pickens demanded a greater say in the management of the company, including a seat on the board. The company's management refused to accede to this demand, raising questions about where Pickens had bought his stock and how—or whether—he had paid for it. These questions Pickens consistently refused to answer, but it eventually became apparent that he had purchased the stock from a well-known Japanese "greenmailer" and that Pickens had borrowed from the seller in order to finance the acquisition. Koito raised important questions about whether Pickens could legitimately be said to own the stock, or whether he was simply being used as a front by the Japanese businessman.

There followed a number of stormy scenes at which Pickens publicly pressed his demands, including one, at a shareholders' meeting, in which Pickens was booed and heckled by a group of obviously hired toughs. Pickens, although perhaps not ideally qualified for righteous indignation, expressed outrage that Japanese buyers were able to exploit the fairness of the American system while denying American investors even basic shareholders' rights. The issue was even absorbed into the general trade talks between the two countries for a while. But in the end Pickens accepted defeat, and he finally sold his stake in Koito back to its original owner.

2. Japanese industries are out to destroy their American rivals. There is a school of American critics who contend that Japan should not be allowed to play by American rules in the United States, because Japanese companies are playing a different game. In the West, a tradition of acceptable business behavior has evolved over the course of centuries that might best be summarized as a code of "fair play." This code or tradition recognizes that companies are basically motivated by self-interest, but it encourages certain checks and balances that prevent companies from inflicting gratuitous harm on their rivals. The majority of the rules of fair play, such as the rule which prevents companies ganging up to eliminate rivals, are codified by the law. However, it is argued that even the letter of the law requires acceptance also of its spirit—a spirit which the Japanese are accused of lacking.

What the critics particularly point to is the apparently destructive nature of competition as understood by the Japanese. Japanese companies are accused above all of giving higher priority to the elimination of rivals than to their own profits. At its most conspiracy-minded, this school of critics argues that Japanese companies are actually in league in a sort of nationalistic plot to destroy foreign industries.

Whatever the motivations of the Japanese, the results are only too plain to see. Take the consumer electronics industry. In 1970, American companies dominated the world in this fast-developing field. American companies invented color television, stereo sound reproduction, and a host of other fundamental advances in the industry. But by 1985, there was only one domestic manufacturer of televisions left, and that was Japanese owned. By aggressive pricing and superior product characteristics, the Japanese succeeded in demolishing a major American industry. This pattern was in fact repeated in other countries around the world, making Japanese companies global leaders.

The same phenomenon may now be taking place in another vital industry, automobiles. Japanese companies now have substantial automobile manufacturing capacity in the United States. The Japanese plants were built to some extent to ward off retaliation for Japanese companies export successes. But the companies must have been aware as they built their U.S. plants that they were creating far more capacity than the American market can realistically absorb. A large amount of capacity will undoubtedly have to be closed down, and there is little doubt which nation's manufacturers are the more threatened.

There are those who argue that Japanese manufacturers are, so to speak, killer bees in the American worker bee community. A common response is to argue that American industries should be given a degree of government protection in fighting this threat. A very few go so far as to argue that the Japanese should therefore not be given access to investment opportunities in America according to the same rules that domestic companies enjoy.

But the theory that Japanese companies are out to destroy American industry is itself highly questionable. The American code of business ethics is essentially captured in the legal code. If an action is not illegal, few would convincingly argue that it can reasonably be condemned. American companies can and do compete using whatever weapons the law allows. Japanese companies have not been shown to have broken the law more than their American competitors. Moreover, the kind of destructive competition that the critics assert would require the Japanese companies to be acting in league against their American competitors. The reality is that Japanese companies compete fiercely with each other as well as with foreign rivals, as is amply shown by the history of industrial competition within Japan.

3. Japan is stealing key technologies and reducing America's defensive capabilities. Japan has in the last decade built an enviable base of high-technology leadership. In 1980, America was unquestionably the leader in most high-tech industries, from supercomputers to biotechnology. However, during the course of the decade, Japanese firms mounted strong attacks on some American strongholds. Their biggest success was in semiconductors, the raw building blocks of computer technology. The quantity of data that can be stored on a semiconductor "chip" has grown phenomenally during the last decade—approximately doubling every two years. The cost involved in developing and manufacturing each new generation of chips has grown proportionately. As the price tag has risen, the pool of competitors in this field has proportionately shrunk. Many of the casualties have been American.

American companies accuse the Japanese of acting in league, with government backing, while American firms have been competing individually with no government support. The Japanese retort that this shows a lack of intelligence on the part of American firms and the government. Americans accused the Japanese of trying to force them out of the market by dumping chips on the U.S. market at uneconomically low prices, forcing American firms to sustain losses or get out of the business. The Japanese have had to defend themselves in court against this charge. But during the decade, Japanese companies have stolen an inexorable lead from their American rivals.

Clearly, Japanese technology companies pose a competitive threat to their American rivals. In addition, there may be a political threat. It is perhaps best expressed by a Japanese politician, Shintaro Ishihara, in the now-notorious book, *The Japan That Can Say No.*[2] In the book, Ishihara argues that Japan has gained immense political power through its dominance of new technologies, and that Japan should use this power to assert its wishes more forcefully.

> While U.S. companies may already have the technological know-how for advanced chips, only Japanese electronics firms have the mass-production and quality-control capability to supply the multimegabit semiconductors for the (latest) weapons systems and other equipment.[3]

In short, without using new-generation computer chips made in Japan, the U.S. Department of Defense cannot guarantee the precision of its nuclear weapons. If Japan told Washington it would no longer sell computer chips to the United States, the Pentagon would be totally helpless. Furthermore, the global military balance would be completely upset if Japan decided to sell its computer chips to the Soviet Union instead of the United States.[4]

In spite of the Soviet Union's demise, this is truly a chilling scenario, especially in the mouth of a Japanese politician. Its threat is further confirmed by an internal Pentagon analysis, which concluded that the United States no longer has a leadership position in 25 of 28 technologies considered essential for American defense.

How does this threat affect Japanese investments in the United States? Japanese companies have major investments in American high-technology companies. The chairman of a major Silicon Valley firm said recently that "any company in Silicon Valley that does not have Japanese backing may not survive the decade." Japanese companies have become essential suppliers of capital to America's high-tech industry. In exchange, they are gaining access to America's leading-edge technologies. Arguably, if there were a security crisis, the Japanese could use this access to deny essential technology to American defense.

To ward off this threat, the Exon-Florio amendment to the Defense Production Act was passed by Congress. Based on this amendment, any acquisition by a foreign company that may threaten the nation's defensive capability must be reviewed by the Treasury Department's Committee on Foreign Investment in the United States (CFIUS). The committee has found some proposed acquisitions to be threatening to U.S. defensive capabilities. In recent years, the stance of CFIUS has reportedly become much tougher. America does therefore have a defense against the political threat posed by Japanese technological leadership—at least from the point of view of cross-border acquisitions. Nevertheless, there is ample evidence that the Japanese lead is being forged more through independent R&D activities than through purchases of U.S. companies.

4. Japanese employers are racist and sexist. There have been all too many instances of remarks or actions by Japanese managers, politicians, or companies that showed clear underlying prejudices against women and minorities. That's not to say that the Japanese have a monopoly on such prejudices.

Charges of racism are frequently leveled against Japanese politicians. The most famous incident was when Prime Minister Nakasone stated in a speech that Japan's success was due in part to the fact that Japan was not "hampered" by the presence of minorities. This remark caused outrage in the United States, and Nakasone was forced to make a humbling public apology.

In the United States, several lawsuits have been filed by minorities and women against Japanese companies. Best known was the suit filed by a group of women employees of Sumitomo Bank, who argued that they had been excluded from responsible positions purely because they were female. The case was settled out of court, reportedly with a substantial payment by Sumitomo.

However prejudiced the Japanese may be—and of course in reality some are much more than others—it must be noted that Americans working for Japanese companies in the United States are protected by just the same laws that would protect them working for an American company. If the law has any meaning, such prejudices should not be taken as a reason to exclude Japanese companies from the United States. Moreover, the majority of Japanese companies in the United States are highly conscious of the possibility of lawsuits (with their attendant unfavorable publicity) and, for this reason or out of innate fairness, most companies treat American employees regardless of race or sex with scrupulous fairness.

5. The Japanese incursions into the United States are part of a plot to gain world domination. This is the most extreme position taken by American critics of Japan, and, but for the fact that it is taken seriously by a large segment of the population, it might be termed the lunatic fringe. For all the hysteria associated with this view, however, its proponents have raised some serious issues.

The Coming War with Japan, by George Friedman and Meredith LeBard,[5] has been a runaway best-seller in Japan. This book takes a hard-headed and somewhat bleak look at the current worldwide political and military situation. According to the authors, the recent collapse of Soviet Communism will have profound effects on postwar military alliance structures, including that between the United States and Japan.

The authors' thesis is that the free trade system that has been so effective in promoting world prosperity since the war was really a political invention of the United States to cement its alliance system. Since it has worked generally to the disadvantage of the United States, creating huge deficits while countries like Japan have benefited enormously, the authors see the free trade system as one of the costs of the cold war against the Soviet Union, a cost that the U.S. was willing to bear as long as the cold war continued. Another cost, of course, was massive U.S. arms spending—6% of GNP in the United States, compared to less than 1% in Japan.

Now that the cold war has ended in American victory, say the authors, it is no longer in the interests of the United States to promote free trade, or to defend Japan at America's expense. In fact, the authors assert that it would be folly to allow the Japanese to continue to build their financial and industrial lead. Now that the cold war threat has passed, say the authors, the interests of Japan and the United States are fundamentally opposed.

Moreover, the United States has emerged from the cold war victorious, and is now the only superpower in the world. According to the authors, it is inevitable that the United States will recoup the cost of building its power (the arms race, plus trade deficits) by exerting pressure on its former allies. The authors point out that Japan is utterly dependent on the United States for the security of its shipping lanes, a vital lifeline for a country with few natural resources. "Thus far, the United States has used (its) power to strengthen its alliance system, but there is no intrinsic reason why this same power cannot be used, now that there is no other global power to contend with, to enrich America and impoverish America's enemies."[6]

The authors point out that the situation for Japan now is in many ways similar to that prevailing before World War II. The strategic realities of Japan's situation, while distorted for five decades by the cold war, will now reassert themselves.

Japan is highly vulnerable. Lacking basic resources, she is totally dependent on the goodwill of the Western powers to allow access to her goods and freedom to purchase raw materials. If such access is denied—as it was before World War II—then Japan has (the authors argue) no choice but to create her own sphere of influence—and, as before the war, the logical location of this sphere of influence is the Western Pacific. If Japan has access to Indian minerals, Indonesian oil, as well as the growing markets of the newly developed Asian economies, then some sort of status quo may be possible.

But in order to create such a sphere of influence, Japan will have to become a military power. It is a central belief of the authors that economic strength is ultimately inseparable from military power. They point out that Japan has already taken giant steps toward rebuilding its military. In spite of the clause in its constitution renouncing war, Japan now has the third most powerful military force in the world, and it is the third biggest spender. Additionally, Japan has for decades concentrated on acquiring essential technologies for a rapid military expansion.

Accordingly, say the authors, the stage is now set for a remilitarization of Japan. The authors do not in fact condemn Japan for this. Rather, they see it as the only prudent course of action. "No nation" they say "should place its national survival in the hands of another nation."[7]

The problem is that once Japan has rebuilt its military strength, it will come to be seen as a threat by the United States, particularly if it tries to exclude the United States from its Asian sphere of influence. The United States may retaliate by restricting Japan's supplies, forcing Japan to take bold actions to secure her position. This would be a replay of the events that led up to Japan's entry into World War II.

While the title of this book seems highly sensationalist at first glance, the book contains some thoughtful and chilling insights. The authors argue that we have grown comfortable with the idea that economics, rather than armies and power politics, are the forces that dictate events in the developed world. But, say the authors, it is naive to think that economics can be separated from the realities of political and military power. We have been protected for decades by a highly effective alliance, which, by ensuring a united stand against the Soviet threat, allowed Western nations to focus on economic competition. But that protection, argue the authors, was a distortion of the realities of political life that lasted just as long as the need for a cold war alliance. Now that that need is over, the alliance structure of the world will inevitably change to reflect a new, and in many ways harsher reality.

Doves

1. Japanese companies are creating jobs in the United States. Ask anyone in Smyrna, Tennessee, whether Japanese investment is a good thing. The Nissan car plant in that town has created 10,000 jobs—good jobs that probably would not exist were it not for Japanese investment. In all, Japanese companies employ an estimated 500,000 Americans. When Japanese companies have acquired American firms, job security has tended to increase for the employees of the firm that was bought. That's a very different story from many American or European buyers, whose first move is to trim staff drastically.

A large percentage of Japanese investments in the

United States is made with the objective of localizing production, part of a worldwide move toward global organization structures. Put simply, automobiles which are made in the United States do not need to be imported from Japan. As it happens, Japan is suffering from an acute labor shortage. So it makes sense for Japanese companies to export jobs overseas. Instead of stealing jobs from Americans (the old complaint against free import policies), the Japanese are creating them.

2. Japanese companies are improving the quality of manufactured goods. Japanese automobiles consistently win awards for customer satisfaction. Few would dispute that the Japanese have raised the standard of products available to ordinary Americans. With their extraordinary achievements in quality control and their innovative manufacturing techniques, Japanese companies have redefined many aspects of manufacturing technology.

American companies have been forced to follow suit. Just-in-time production and other Japanese-pioneered techniques are now routinely studied by American managers. Of course, the process has been painful for many American companies that have not been able to adapt to change. But do we want to accept second-rate products in order to protect our industries? As Eastern Europeans have discovered, sooner or later that policy would come home to haunt us.

The study of how the Japanese manage to do things so well became immensely popular from the early 1980s. Techniques ranging from *kanban* to Zen were reported and, in some cases, incorporated into the American way of doing things. But the more that American observers attempted to isolate the essence of Japanese success, the more they were forced to recognize that a great deal of that success depended on the complex and unique characteristics of Japanese society itself. Japanese people work harder than Americans. They show more empathy with the goals of their employer. They are better educated to assume responsibility for their allotted tasks. They tend to accept the subservience of their individual interests for the common good. They value loyalty. They accept discipline. They have comparatively recent memories of hardship and suffering. They tend to work toward long-term goals and are ready to sacrifice short-term benefits. They place a high value on consensus. All these characteristics and many more have been credited with contributing to the remarkable commercial success of the Japanese.

Of course, some of these are all but impossible to reproduce on American soil. In particular, there seems to be a fundamental clash of cultures between the consensus-driven, corporatist approach of the Japanese and the individualistic ideals of the Americans. While some Americans may lament the effects of lack of discipline on their children's education, most would probably not want to sacrifice the creative freedom and individual opportunity that characterize American society. However, it would be rash to assert that American society has not been influenced by the success of Japan's peculiar social makeup. Americans are said to work much harder today than they did ten years ago, at which time the expectation was that the reverse would transpire. Nobody seems quite sure why Americans have become so much more absorbed in their work and careers, but the pressure of foreign competition is surely a plausible explanation.

American schools are also making an increasing effort to react to the demonstrably superior educational standards of Japanese children. Studies highlighting the differences are being used as an essential tool in the development of a more effective educational program for future generations of Americans.

If we are going to remain competitive in global industries, say the supporters of free links with Japan, we have to compete with the best. And if we are to compete with the best, we should not be afraid of allowing foreign companies access to our consumers—least of all when they are establishing manufacturing centers in the United States, from which knowledge is more likely to flow to Americans.

3. Our politicians and businesspeople are begging the Japanese to invest. Fact: More than half of the state governors have been on missions to Japan to encourage Japanese investment in their states. Fact: the sellers of Rockefeller Center approached 22 different Japanese firms before accepting an offer from Mitsubishi Estate.

The fact is that the Japanese are receiving very mixed signals about their investment in the United States. On the one hand, they have American businesspeople and politicians beating a path to their door asking for their investment money. On the other hand, the American public, and sometimes the same businesspeople and politicians, condemn Japan for "buying up America." Many Japanese businessmen profess to be confused and angry at the double standard employed by Americans, especially by American politicians.

4. The Japanese pay top dollar. Why do American businesspeople seek Japanese acquirors? One compelling reason must be that historically, Japanese companies have paid top prices for their U.S. acquisitions.

The Japanese say that they have a long-term outlook, and apparently that has been used as a justification to ask them for higher prices—on the theory that they will not mind waiting longer to get a return on their investment. There is some talk that Japanese buyers are getting wise to the so-called "Japanese premium." But prices paid to American shareholders continue to be very high.

Arguably, the funds received by American sellers will be reinvested in the American economy, which will have gained in overall value through the transaction. Whether or not this is the case, Japanese buyers have certainly made a lot of American share owners happy.

5. National boundaries are irrelevant in a global economy. In his book, *The Borderless World*,[8] Kenichi Ohmae, managing director, McKinsey & Co., Inc., Japan, argues that advanced economies can no longer look at investments and corporate ownership in terms of national boundaries.

Major industries of the coming decade will be characterized by converging consumer tastes throughout the developed world—particularly in the three "Triad" regions of Europe, North America, and Japan. Improvements in communications media ensure that governments are powerless to prevent their citizens understanding and demanding the top quality at the best possible price, regardless of the country of manufacture. But in order to get close to consumers, and to provide for subtle variations in local tastes, companies will increasingly locate research and manufacturing inside each of the major market areas.

Accordingly, the economic system of the future will include giant, essentially stateless companies that manufacture locally in all major market areas, rendering the old concept of export-dominated economies virtually irrelevant. According to Ohmae, the trade deficit with Japan is anyway greatly overstated, since the figures do not include profits of U.S. companies manufacturing in Japan.

6. Americans are racially motivated when they condemn the Japanese. This is one of the most disturbing accusations leveled against the Americans—disturbing because it has an unpleasant odor of truth to it.

During the last decade, Europeans have consistently outinvested the Japanese in the United States. For example, British investment continued to outpace Japanese investment during the 1980s. Yet how often do we hear an outcry against a British takeover in the United States? That's in spite of the fact that Europeans tend to be much more callous owners than their Japanese counterparts, often selling assets and laying off workers without hesitation.

Why are the Japanese singled out for blame? The Japanese themselves ask this question repeatedly. Here is the conclusion drawn by Shintaro Ishihara in *The Japan That Can Say No* in a chapter entitled "Racial Prejudice: The Root Cause of Japan-Bashing":

> In World War II, the United States bombed German cities and killed many civilians but did not use atomic bombs on the Germans. U.S. planes dropped them on us because we

are Japanese...We should never forget this. The same virulent racism underlies trade friction with the United States.[9]

American readers may take this to be a somewhat extreme view, but we would do well to remember that Ishihara's sentiments are shared by large numbers of educated Japanese. The reason for this is the history of treatment of the Japanese by America. Americans should be especially concerned not to perpetuate the discrimination that has undeniably permeated past dealings with Japan.

7. The Japanese are good citizens. Perhaps aware of their poor public image, Japanese companies have become significant givers to American causes in recent years. Recipients have ranged from major universities to local fire departments. At least one major advertising campaign focused not on the superior products that a Japanese company offered, but on the fire engine that the company had bought for a small town in Tennessee. The Japanese, in fact, desperately want to be seen as good citizens.

Okay, so a lot of this may be public relations. But two important points should be considered. First, Japanese companies have become important contributors to American arts, sports, and social causes. Second, due to their sensitivity about public image, Japanese companies are far less likely than American companies to become involved in underhand dealings that might further tarnish their image. Their good citizenship is probably no more self-motivated than that of any other big company, and perhaps it's a great deal more sincere.

8. Japanese investment cannot harm the U.S. economy. Although it is easy to become concerned at the Japanese acquisition of "trophy" assets like Columbia Pictures or the Rockefeller Center, leading academics who have studied the issue conclude that there are few adverse effects from foreign acquisitions of U.S. assets.

The deepest fears are perhaps emotional more than rational. We see foreigners able to buy prized assets at prices that Americans apparently cannot match, and so we fear that America is becoming a second-rate power. The acquisitions have come to symbolize America's decline. On a more hard-headed level, some critics assert that Japanese investments will lead to an exporting of American technologies, leaving Americans with the more menial tasks while high value-added tasks will continue to be performed in Japan.

But as Edward Graham and Paul Krugman (a professor of economics at MIT) summarize in their landmark work, *Foreign Direct Investment in the United States*:

> A careful assessment of the evidence on foreign direct investment (FDI) in the United States does not justify great concern about its effects. Foreign firms do not shift high-value or high-compensation activities to their home countries, nor do they perform less R&D in the United States than their U.S. counterparts . . . There is little evidence to suggest that affiliates of foreign firms make less of a contribution to the U.S. economy than do U.S.-owned firms in the same industry.[10]

Historical Perspective

One of the most provocative facts underlying the relations between the United States and Japan is that, in spite of the immense cultural and geographic distance between the two countries, they are in fact neighbors. In the years of Japan's isolation, commerce with foreign nations was prohibited regardless of location. But in the twentieth century the proximity of these nations, magnified by the scope of modern communications, has become a crucial determinant of modern history.

The first official exchanges between the two countries did not occur until 1866 when, shortly after Japan reluctantly opened her ports to the outside world in response to a massive show of force by American Commodore Matthew Perry, the government of the still-feudal country began issuing passports for foreign travel, ending a 250-year ban on foreign intercourse.

The opening of Japan came at the time of America's

greatest period of expansion. While the Eastern states were developing industries that would propel the nation to world greatness, the West was opening its limitless spaces to settlers who advanced with the newly built railroads.

The whole nation needed labor, and the waves of European immigrants fleeing the turmoil of their homelands were welcomed and speedily integrated into the burgeoning economy. In the West, where access to European labor was far more restricted, the farms and railroad companies had for some time been looking to China to provide their desperately needed labor resources. Immigration was at that time unrestricted by legislation, and between 1860 and 1890 the number of Chinese residents in the West grew from 35,000 to 108,000.

But as the Chinese presence grew, and as the West suffered periods of economic difficulty, settlers of European stock found themselves competing with the Chinese for increasingly precious jobs. Resentment against the Chinese grew, as they were reputed to be ready to accept subhuman living conditions and rock-bottom wages, thus allowing them to undercut Americans in the labor market. Moreover, some Chinese were becoming successful businessmen and farmers, competing with American-born settlers for the region's commerce.

In 1877, the Workingman's Party of California was formed to lobby for restrictive legislation, and their efforts were rewarded with the passage in 1882 of the Chinese Exclusion Act, which banned further Chinese immigration and prohibited naturalization of those Chinese already in the United States.

It is an extraordinary fact that there are no clear guidelines in the Constitution on the question of race. American policy has developed based on the dictates of the philosophy current at the time. In the 1880s, it was acceptable to exclude the Chinese on the grounds of their inherent undesirability as U.S. citizens, and the Japanese were eventually to suffer the same discrimination.

In the short term, Chinese exclusion actually opened

the door to an influx of Japanese labor. Japan itself was undergoing radical social and economic changes which were producing great hardship among parts of the rural population at home. In the 1880s a small number of Japanese laborers, some of them on limited-term contracts, took up jobs on farms and at the railheads. The numbers were truly tiny: 859 laborers entered the United States during the entire decade. The total Japanese population in the 1890 census was 2,039. During the 1890s, the influx accelerated somewhat, with 8,445 Japanese laborers entering the United States. But even these numbers were far below the scale of the Chinese influx.

Laborers were not the only class of Japanese coming to the United States during this period. During the 1880s, 1,340 students came to attend American schools and colleges. These were generally members of a privileged elite who returned to Japan on completing their studies, to assist in the task of transforming their country into a modern industrial state. Some wealthier Japanese also came for reasons of political misfortune or economic opportunity. An early attempt to found a tea- and silk-growing colony in El Dorado County, California, ended in failure in spite of the enthusiastic support of the local population. A group of defeated samurai from Japan's 1868 civil war leased a farm east of the San Francisco Bay. A number of wealthy entrepreneurs attempted to establish rice- and fruit-growing plantations in Texas. In New York, a few adventurous Japanese established offices to promote trade with family ventures back home. One of these, Ryoichiro Arai, who came to New York to sell silk at the age of eighteen, became known as the "father" of U.S.-Japan trade. He founded the prestigious Nippon Club, and his granddaughter, Haru Reischauer, was the wife of America's Ambassador to Japan.

But as demand for Japanese labor remained strong, the uneducated component of the Japanese influx gained numerical ascendancy toward the end of the nineteenth century. The Japanese government, eager to be accepted as an equal by the Western powers, was embarrassed at the growing perception of Japanese as low-paid laborers. Even more humiliating was the low life into which many of these people drifted. In 1891, the secretary of the Japanese consul in San Francisco reported on a trip to Seattle that "Of 250 (Japanese) residents, only forty have steady jobs as proprietors or employees of the grocery store and several restaurants. The remaining two hundred are, if not prostitutes or proprietors of houses of pleasure, either gamblers or pimps."

The Japanese immigrants were also increasingly unpopular with the local communities, though for different reasons. Once again, the more hardworking among them were proving that they could not only work for but also compete with established local businesses. Hired farmhands began to lease their own plots (land ownership by aliens was forbidden in most states) and were soon able to outbid their less frugal neighbors. And as the labor shortage eased, the Japanese came into competition with American-born workers for increasingly valuable jobs.

The Japanese were subjected to discrimination in the United States from the very outset. They were, like other Asians, ineligible for U.S. citizenship. This stigma was only once subjected to legal challenge, in 1922, when the Supreme Court ruled that Congress had, in a statute of 1790 amended once after the Civil War, limited naturalization to free "white" persons and those of "African nativity." Asians were not eligible. It was not until 1952 that a native-born Japanese was given the right to U.S. citizenship. But even in their small numbers and with the restriction imposed on them, they rapidly fell victim to the racial antagonism of the more established ethnic groups. Labor unions and the newly formed Japanese and Korean Exclusion League fanned the flames of prejudice, publishing such statements as

> The American workman is compelled to maintain his family and provide for the education and improvement of his children and the maintenance of his home at a cost not to be

compared with the expense of the living of people of other races . . .[11]

and

The . . . Japanese are not bona fide citizens. They are not the stuff of which American citizens can be made.[12]

While their persecutors had powerful connections the Japanese, who were few in number and ineligible to vote, were able to muster little political support. Their most powerful helper, the Japanese government, was restrained by its intense desire to gain acceptance by the club of industrial nations. This led it to subscribe in 1907 to a secret "Gentleman's Agreement," by which Japan stopped issuing passports to emigrant laborers.

However, the people of California were not informed of this agreement, and therefore not appeased by it. Although laborers were no longer entering the country, the number of immigrants, mostly brides married by mail after an exchange of photographs, continued to increase. This influx was necessary to redress the unacceptable imbalance of the sexes (24 males for every female in 1900), but it added to the fears of Californians who were not only horrified at the method of selecting the brides, but who also spoke of a plot to subvert the immigration restrictions by breeding new generations of Japanese who, born in the United States, would automatically be citizens.

The anti-Japanese lobby would not be gainsaid. Their concerns happened to coincide with those of racial purists on the East Coast who were seeking to restrict immigration from Eastern and Southern Europe, in an overt movement to maintain the Anglo-Saxon supremacy within the nation. The combined pressures led the government, after a series of interim measures, to enact in 1924 a sweeping new immigration law, which both rolled back Slavic and Mediterranean immigration and prohibited all further immigration of "aliens ineligible to citizenship." From that time until 1952, Japanese immigration was completely prohibited for any cause.

Why were the Japanese singled out for such harsh

treatment? Certainly, there is no statistical justification for the premise that the Japanese threatened to inundate the West Coast. Of some 26 million immigrants to the United States between 1860 and 1920, only 250,000 were Japanese—less than 1% of the total. The Japanese government had done everything possible to prevent any mass exodus of Japanese, and such a movement, while perhaps plausible in the light of poor social conditions and overpopulation in Japan, was never in fact threatened. All other arguments rested on purely racial grounds such as the supposed unworthiness of the Japanese (and Chinese) for the dignity of American citizenship, and a series of confusing but highly biased interpretations of the intentions of the founding fathers and subsequent Congresses as to the racial complexion of the United States. If the policies seem lamentable by the values of a half-century later, it must be remembered that multiracial societies were virtually nonexistent at this time, and the relations between the nations of the world were characterized by an extremity of racial oppression.

In terms of the statistics of population movement, the Exclusion Act of 1924 was actually insignificant. Immigration from Japan in the first four years of the decade was a mere 33,000. But the political consequences, for Japanese-American relations, and the social consequences, for the Japanese already in America, were profound and highly detrimental to all parties. Japanese national pride was intensely hurt by the arrogance of this act, with its barely veiled implication of Asian inferiority. It is often suggested that the outrage that swept Japan was a direct cause of the political radicalization of the country which ultimately led to the attack on Pearl Harbor.

Even today, the bruises from this past discrimination are not completely healed, and necessary dialogue between Japan and America is apt to become clouded by emotive racial concerns. Indeed, it is not hard to see parallels between American fears at the Japanese influx at the turn of the century, and fears today of a new, economically driven influx.

For the Japanese remaining in the United States, as well as for their American-born children, life remained fraught with discrimination and hostility. The situation of this community, now numbering some 140,000 in total, actually became more difficult as the threat of aggression from the expansionist Japanese Empire increased through the 1930s.

By most accounts, the Japanese made almost pathetic efforts to assimilate and demonstrate their loyalty. For the children, the situation was particularly difficult. They were Americans—most of them had never seen their parents' country—and yet they were not accepted in America. Moreover, the hardship that they suffered was material as well as emotional: in the prevailing anti-Japanese climate, jobs were all but impossible to find in the Depression years. Increasingly, Japanese-Americans came to depend on each other for mutual support in making sense of their lives in this strange limbo. In 1930, the Japanese-American Citizens' League was formed to offer a social and political focus for the Nisei (second-generation) community.

Yet all these concerns paled against the disaster that befell the Japanese-Americans in 1941, when Japan attacked Pearl Harbor. Overnight, the Nisei's parents became "enemy aliens"—although some had lived for up to 60 years in the United States. Their funds were frozen, and many were taken into custody by the FBI on suspicion of complicity. Hard as they were, these actions were perhaps understandable in the context of the impossible situation that had arisen. But there followed one of the most shameful events in American history. Within two months of the outbreak of war, an order was issued for all those of Japanese descent living on the West Coast (the great majority of the Japanese-American population) to be interned. They remained in concentration camps until almost the end of the war.

Ostensibly, the internment order was a safety measure, to protect the West Coast against fifth-columnists in the event of Japanese attack. The coastal areas were designated a war zone. But on what basis were American citizens assumed to be disloyal? The military commander who initiated the evacuation, General DeWitt, used the notoriously disingenuous argument that "the very fact that no sabotage has taken place to date is a disturbing and confirming indication that such action will be taken."[13] When asked why Nisei were being singled out and not Italians or German-Americans, California's attorney general (Earl Warren, later Chief Justice of the Supreme Court) replied:

> We believe that when we are dealing with the Caucasian race we have methods that will test the loyalty of the. . . . But when we deal with the Japanese we are in an entirely different field and we cannot form any opinion that we believe to be sound.[14]

The internment order was carried out with strong public approval on the West Coast and a willingness to accommodate on the East. In the process of approving the measure, there seems to have been remarkably little concern over its constitutionality—in particular, the apparent violation of the Fifth Amendment, guaranteeing that no person could be deprived of his or her liberty without due process of law, and the Fourteenth Amendment, guaranteeing equal protection under the law for all citizens. The assistant war secretary, John J. McCloy, a key figure in the internment, is quoted as saying: ". . . if it is a question of the safety of the country (and) the Constitution . . . why the Constitution is just a scrap of paper to me."[15]

By the end of the war, the legality of the internment was to be effectively discredited in the courts. But the Japanese-Americans themselves chose to show their loyalty in the only way left open to them at the time, by complying obediently with the internment orders. Although the evacuation took place over a period of months, Japanese-Americans in any given area were furnished only a week's notice before they had to appear at relocation stations equipped with no more than they could carry in a suitcase. Businesses and property that had been built up over painful decades was relinquished at distress prices. The evacuees were escorted under armed guard onto trains and buses for a grueling journey of 72 hours or more. Altogether, over 100,000 Japanese and Japanese-Americans were evacuated in this way, to 11 concentration camps in the desert lands of the Southwest.

By the end of the war, the unfairness and probable illegality of the internment were widely acknowledged. But it was not until 1988, 43 years after its end, that the U.S. Congress voted to provide a tangible gesture of apology to the victims, in the form of a $20,000 cash payment to every surviving internee (due to budgetary restrictions, the settlement has yet to be paid). One cannot help wondering if this gesture against past discrimination may not be connected with the vital role in America's economy that Japan has recently come to play.

As a way of proving their loyalty, the Japanese-Americans' acceptance of internment was, if personally painful, hardly convincing for the rest of the nation. It appeared, after all, to constitute an acknowledgment that they did indeed present a security threat. However, in 1943, they were given a chance to make a more compelling impression. A Japanese-American regiment was formed with an initial strength of 4,200, of whom 1,500 were released from internment and the remaining 2,700 were from Hawaii (where, due to the high Japanese component of the population, internment had been impossible). The 442nd Infantry Regiment fought heroically in North Africa, Italy, and France, suffering 9,486 casualties, including 600 dead. The unit won 43 division commendations, 13 army commendations, and 7 Presidential Distinguished Unit Citations, as well as a total of 18,000 individual decorations, including 1 Congressional Medal of Honor and 52 Distinguished Service Crosses. There is no doubt that, receiving as it did intensive press attention during its hard-fought campaigns, the Japanese-American regiment was responsible for awakening Americans to the loyalty of their fellow citizens and to the harsh discrimination to which they had been subjected.

After the war, moves to provide equal treatment both

to Japanese-Americans and to Japanese immigrants were made quite rapidly and to near-universal popular assent. In 1947, a measure was enacted to allow residence in the United States for the Japanese wives of American servicemen. These were the first Japanese to emigrate legally to the United States since the exclusion law of 1924. In 1952, a new immigration law provided the right of American citizenship to Japanese resident in the United States, and further immigration from Japan was permitted under conditions similar to those applicable to other nations. In 1956, a referendum in California to repeal a law prohibiting land ownership by Japanese aliens was approved by an overwhelming majority. (Today, as we enter the 1990s, the wheel may be turning full circle, as a movement grows to place new limits on foreign investment in American land and assets.)

Reconciliation, however, came too late for some Japanese-Americans. Embittered by their treatment at the hands of their countrymen, more than 1,000 chose to renounce their American citizenship and start new lives in Japan. An additional 2,000 American citizens accompanied their parents, who were among the 1,700 Japanese alien residents who chose to give up the struggle in the United States and return to their homeland.

The postwar era has seen a much more complete integration of Japanese-Americans into American society. A number of factors have contributed: the exemplary deportment of Japanese-Americans, in and out of uniform, during the war; the formal adoption by the United States of nondiscriminatory immigration policies; the success of minority rights activists and the growth of the antidiscrimination movement; the high levels of educational and economic achievement of Japanese-Americans; the growth of Japan as a major world power by peaceful means; and the arrival of many more waves of immigrants from other parts of Asia. Today, immigration from Asia constitutes almost 50% of the total influx to the United States. Japan constitutes less than 2% of Asian immigration (the present rate of immigration from Japan is only about 4,000 people a year). On a cumulative basis, Americans of Japanese ancestry (including mixed blood) constitute only about 0.35% of the population, numbering 791,000 in 1980.

But as Japanese-Americans have successfully integrated, and as they have achieved their goals of success in American society, they have also become much less Japanese. The Nisei generation (second-generation Japanese-Americans) are now grandparents, and their grandchildren know as little about their ancestral country as fourth-generation Americans of Polish ancestry might know about theirs. Indeed, the very term "Japanese-American" is losing its meaning, as interracial marriages blur distinctions. Perhaps the present boom in Japanese investment and business development in the United States will lead to a new influx of Issei, or first-generation immigrants, from Japan. But, coming as they do from the world's second-richest nation, their circumstances will be altogether different from those of the humble laborers who started trickling into the country just a century ago.

Endnotes

[1] Clyde V. Prestowitz, Jr., *Trading Places: How We Allowed Japan to Take the Lead* (New York: Basic Books, 1988).
[2] Shintaro Ishihara, *The Japan That Can Say No* (New York: Simon & Schuster, 1991).
[3] Ibid., p. 20.
[4] Ibid., p. 21.
[5] George Friedman and Meredith LeBard, *The Coming War with Japan* (New York: St. Martin's Press, 1991).
[6] Ibid.
[7] Ibid.
[8] Kenichi Ohmae, *The Borderless World* (New York: Harper Business, 1990).
[9] Ishihara, *The Japan That Can Say NO*, p. 28.
[10] Edward Graham and Paul Krugman, *Foreign Direct Investment in the United States* (Washington, D.C.: Institute for International Economics, 1989), p. 64.
[11] Robert Wilson and Bill Hosokawa, *East to America: A History of the Japanese in the United States* (New York: William Morrow, 1980), p. 119.
[12] Ibid., p. 121.

[13] Ibid., p. 234.
[14] Ibid., p. p.197.
[15] Ibid., p. p.196.

3 THE BEST OF BOTH WORLDS

In a successful deal, both sides win. The United States has a lot to gain from foreign investment, both indirectly and directly. Some of the potential gains include

- Continued financing of federal budget deficits
- Reduction of the trade deficit
- Introduction of new technologies
- Increased export potential
- Increased employment

Of course, not all these benefits will be achieved in every case, but equally, it would be unwise for the United States to cut itself off from access to these benefits unless there were very compelling costs to outweigh them.

That doesn't mean there shouldn't be rules of play. The U.S. government has some rules already in place, and it is reviewing others to increase protection of Americans from the damage that could be caused by foreign investment. The measures that the U.S. government should adopt are

1. *Continued screening of foreign acquisitions of U.S. companies for potential threats to U.S. defense capabilities.* Clearly, the United States does not want foreigners—and history has shown that any foreigner, no matter how friendly today, may one day be an enemy—to

control technologies that are vital to national defense, or to have access to United States defense secrets. The Exon-Florio rule provides the necessary protection. This policy is now being fairly applied.

2. *Implementation of antitrust rules.* The United States has tough rules to prevent excessive concentration in industries or the manipulation of prices at the expense of competitors or consumers. The rules apply, of course, to foreigners doing business in America as much as they do to Americans. These rules have been responsible for dramatic restructuring of the shape of American business, such as the breakup of AT&T.

During the past decade, antitrust rules have not been strictly enforced. The attitude of the Reagan administration was often described as laissez-faire and pro-business.

But antitrust rules are our best protection against unfair competition by Japanese-owned companies in the United States. The law has defined what is unfair. All the government needs to do is enforce the law. If a U.S. acquisition would threaten to give a Japanese company undue control over an industry, then the acquisition should be blocked. Similarly, if there is evidence that Japanese companies are engaging in unfair competition in the United States through price-fixing, formation of cartels, or other collusive practices, then these companies can and should be prosecuted. The laws are already in place.

3. *Ensuring full compliance of Japanese firms with U.S. laws.* There are a host of laws and regulations that, if properly enforced, will protect U.S. consumers, and the U.S. economy, from damage that might be caused by foreign buyers. These include equal opportunity laws, which protect U.S. workers from discrimination based on race or sex, and accounting rules, which ensure that companies report their earnings fairly and pay Uncle Sam what they owe. Again, it is compliance

with the law that is at issue: the laws themselves already provide adequate protection to Americans.

Some Japanese companies have complained that they are singled out for excessive investigation under U.S. laws, compared to American companies or other foreign companies. But if the Japanese companies are complying with U.S. law, there should be nothing to fear from a high level of oversight. The public relations benefits could be substantial if Japanese firms show themselves to be free of violations.

But there are any number of expert advisors and concerned citizens providing advice to the government—some free, others for a hefty charge. More important is that individual U.S. businesspersons and business owners should follow a few simple guidelines in assessing the desirability of Japanese investment in their enterprises. An intelligent assessment of the threats to Americans from a Japanese involvement in their company might well head off unpleasant controversy in future. There is a responsible approach to soliciting Japanese investment—one that can maximize the benefits to business owners while protecting ordinary Americans and the American economy.

Here are some guidelines:

1. *Don't compromise your nation's defense.* If you are involved in research or manufacturing that is vital to the nation's defense effort, don't look for Japanese investors or buyers. Chances are the deal would be prevented by the Committee on Foreign Investment in the United States under Exon-Florio. But why subject yourself and your employees to such an inquisition? Presumably the government has found you to be a responsible and patriotic citizen—otherwise, they wouldn't be dealing with you (we hope). You can show your patriotism by keeping your technology and the government's secrets under American control.

2. *Choose a responsible buyer.* There's a difference between selling out to a responsible multinational company

and selling to the *yakuza* (Japan's answer to the Mafia). Responsible buyers are aware of their societal obligations, and they will have proved this through past actions. They will show a commitment to being responsible corporate citizens, protecting jobs, paying taxes, contributing to their communities, and building your business over the long term.

Not all potential buyers fit that description. If someone you're negotiating with has a reputation for stripping companies down and selling off assets (actually more a European practice than a Japanese one), union busting, reselling at the first sign of a profit, holding for capital appreciation without making use of the assets, or using funds borrowed from dubious sources, then consider looking for a more attractive party to deal with.

Naturally, you won't solve the problem just by selling to an American company with the same undesirable characteristics. This guideline actually has less to do with nationality than with common sense and basic responsibility.

3. *Look for synergies.* Business academics often say that four acquisitions out of five don't really make sense. In most cases, the buyer pays a higher premium than will ever be recovered from future improvements in the selling company's earnings. The only acquisition that is really justified on economic grounds is one in which the buying company can add some competitive or economic advantage that will create synergies: the value of the whole will be greater than the sum of the two parts run separately.

Of course, sellers on the whole don't worry too much about synergies: once they've pocketed their cash, they're usually out of the picture. But identification of potential synergies can actually be very useful to the seller. It can help in finding the right buyer, it can greatly strengthen the negotiating hand of the seller, and it can benefit the national economy by increasing efficiency.

Synergies are particularly important if you are planning to stay with the company after the acquisition. You want to preside over a period of rising prosperity, due to the value that the seller was able to add.

Looking for synergies is helpful whether you are selling to an American or a Japanese company. Japanese companies are not noticeably better or worse than American companies at picking acquisitions that make real economic sense. But Japanese companies do have some major benefits that they may offer American acquisition targets, in addition to piles of cash. Foremost among these is access to vibrant Japanese and Asian markets.

The Andrew Jergens Company, maker of a well-known U.S. toiletry brand, was able to introduce some of its specialty products in Japan after being acquired by Japan's Kao Corporation. At the same time, Kao has been marketing its products in the United States through the Jergens network. The result: increased sales for both sides.

Japanese buyers will naturally be impressed when approached with a convincing analysis of how value may be created through a merger. Ultimately, they may not base their purchase decision on this added value—they tend to be driven by longer-term strategic motivations. But the fact remains that it is hard to fault an acquisition where added value was clearly created, and all sides clearly benefited.

4. *Protect your employees.* Some analysts are concerned that foreign acquisitions will have the impact of reducing American employment as jobs are shipped abroad. Particularly alarming is the idea that the most valuable jobs—research and development (R&D), for example—will be the first to go, leaving a marginalized, semiskilled work force in place.

In fact, most Japanese buyers are extremely anxious to retain employees in businesses they acquire, in order to maintain continuity and minimize disruption. Unlike many acquisitions by American companies, wholesale layoffs are not usually the first action taken by Japanese buyers.

But, to ensure that your employees do not suffer from falling into the hands of a Japanese buyer, there is no reason not to negotiate on behalf of employees' rights in the purchase agreement. You may seek commitments to provide minimum levels of job security, to avoid layoffs, or to continue research and development activities. From the Japanese point of view, there may be considerable public relations benefits from publicizing these kinds of clauses in a purchase agreement, which only formalize what the buyer probably intended to do anyway.

5. *Don't sell technology too cheaply.* The Japanese are well known for being adept negotiators. According to one analysis, Japanese companies paid only $17 billion for 34,000 license agreements during the past four decades. That represents only a fraction of one year's R&D expenditure in the United States. Certainly, there was a tendency in the past to underestimate the threat from the uses Japanese companies might develop for American technologies. But U.S. companies should by now have their eyes fully opened.

Some American high-tech companies are so desperate for capital that they would effectively sell all their secrets in exchange for a few million to tide them over the next fiscal year. Unfortunately, the U.S. venture capital system works only sporadically and is subject to cyclical droughts as investors and banks shy away from the risks inherent in high-tech investing.

It's hard to argue with a company that accepts Japanese money because without it, it would be forced to close down. If you are in that situation, you may literally have no choice, and we just have to blame the system if the Japanese walk off with an important new technology as a result.

But if you have any room for maneuver at all, remember that the technology you are developing is a precious national asset, and do your best—for your own sake as well as your country's—to protect it as such. That means if you are going to sell it to the Japanese, sell it for a price that compensates for the benefits it may create for Japanese industry, and for the threat it may create for American industry. Make sure that the benefits will remain available to Americans. Ensure that research will remain on American soil, and that access will be guaranteed for American buyers in the future.

6. *Consider other options.* All too many American concerns are lured by stories of massive premiums paid by Japanese buyers, to seek a Japanese investor without exploring other alternatives.

That is just not good business sense. There may be viable alternatives that add up to a better deal than the Japanese can offer. At the very least, you may be able to use an alternative offer as a bargaining chip.

Before entering into serious negotiations with Japanese investors, answer to your own satisfaction the following questions:

- What are my goals in seeking a buyer? Is it just to cash out? Are there other ways to do that, for example, American buyers, public stock offerings, special dividends, and so on?

- What synergies will be created by selling to a Japanese investor? Is there an American buyer for whom the synergies would be greater?

- Are there alternatives to outright sale, for example, joint venture, partial divestiture, or reformulated business strategy?

Although the Japanese have become well known for paying high prices, a Japanese buyer may not be the answer for your particular situation.

Case Studies

In a successful deal, both sides win. Of course, it's possible to make a killing at the expense of the other party. But how many long term business relationships are based on that kind of an approach? If both sides come out winners, nobody can complain.

Let's look at three case studies of Japanese investments in American companies where clearly everyone benefited.

New Faith in Manufacturing: Firestone Tire Plant in LaVergne, Tennessee

When Firestone Tire and Rubber Company built a new plant in a quiet town near Nashville, the future looked bright for the community and for the industry. The year was 1972. Demand for automotive products had been growing throughout the boom years of the 1960s, and the new plant would help meet the demand in the fast-growing radial truck tire segment. The "greenfield" site (i.e., built from nothing) in the newly developing sunbelt was to be a symbol of good labor relations and the benefits of industrial investment in a rural community.

Those hopes were never realized. For a variety of reasons that perhaps represent the story of America's industrial problems in microcosm, the plant never reached profitability, and in 1981 the company decided they must either sell it or close it.

The oil crisis was the first setback. When oil prices shot up in 1973, demand for new vehicles plummeted. Truck owners, faced with a crisis of costs brought on by high fuel prices and a shrinking economy, became far more conservative in their use and replacement of tires. This was a particular problem for Firestone, because tires made at the LaVergne plant were good only for two retreads, while some competitors' lasted through three or four.

Product quality was another problem. Radial tires require a very high standard of manufacturing precision compared with the traditional "bias" tire design. Firestone was relatively inexperienced at large-scale production of radial truck and bus tires. In spite of intensive efforts to monitor product quality (there were 18 roving inspectors in the LaVergne plant alone), quality problems were endemic. In the automotive division, Firestone had to recall 14 million radial passenger car tires due to failures that had allegedly caused 41 deaths. In the truck division, the company started losing customers to highly aggressive competitors.

Labor relations was another factor in the developing fiasco. Originally nonunion, the work force gradually came under the influence of the United Rubber Workers union, which eventually demanded formal recognition. When management refused, the work force came out on strike. Another equally bitter confrontation occurred when union and management failed to agree on a contract.

All these problems were compounded by the distance of the senior decision makers, who remained in Akron, Ohio, at the Firestone corporate headquarters. Even minor decisions often had to be made or approved by Akron, causing constant delays and misunderstandings.

By 1981, the LaVergne plant was still operating at only 50% of capacity. Management decided to offer the plant for sale, and eventually laid off two-thirds of the work force in 1982. For Firestone, this was just one episode in a painful long-term contraction that left the company with only five plants and half the work force of a decade earlier at the time of its ultimate sale to Bridgestone Corporation in 1988.

The LaVergne plant was offered to Bridgestone, which at that time had no connections to Firestone. Bridgestone can hardly be said to have jumped at the chance to buy the ailing, strife-ridden plant. It was on the block for a year before the Japanese came to look at it. When Bridgestone finally entered into negotiations with Firestone (in spite of their similar names, the two companies were unconnected) in late 1981, the Japanese made it clear that any purchase would be contingent on gaining a satisfactory contract with the labor force.

Finally, in the summer of 1982, a delegation from Bridgestone came to visit LaVergne to discuss matters directly with the union. The meeting was a disaster.

The president of the union local became overheated during the debate, and when the Japanese would not yield a point, he told them that in that case they might as well just go back to Japan. They did. The next morning when the union official tried to call them to smooth things over, he was told they had already checked out and left.

That was really the last thing that the union members wanted. If Bridgestone did not buy the plant, it would almost certainly be closed. The union eventually invited Bridgestone back to the negotiating table and offered certain changes in work rules.

The last obstacle cleared, the deal was signed in January 1983. Bridgestone bought the LaVergne plant for $52 million.

The new Japanese owners didn't fire a single worker or manager. Rather, they recalled all the workers laid off by Firestone. They accepted union representation. Yet within four years, output at the plant quadrupled, productivity increased by 70%, quality problems decreased by 60%, and injuries dropped to one of the lowest levels in the industry.

Plant managers were expecting the Japanese to send in an army of new managers and effectively start things off with a clean sweep. They didn't. Instead, they sent in a team of six managers and 30 "advisors." Mostly young technicians dedicated to the concept of "total quality control," these advisors saw their role as sharing a technology and working on specialized problems, rather than handing out orders. As one American manager put it, "They'd make you think. They'd give you a bunch of scenarios—"Have you thought about this?"—They wouldn't tell you what to do." The advisors insisted on confronting problems and working out solutions.

A huge emphasis was placed on training. Aided by a $300,000 subsidy from the state of Tennessee, Bridgestone devoted 50,000 person-hours over a period of five years to training its work force. For many employees and managers, training included a visit to Bridgestone's headquarters and plants in Japan. There, they saw how Japanese management concepts had reduced unnecessary tasks, automated labor-intensive processes, and ensured a standard of cleanliness high enough that carp were kept in ponds full of water recycled from the plant.

Bridgestone took a number of actions to demonstrate commitment to the manufacturing process. Reserved parking spots were eliminated: Managers and employees were now treated equally. Partitions were removed so that engineers, managers, and administrative staff now visibly shared space with their production line colleagues.

Using charts and other quantitative measurement techniques, the Japanese advisors showed their new colleagues how to observe every step in the manufacturing process and to devise new methods of improving efficiency and making workers' jobs easier (and therefore more productive). A group of observers would congregate behind a worker and watch his or her task being performed. As they watched, they would take notes, recording any and every idea that came to them with regard to the process they were watching. Afterward, the observers would get together in a meeting room and discuss their ideas. More often than not, substantial improvements were made in the process. All along, the emphasis was on small, incremental improvements, preferably emanating from the employees themselves rather than on radical change.

The improvements made by Bridgestone did not come cheaply. The plant remained unprofitable for two years, while the new owner pumped in $68 million for training and upgrading of equipment. But the changes, once made, have been long lasting, primarily because they involved a radical adjustment of the attitudes and philosophies of the workers themselves.

Not to say that everything has been perfect between owners and staff. Employees have resented the abandoning of Firestone's suggestion system. Under the previous system, employees were rewarded for a suggestion with 10% of the first year's savings resulting from the suggestion. Bridgestone replaced that with modest dollar awards at the discretion of management. And management has not succeeded in getting all workers interested in so-called "employee involvement groups." Only 30% of the work force regularly participates. Nevertheless, the acquisition of the LaVergne plant by Bridgestone has demonstrated clear benefits for all.

First, Firestone benefited. The company had planned to close down the LaVergne plant. That would have involved large outlays on severance, disposal, and administration of the closure. Instead, Firestone was able to bank $52 million and get the problem off its back at the same time. No American company was willing to step up and offer such a deal.

Then, most important, the employees of the plant. Their jobs were safeguarded—they probably have greater job security now than ever before—and those production employees who had been laid off were called back to work. Since the takeover, employees have been given substantially greater responsibility over their jobs, with a concurrent rise in job satisfaction. More subjectively, the workers now belong to a winning team. The effect on morale is judged to be substantial.

Then the people of LaVergne benefited. A plant that was vital to the local economy has been saved and continues to generate jobs and business for local suppliers.

Last but not least, Bridgestone Corporation itself benefited. Bridgestone had good commercial reasons for wanting to acquire a plant in the United States. Local production eases supply logistics, protects the company against currency fluctuations, and helps ward off protectionist threats. Tennessee was in many ways an ideal choice for Bridgestone to invest in. The state has aggressively sought out Japanese manufacturers, offering generous subsidies and other incentives. Bridgestone benefits not only from state incentives, but also from the proximity of other Japanese companies, such as the Nissan car company, that is located just down the road in Smyrna. Finally, compared to the potential cost of building a plant from nothing, Bridgestone's investment probably represents a bargain, from which the company may reap benefits over many profitable years.

A Friend in Need: Materials Research Corporation

Dr. Sheldon Weinig is a model of the American entrepreneur. Asked to introduce himself, he starts by saying: "I think I'm the last remaining native New Yorker." In the study of his comfortable Manhattan apartment, looking down over a silver-gray stretch of the East River, his feet propped on a footstool and his pedigree dogs at his side, Dr. Weinig exudes belonging. But the story of his attaining the easy comforts of his present life-style is one that he himself says could happen only in America.

Born into a modest family, he attended New York City public schools, including the acclaimed Stuyvesant High. After the war, he earned a B.S. degree from New York University, followed by a Ph.D. in metallurgy from Columbia. He joined the faculty at Columbia, eventually transferring to a professorship at NYU.

But after some teaching and academic research, Weinig quit to start his own company. "It wasn't the money that got me down about academic life: I had a lucrative consulting practice on the side. The problem was the bureaucracy."

With a minimum outlay, Weinig rented rooms over a yo-yo factory in Yonkers, New York, and started Materials Research Corporation (MRC). The company was conceived as a consulting enterprise, whose mission was to help improve the quality of materials used by high-technology companies. Weinig's axiom was, and remains, that "materials are the keyhole to the advance of all technology." Advances in semiconductors, ceramics, and superconducting materials have more than confirmed this premise.

MRC's business soon expanded to lab work. In new premises in Orangeburg, New York, MRC became a pioneer in the creation of highly pure materials for industrial use. During the 1960s, the company developed expertise in the manufacture of "thin-film" coatings that proved vital to the semiconductor industry. MRC developed important relationships with IBM and Texas Instruments. The company also assisted Gillette in developing platinum-coated razor blades.

MRC went public in 1970, and by the mid-1980s had become a $150-million-a-year company with plants in the United States, Europe, and Japan and over 1,500 employees. The company's growth had been financed through stock offerings and borrowing, and for a while MRC was a darling of the Wall Street financial community. During the course of this growth, Sheldon Weinig became a wealthy man.

But although his company had grown beyond the wildest dreams of its early days in a cramped room in Yonkers, MRC remained a small company by the standards of the immense outlays required for high-technology development. A single mistake could floor the company.

One nearly did.

In 1983, MRC engineers developed a machine called the Waferline that was intended to set a new standard in thin-film coating. Initial sales were promising, and Weinig was buoyed by the immense prospects for the technology. But before long, a problem became apparent. The Waferline machine was so sophisticated—or so complex—that users were unable to operate it without MRC's assistance. Minor bugs were constantly surfacing, and the only way MRC could assure smooth operation was by supplying a technician to supervise use of the machine. "A critic summed it up nicely when they said that the machine was great so long as you had a neurosurgeon and a psychiatrist to keep it running," says Weinig, without specifying whether the psychiatrist was needed for the machine or the user.

Weinig sunk more money into improving the Waferline. It had become so important—and expensive—that the company's future depended on it succeeding. But finally, in 1986, Weinig conceded that the machine was a failure. Faced with losing his most valued customers, he agreed to buy back all the Waferlines that MRC had sold. The buyback cost millions, and the company was financially devastated by it.

But Weinig would not admit defeat. "My theory," he says, "is that a huge failure like the Waferline can have two effects on a company. Either it goes under, or it comes back stronger than ever before, having learned its lesson in the hardest possible way." Weinig cites the example of Sony's Betamax video system. "Sony tried to go its own way, and it took a severe beating as a result. So when it developed the 8-millimeter format, it made sure that its competitors had access to the technology. Now everyone uses the same standard, and the product's been a wild success." MRC developed a new thin-film coating machine called the Eclipse, and this time the market's reception was enthusiastic.

However, the Waferline fiasco, and an expensive voluntary retirement program that followed it, had sapped the company's financial resources. MRC lacked the working capital to build Eclipse machines fast enough. (They sold for up to $2 million each.) By 1989, it became apparent that MRC was on the brink of collapse.

Weinig was not without friends. New York's money center banks had been assiduously pursuing MRC for years, and Chase Manhattan had made such an impressive pitch that Weinig had made them his lead banker. So he turned to them to help him in his hour of need. But bankers have a tendency to fall in love with success and to shy away from riskier ventures. MRC's recent history had given Chase cold feet. Anyway, said the financial giant, Chase was "getting out of the high-tech business," at least for small and midsized firms.

Although this was the height of the Reagan-era boom, and the investment market was as strong as it had ever been, technology companies were out of favor. They had never recovered the heady status they had achieved prior to the 1987 stock market crash. And MRC's glory days had been soured by the Waferline episode. When Weinig turned to Wall Street for assistance, he was given the cold shoulder again. The outlook for a share issue was very poor. Drexel Burnham Lambert suggested a "junk bond" issue, but even as a Wall Street outsider, Weinig could see that the high fixed interest costs were not appropriate for a growth company like MRC. Another investment bank proposed liquidating MRC.

Disheartened and increasingly desperate, Weinig turned to his customers. He realized that he would have to sell some or all of the company in order to save it. IBM had invested $250 million in Intel to see it through a similar problem period, and had eventually sold its stake for a 400% gain. Weinig approached IBM and other large customers to discuss a similar investment. But all declined.

Finally, Weinig hired an investment bank that specialized in German and Swiss acquisitions to negotiate the sale of MRC to a Swiss conglomerate. Negotiations proceeded relatively smoothly, but Weinig was less than enthusiastic about the deal. "As things went on, I saw that this was not going to be a happy marriage. The people we were dealing with just had different interests from those I foresaw for the company." Finally, as negotiations with the Swiss company reached their climax, Weinig thought of an old acquaintance and fellow-physicist who was now vice chairman of Sony USA, Dr. Michael ("Mickey") Schulhof.

Schulhof and Weinig had recently been discussing the application of MRC's thin-film technologies to compact audio and optical discs manufactured by Sony. They had also discussed the long-range prospects for Sony investing in MRC. But Sony was not a significant customer of MRC, nor was there any existing relationship between the two firms.

Weinig takes up the story: "I picked up the phone and called Mickey on a Tuesday. I reminded him that we had once discussed Sony making an investment in the company when the time was right. 'Well,' I said, 'the time is right.' 'Great,' says Mickey, 'I'd love to look at the idea. Of course it's August now and nobody much is around, but if you send me some information, I'll get back to you in a few weeks.' 'No Mickey,' I reply, 'you don't understand what I'm saying. I mean the time is right . . . NOW!'"

Weinig sent Schulhof all the documents that had been prepared to assist the Swiss company. On Thursday, the Swiss company made its "final offer" and demanded a response by Monday. "Mickey Schulhof and his investment bankers were examining the data we'd sent them around the clock. By the weekend, they were ready to recommend making an offer. The problem was, no offer could be made until the decision was ratified by the Management Committee of Sony in Tokyo, which meets on Tuesday mornings. That's Monday evening, New York time."

An assistant in Sony's New York office spent the whole of Sunday night faxing documents to Tokyo. On Monday morning, Weinig convened with his lawyers and financial advisors. A call soon came from the Swiss company, demanding the response to their offer. "We just kept stalling them, through the day," admits Weinig. Finally, at 7:00 P.M., word came that Sony's Management Committee had approved the purchase of MRC. The letter of intent was signed that same evening. The whole acquisition had been put together in only six days.

The purchase price for the company was $56 million. But the company also had substantial debt, and needed an immediate cash infusion. Weinig puts the total initial investment by Sony at close to $100 million.

"Once the deal was made public, the proverbial 'blank' hit the fan," says Weinig. "When the company was up for grabs, no one was interested. Now that it's being sold to the Japanese, oh my, our high-tech industry is being sold off to the enemy. MRC is a national asset. Our national defense capability is being threatened. What I want to know is, where were all these voices when my company was threatening to close down altogether?"

Weinig was required to testify before the Exon-Florio Committee, which reviews acquisitions that may pose a threat to national security. Weinig pointed out that the alternative to the sale was probably closure. He also argued that the technology would remain in the United States and would still be available to existing customers. Employees and managers, including Weinig, who signed a five-year contract, would still be American. "I told them that if there was a real case of national emergency, the company would still be here for the government to nationalize." The sale was approved—as it turned out, it was the last such deal to be approved before the committee adopted a much tougher stance against high-tech acquisitions.

Once the deal closed, the staff of MRC waited in trepidation for the changes that the new ownership would bring. In the event, all that happened was that Mickey Schulhof arrived in a corporate helicopter and threw a welcoming party for the entire staff. As a "party favor," all employees were given an extra week's pay.

Since the acquisition, change at MRC has been hard to discern, and, says Weinig, such change as there has been is all positive. Unlike the case of Bridgestone, Sony has left management at MRC completely untouched. There is only one Japanese employee on Weinig's staff: a Sony man, who is assigned to ensure adequate liaison with Sony in Tokyo and New York. "Actually," says Weinig, "I wish at times that Sony would get a little more involved with the management of MRC. I feel at times that we're not really being integrated into the family." In particular, Weinig feels that MRC is left out of Sony's long-term planning process. "We don't yet share their vision of the future."

But Weinig has no complaints about the tangible encouragement he receives from Sony. "Our R&D budget has tripled since the acquisition. And our staff had increased by 25%." MRC was able to take advantage of recession in high-tech industry to hire top quality staff from competitors. "Thanks to Sony, we are able to pursue our mission, which is to be leaders in creating excellence in thin films."

In addition Sony, which is the largest user of thin-film coatings in the world, has become a major customer of MRC, funding special research projects to develop more new technologies. Weinig emphasizes that Sony is by no means an easy customer in spite of the corporate relationship. "They are so demanding that they set new standards for our managers and designers." Weinig adds: "There is no guarantee at all that Sony will use us to fill their needs. We have a banner in our headquarters that reads simply 'WIN SONY.' It means just that." Weinig worries at times that the rigor of Sony's demands as a customer may be counterproductive. "They never pat you on the back. If they ask for something with a standard of, say, 80, and your people stay up all night busting their guts and give them 90, they'll come back and say: 'Now why can't you reach 95?'" Nevertheless, the benefits from the Sony acquisition are clear.

First, MRC was saved from possible collapse and was permitted to carry on its mission of leadership and excellence in thin-film technology. No American company or financier would make that possible.

Next, Sheldon Weinig made a small fortune from the sale. He also continues to manage the company.

Then, the company was given access to massively increased funding as well as an entirely new customer base, although Weinig feels more could be done to expand business in Japan through Sony's contact network. All this without any layoffs, disruptive management changes, or onerous interference from the new owner. Moreover, the company has retained all its important customers. "If anything, our relations with them are enhanced," says Weinig. "They see us as a stronger player now."

From Sony's point of view, MRC represented an opportunity to buy a leading research arm in a technology that is crucial to its future product strategies. Weinig explains the importance as follows: "Sony is traditionally perceived as being in two industries: audio, with CD and cassette players as hardware, and with CBS Records providing software; and video, with televisions and VCRs as hardware, and with Columbia Pictures providing the software. But in reality, there's a third layer. Sony is a worldwide leader in manufacturing technologies. In addition to CD players and televisions, Sony sells its manufacturing process technologies to its competitors. Its competitive advantage in this field is key to its success."

Although Sony did not enter the deal with an expectation of immediate profits from MRC, in the event MRC's potential has been strongly realized since the acquisition, and the company has had record sales and earnings. Although he would not give specific figures, Weinig maintains that the acquisition has been profitable to Sony from a return on investment perspective.

Turning the Tables: NUMMI

Even more dramatic has been the success of Toyota's NUMMI joint venture with General Motors.

In 1982, the General Motors plant in Fremont, California, was a veritable symbol of industrial decline. Productivity was dismally low and was actually declining. Absenteeism ran at 20% or more. There were no fewer than 5,000 worker grievances on the union's agenda. Bitter strikes were a way of life, often flaring over trivial causes, and frequently erupting into violence. Communication between management and workers was virtually nonexistent. In that year, General Motors decided to abandon the struggle, and the factory was closed, ostensibly for good.

But a year later, General Motors entered into a joint venture with the Toyota Motor Company, named New United Motor Manufacturing, Inc., and generally known as NUMMI. The Japanese partners agreed to reopen the Fremont factory, under Toyota management, to make a Chevrolet Nova that was modeled on the Toyota Corolla.

Many skeptics were convinced that Toyota had bitten off more than it could chew—it would take a miracle to bring the factory up to industry standards.

But Toyota not only undertook the task, it even hired back 2,500 of the militant United Auto Workers Union members who had precipitated the demise.

Within three short years, the Fremont plant became the most productive automobile factory in the United States, producing 63 cars annually per worker, or 40% above the national average. The Toyota-produced Nova takes just 21 person-hours to assemble, compared with 38 for GM's most comparable model, the Chevrolet Cavalier—and this in a relatively nonautomated plant. And NUMMI workers work on average for 55 seconds out of every minute, compared to 46 in comparable GM plants.

Toyota abandoned GM's cumbersome system of over 100 job classifications in favor of a team approach, with members trained to perform several tasks. Managers abandoned their traditional perks such as privileged parking lots and private dining rooms. Workers were encouraged to take responsibility for their own tasks, and have often devised much more labor-efficient procedures. Absenteeism now runs under 2%, and it was recently reported that only two worker grievances were outstanding.

Toyota managers were on an absolutely level playing field in proving their skills: The plant has the same workers, the same technology, the same buildings and equipment; only the managers have changed. Yet the difference between the factory before and after the change seems truly miraculous.

Certainly, General Motors has benefited from NUMMI's success in producing efficient, low-cost automobiles. But the benefits may ultimately be much more profound. GM has had an opportunity to see Japanese management practices in action, and the auto giant has evidently taken many of the lessons to heart. GM's latest venture, the Saturn project, has incorporated many of the practices that GM observed working so well in NUMMI.

The entire management technology of America's largest company has been profoundly affected. Unfortunately, changes have not come in time to prevent severe retrenchment at GM, which recently announced a wrenching program of layoffs.

Toyota also benefited by gaining knowledge of manufacturing in an American environment, before launching a full-scale manufacturing operation in the United States.

Conclusion

The lesson from these three case studies is that both sides can win from Japanese investment. Japanese companies have more than just money to offer. In a well-conceived transaction, U.S. companies can benefit from Japanese management skills and technical know-how, as well as from the vast capital resources and market opportunities offered by Japan. Nobody lost from these deals—not the participants, not the U.S. taxpayer, and certainly not the workers who would otherwise have been out on the street. Not all deals will result in the near-miraculous benefits described in these cases. But in a well thought out, carefully constructed deal, all the parties should be winners.

4 WHY HERE?

Why are the Japanese buying American companies?

It's important to know the answers to this question for two reasons. First, it's impossible to form any meaningful conclusion in the debate about Japanese investment without first understanding the underlying causes of the investment and the implications of those causes for future trends.

Second, understanding what the Japanese want will help American businesspeople identify opportunities to find the right deals on the best possible terms: deals that satisfy the needs of Americans and Japanese alike.

As one might expect, the reasons for the increased Japanese investment in the United States are not always simple or clear cut. Analysts have at times disagreed sharply over the motivations of Japanese buyers. In the final analysis, perhaps even the buyers themselves do not always fully understand the reasons for their actions.

Some of the reasons are financial, others strategic.

Financial Motives

Japan has been creating cash on a vast scale through the 1980s, more, perhaps, than the Japanese know what to do with.

The situation is in some ways reminiscent of the Arab wealth of the 1970s. When the price of oil leaped up in 1973, millionaire Saudi princes suddenly became multibillionaires. Exasperated buyers were pouring millions of dollars every day into the oil producers' pockets. Westerners quickly became accustomed to the sight of shiny limousines spilling white-robed men and veiled women onto the sidewalks in front of the world's great shopping districts.

But there was a limit to what the princes could buy with this gushing stream of cash. Where was the money to go? The princes already enjoyed nearly-absolute power in their own countries: there was little more that money could buy. There was little or no domestic industry in which to invest the surpluses. The Saudis, Kuwaitis, Bahrainis, and others found themselves sitting on huge, dollar-denominated bank accounts that they could not possibly spend on their own. Meanwhile, the dollar was losing its value due to the inflation created by the Arabs' own price hikes.

The Arabs had to invest the money, and they chose two ways to do so. First, they invested vast sums to turn their desert countries into modern industrial states. Not only did they make life more comfortable by building air-conditioned offices, water desalination plants, and superhighways; they also bought insurance against future downturns in oil revenues by diversifying into other industries, such as refining and agriculture. Even these huge expenditures did not sop up all the revenues, especially in the smaller Gulf states. The remainder, the princes invested in the Western industrial system, buying stocks and bonds and taking direct stakes in industrial enterprises. Kuwait's $100 billion nest egg served her in good stead during and after the agony of the Iraqi invasion.

The Japanese export boom of the 1980s is in some ways similar to the oil boom of the 1970s. The extraordinary successes of Japan's industrial concerns have created vast surpluses that have to be, so to speak, recycled. Like those of the Arabs in the 1970s, Japanese companies' bank accounts are bulging with dollars.

The amount of money created has been so great that the Japanese economy simply cannot absorb it. Domestic spending has been growing rapidly as consumer demand has surged. And Japanese companies have been investing unprecedented amounts in capital equipment as well as research and development. These investments almost guarantee that Japanese companies will continue to play a leading role in world industry. But they are not enough to mop up the surpluses caused by record profits and massive exports. The recent collapse in the Japanese Stock Market has substantially dried up liquidity in the short-term, but exports and cash balances remain high.

And the surpluses are only a part of the problem. To them, we must add at least three other related factors which have added to Japan's huge cash hoard.

1. *Savings.* The average Japanese family saves about 20% of their after-tax income. That gives Japan the highest savings rate of any country in the industrial world. By contrast, Americans saved only an estimated 3% of their 1990 earnings. Japanese savings are primarily sitting in post office and bank savings accounts (the Japanese post office, if it were counted as a bank, would be the largest in the world). What happens to these funds once they are on deposit? Naturally, they become available for investment in business and economic development—in other words, they add to the cash pile.

2. *Pensions.* Like America, Japan had a baby boom after the war. Only Japan's was even more explosive. Members of the baby boomers are now in their prime earning years, and as the Japanese economy has also grown, the value of their contributions has become immense. Meanwhile, the number of older people that must be cared for out of pension funds is relatively small. Add to that the recent liberalization of the Japanese investment system, which now gives pension funds much more leeway in selecting investments. The result is a massive addition to the nation's liquidity. This liquidity will start to dry up as the baby boomers reach pensionable age—they will then become net consumers of pensions. But that won't start to happen until the turn of the century.

3. *Cheap Money.* For a variety of reasons—including the large amount of funds chasing limited investment opportunities, the government's conservative financial policies, a low inflation rate, a booming stock market, and the very high credit rating of Japanese companies—interest rates were for much of the 1980s among the lowest in the world. The average cost of capital during the period 1984-1988 has been estimated as low as 2%.

Thus, in addition to internally generated funds, Japanese companies have had access to virtually unlimited financing. If they did not borrow money from their own bank, companies could tap the international capital market, which was more than willing to finance the world's strongest enterprises. As another alternative, companies could tap the Japanese stock market, which for much of the decade put an extraordinarily high valuation on companies, allowing them to access one of the cheapest sources of capital in the world. Many large companies took advantage of this simply because it was too good an opportunity to miss.

Since 1988, interest rates have risen substantially, and the stock market has recently experienced a steep decline. These factors may contribute to a slow-down in the Japanese spending spree. But many companies remain in possession of some of the largest accumulations of cash in the world. For example, the Toyota Motor Company reported cash and short-term investments totalling $14.4 billion in its 1990 annual report. With that kind of money, Toyota could buy out virtually any company in the world.

All these, we might call macroeconomic factors that have made foreign investment more likely. We should add to these another vital factor. In 1986, the yen started out on a sustained rise against the dollar. By 1987, the dollar had plunged by 50% against the yen, from a high of 240 yen to a low of 121 yen. This adjustment in values was strongly desired by the U.S. government, in order to give a boost to U.S. exports and to help reduce the U.S. trade deficit. For many Japanese companies it was a disaster, as they found they could no longer offer products at competitive prices—although most companies rapidly adjusted to the more competitive environment.

But the cloud had at least one silver lining. Relative to American acquisition opportunities, Japanese cash had doubled in value. America suddenly seemed like a Japanese shopper's paradise. It is surely not a coincidence that the real surge in Japanese acquisitions started in 1988.

A Question of Returns

These macroeconomic factors have undoubtedly influenced the overall trend toward increased Japanese investment in the U.S. economy.

But individual companies are not generally guided by macroeconomics in their decision making. Their actions are usually prompted by their own individual circumstances.

The key to the vast majority of Japanese investment in the United States is that for much of the 1980s, the United States has offered higher returns than those available in Japan.

Let's take interest rates. From 1984 through 1989, the interest available on U.S. government securities was about five percentage points higher than the interest available on equivalent Japanese securities. The differential for corporate debt was even greater: a Japanese corporation might not be willing to pay more than 3% to 4% on a bond issue, while U.S. corporations with similar credit ratings were paying 10%. For bolder investors, junk bonds were available with coupons up to 15%. These kinds of returns were obviously attractive to Japanese companies, and they explain why the Japanese were huge investors in U.S. Treasury and corporate debt securities during much of the 1980s. So large was their contribution, in fact, that the Japanese played a major role in funding the trade and budget deficits that were the hallmarks of the decade.

Other passive investments, such as stocks and real estate, were also more attractive in the United States. During much of the 1980s, Japanese stock prices were soaring through the roof. The average price/earnings ratio of Japanese stocks reached a high of 70 in 1989. At the time, the U.S. ratio was 15. As a general rule, stock prices go up when interest rates fall, and since Japanese rates have increased, stock prices have indeed moderated. But during much of the decade, American stocks must to Japanese eyes have seemed a very good buy indeed.

Real estate was even more compelling in the United States. Japanese real estate prices went sky-high in the 1980s, with the result that investors have been virtually unable to get any significant return from income-oriented investments. The rents, for example, on an office building would provide a minuscule return on the cost of buying that building.

Although Japanese companies continued to buy real estate in Japan—both to develop it for consumer and commercial markets, and as a speculative investment—many American properties seemed unusually attractive by comparison. A number of large investments were made by Japanese companies in prestigious, top-quality American properties—Rockefeller Center being the best-known example. Real estate investments were estimated as high as $14 billion a year in 1988 to 1990. Although in many cases the Japanese buyers paid extremely high prices by American standards, the returns on these properties may still have seemed attractive when compared with the returns on equivalent investments in Japan.

Strategic Motives

Financially, the time was right. Looked at from this perspective, the surge in Japanese acquisitions in the late 1980s was a logical response to the prevailing financial conditions.

But while the financial picture may explain passive or indirect investments in such instruments as stocks or bonds, it goes only a small way toward explaining why

Japanese companies are making acquisitions in the United States.

Buying a company is not like buying a Treasury note. Once bought, a company must be nurtured and developed. Management problems must be resolved, and a smooth transition ensured to the new ownership. Difficult labor relations issues must be addressed. And a strategy must be developed for integrating the parent with the new subsidiary. Anyone who has gone through an acquisition knows about the enormous expenditure of time and patience required to make the transition successful.

Acquisitions are not normally made for financial motives. Certainly, there are exceptions to this rule. Many so-called "corporate raiders" look for undervalued companies that they can buy and then disassemble, selling the parts for more than they paid for the whole. But that has not yet been a tactic employed by Japanese acquirers. Of course, buyers, including Japanese buyers, expect to receive a return on their investment. But the primary motivation for a corporate acquisition is usually strategic.

What kinds of strategies prompt Japanese acquisitions of American companies? Of course, each case has its own unique features, and the choice of specific targets may have tactical as well as strategic elements.

But the majority of acquisitions are motivated by one or both of two overriding strategic considerations: globalization and technology.

Globalization

"Globalization" has become a buzzword in recent years. Self-respecting analysts, as well as executives of multinational companies, don't like to complete a paragraph without a reference to this fashionable concept. Yet perhaps nobody knows exactly what globalization means.

Japanese companies have been global—in some senses of the word—for most of their history.

When Japan emerged in 1860 from three centuries of self-imposed isolation, she found that to overcome the problems that were besetting her decaying social and economic systems, she had to look outside. Early Japanese delegations studied the political systems of Western nations and eventually drew up a constitution based on the Prussian model. Industrial technologies were imported, as well as the entire paraphernalia of a modern industrial state: railways, telecommunications, architecture, urban planning. By the end of the nineteenth century, Japan had mastered the Western models so effectively that she was able to defeat Russia, one of the great world powers, in a devastating naval confrontation.

Ever since Japan's emergence into the modern era, the lifeblood of that nation's prosperity has been trade. Japan was, until very recently, a poor nation in terms of per capita income. And she remains desperately poor in natural resources. In order to live the life of a modern state, in order to pay for the import of essential raw materials and even food, the Japanese have had to export. In the devastated aftermath of World War II, the need to export became even stronger. There was virtually no domestic market to sell to.

In his book *Made in Japan*,[1] Sony Chairman Akio Morita describes the development of his company from its founding in a bombed-out department store in 1946. The company's first successful product was a magnetic tape recorder, built for sale to the domestic market. But the second major product introduction—the transistor radio introduced in 1957—was a global product. "It was the consensus among Japanese industrialists," comments Morita, "that a Japanese company must export goods in order to survive." With virtually no overseas experience, no marketing training, and limited English, Morita traveled to the United States and personally hawked his company's product around the nation. He relied on the quality and innovativeness of the product to sell itself.

Sony's story is paralleled by those of countless Japanese companies. Throughout the postwar era, it was not uncommon for Japanese companies to have much greater sales abroad than domestically.

So Japanese companies have been globally oriented for decades. Why, then, the sudden emphasis on the concept of "globalization" and the accompanying spate of overseas acquisitions?

One reason is the changing nature of competition. As an exporter, Japan was able to rely on low labor costs at home, and therefore the main strategy used to develop export markets was low prices. The Japanese, effectively, undercut the competition. (Sony was an exception. It has always sold higher-priced products that have unique technological benefits.) However, in recent years Japan has lost its cost advantage. Labor in Japan is now comparably priced with other industrial nations, and many other costs—especially land for building factories—are much higher. Meanwhile, newly developed countries such as Taiwan and Korea have lower labor costs than the Japanese.

An initial response by many Japanese companies was to move production offshore—to open factories in countries where labor was cheap. This may be seen as the first step down the road to globalization.

But American and European companies are also able to open factories in low-cost countries. So the playing field has in some ways been leveled. Instead of labor costs, the Japanese have had to focus on manufacturing costs, working to improve productivity and process efficiency. But many American and European competitors have been hard on their heels in making these improvements.

Instead, the attention of competitors has turned increasingly to the product itself. According to the global concept of doing business, to be successful, a company must provide its customers with the products that they want or need in their specific regional market, at a competitive price. Customer needs may vary from country to country; hence the most effective competitor will be the one which best understands and provides for the local needs of individual markets. The best way to meet these needs is to have a local presence both for marketing, design, and manufacturing.

The concept of globalization has been expounded by many influential academics and business analysts, including the noted Japanese management "guru," Kenichi Ohmae. Ohmae, managing director of the consulting firm McKinsey & Co's Tokyo office, described a strategy which he called "triad power."[2] According to Ohmae, the successful corporations of the 1990s will have the ability to compete fully with domestic manufacturers in the three key regions of North America, Japan, and Europe.

In some ways, the Japanese are still very far from being global companies. Let's briefly compare the examples of two companies, Ford and Toyota.

The Ford Motor Company, which enjoyed a huge success in introducing mass-produced cars in the United States, was looking to consolidate its successes overseas. And after the allied victory in World War II, Ford, like other U.S. multinationals, moved quickly to expand its position in the newly growing markets of Europe. Hiring local management, Ford expanded its plants in Britain and West Germany, becoming the number two carmaker in both those countries. Manufacturing now takes place on a global basis.

In postwar Europe, the demand was for very different types of cars from those sold in the United States. Roads were narrower, gasoline was scarcer, and income was lower than in the United States. Thus, from a very early stage, Ford located the design of its models in the region of manufacture, making models appropriate for the individual market. In spite of some recent successes in promoting the "world car" design concept, Ford remains highly sensitive to the differing needs of its various markets.

Moreover, Ford's overseas subsidiaries have come to be seen as national assets in many of the countries in which they operate. Ford is now the only privately owned major British carmaker. The senior managers of Ford of Britain are primarily British (though its head is often American), and they enjoy considerable mobility throughout the Ford group. Many Europeans enjoy top positions within the

American parent. The company's stock is widely traded in Europe as well as in the United States. In short, the American identity of the company has become increasingly blurred, to the point where it is no longer an essential characteristic of the company. Looking at it another way, the Ford Motor Company could move its headquarters to, say, Germany, and in all probability it could continue to function as effectively as it does now. Ford has become a truly global company.

Toyota's overall sales are roughly equivalent to those of Ford. Like Ford, about half of its sales are outside its home country. But there the similarities end.

Until the mid-1980s, Toyota had no major production facilities outside Japan. Although it operated some plants under license in Asian countries, this was primarily to overcome import restrictions. The plants were generally limited to assembly operations. Toyota grew into a global giant almost exclusively through exporting from its home base in Aichi Prefecture, Japan.

But as Toyota's market share grew worldwide, the company recognized the limitations of the export method. Perhaps the greatest threat was from the potential for growing import restrictions, both in the import-saturated United States, and in the newly emerging united European market. But in addition, the company recognized that it could not continue to cater to the tastes of consumers as the company's market share continued to grow worldwide. Another factor was the increasingly severe labor shortage in Japan.

In 1983, Toyota initiated its first manufacturing facility in its biggest overseas market, the United States, through the NUMMI joint venture with General Motors. In 1990, the company broke ground on its first major European production facility. In addition, Toyota acquired a design company in California that provided an innovative minivan design that has been a success both in the United States and Japan.

Toyota's 1990 annual report is highly focused on the

increasing globalization of the company's operations. The concept of contributing to local communities is also good public relations. The report states: "Time was when our cars were about the only thing outside Japan that we could point to and say, 'Look, this is us. This is what Toyota looks like.' Now we can point to ourselves. There are thousands of us now: Americans, Australians, Belgians, Brazilians, British, Canadians. . . . We are thousands of members of hundreds of communities in scores of nations worldwide."

However, a glance at the back of the same annual report shows that the entire senior management group of the company, as well as the entire board of directors, remain Japanese. When I interviewed a Toyota manager recently at the company's Toyota City headquarters, he posed the question: "Are we really a global company?" An examination of the company's organization structure reveals that every single major division is headquartered in Japan—either in Tokyo or Toyota City. That includes the divisions responsible for U.S. production, sales, and marketing.

Toyota is moving in the direction of globalization, and has clearly targeted globalization as a primary strategy. But Toyota is in many ways far behind Ford and other U.S. multinationals. The same is true of most of Japan's other powerhouse manufacturers. Although they have racked up massive worldwide sales, they remain in many ways surprisingly insular. The top 50 Japanese corporations have less than a dozen foreign board members among them.

It is not surprising that the most forward-looking Japanese companies—in terms of the shift toward global structures—have also been among the biggest buyers of American corporations. An example is Sony Corporation. Sony was for decades something of an outsider in Japan. Started after World War II, Sony lacks the pedigree of the established older Japanese firms. It also lacks the entrenched network of affiliate relationships that can prevent Japanese firms from forging new alliances. Sony has always survived by being a step ahead of the competition. It was among the first Japanese companies to accept a foreigner onto its board of directors. And with its acquisitions of CBS Records and Columbia Pictures, Sony has committed a large amount of its future to non-Japanese operations. Honda, another maverick in Japan, was the first Japanese automaker to build its own factory in the United States.

But if Japanese companies are behind in the move to globalization, they nevertheless recognize the need to catch up. That is one of the root causes behind the growth in acquisitions of American companies by the Japanese.

Technology

Another strong driving force behind recent Japanese investments in the United States has been the desire to acquire U.S. technology.

The Japanese have always been intensely eager to gain access to U.S. technologies. After World War II, Japan trailed far behind in virtually every leading technology. It was a struggle just to find rice for the people's mouths. But even though companies and individuals were desperately short of cash, from the very beginning Japanese companies were ready to pay to gain access to new technologies. For example, Sony was one of the first overseas companies to license the new transistorized circuitry after it was developed by Bell Laboratories in the late 1940s. Japanese companies purchased the rights to make monochrome televisions as the Americans moved into color technology, and then acquired the color technology early enough to beat the American manufacturers in the development of a solid state color television set.

The Japanese were ready to pay for these technologies, even at a time when capital was scarce and results uncertain. Americans, seeing perhaps the pitiful state of the Japanese economy and the limited potential of the Japanese market, tended to sell their technologies relatively cheaply. According to James Abegglen's *Kaisha*,[3] over a period of 30 years Japanese companies entered into a total of 42,000 licencing agreements for a total in fees and royalties of $17 billion, a fraction of the amount spent by U.S. firms on research and development (R&D) in a single year. In exchange for their investment, Japanese firms have gained access to technologies that have helped them put entire American industries out of business.

But in spite of the success of Japanese companies' license purchasing polices, they are of limited use in today's industrial climate. First, American firms are far more aware today than previously that licensing their technology to foreign companies may eventually put them out of business. Second, licensing is primarily useful for companies that are followers in new product development. By definition, licensed technologies have already been invented by someone else. Japanese companies are now making the transition to a leadership role in technological innovation. One manifestation of this is the vast amounts now being spent by Japanese firms on research and development. Another is the increase in acquisitions of American high-technology companies.

For all its failures in the race to dominate new industries, America remains a powerhouse of innovation. American scientists have claimed the majority of the Nobel science prizes awarded since the World War II. While Japan produces more engineers than the United States in spite of its smaller population, the United States still produces eight times as many science and math graduates as Japan. U.S. research institutions continue to attract the best minds in the world. American start-up companies remain a primary source for the introduction of new technologies.

Now that Japanese companies are flush with cash, America has become a prime picking ground for the purchase of new technologies. The Japanese have become major financiers of university research. The Massachusetts Institute of Technology has at least nine chairs endowed by Japanese firms. Japanese companies have also been providing capital for start-up ventures in Silicon Valley and elsewhere. And they have been acquiring high-technology firms that have had trouble ensuring their survival in the

American system. An example is Materials Research Corporation, highlighted in a case study in Chapter 3. Sony Corporation purchased this leading supplier of top-grade materials when American sources of financing turned their backs on the company.

Buying technology may mean more than simply investing in high-tech scientific ventures. American companies are ahead of the Japanese in many fields, due to the innovative leadership role that American companies have tended to play in recent decades. An example is the financial industry.

One of the great opportunities of the 1990s for the financial industry will be the continuing wave of Japanese investment in overseas assets. But in some ways, Japanese banks are among the least well placed to profit from these investment transactions. Japanese bankers are acutely aware that, although they command access to a vast resource of business contacts and capital, they lag far behind American and European institutions in the expertise required for the lucrative intermediary role in complex acquisition transactions. New York and London are the centers of innovation in the financial world, and Japanese banks are also eager to keep up with the continual refinement of such sophisticated and profitable transactions as interest and currency swaps, convertible debt issues, program trading, options, and futures.

When a Japanese bank hires an American expert, the new employee is likely to find he or she has a dual role: while it is hoped that he (or she) will make money for the employer, the new employee may find that an even more important function is to teach his or her skill to a succession of understudies, many of whom are likely to have been sent expressly from Tokyo. An American currency trader who works for a Japanese bank in New York developing complex computer programs to monitor exchange rate movements complains that he can never secure the services of a qualified assistant. As soon as he has trained one to do an effective job of supporting his activities (this takes about two years), that colleague is transferred back to Tokyo to pass on the word, and a neophyte replaces him.

As a result of Japanese banks' need for access to the latest techniques, several have invested in American securities companies and other financial institutions or formed joint ventures. The Dai Ichi Kangyo bank, for example, has a strong partnership with the New York mergers specialist Dillon, Read and regularly sends executives to U.S. business schools followed by a stint with their American associates.

There is a fascinating interdependence that has grown out of the Japanese quest for a share of the lucrative finance industry. The Japanese themselves represent to American institutions a vast opportunity due to the prodigious capital resources filling their coffers across the Pacific. A joint venture can be the quickest and cleanest way to gain access to these funds. But the Americans are unlikely to forget the danger of being swamped once the floodgates are released. On the other hand, the Japanese banks have a desperate need for American expertise, but their goal is nevertheless to compete in the global marketplace, which means against American banks. The result may be partnerships or joint ventures in which each side has to balance a modicum of genuine cooperation with the compulsion to hide important aspects of their business activities.

In one perhaps typical case, an American acquisitions expert has been seconded to a Japanese joint venture partner in order to build an acquisitions practice. He has a team of Japanese working with him, and they meet twice a week with the bank's senior managers to discuss strategy. The meetings, which are held in English, often seem to dwell inordinately on minor tactical and procedural questions, without tackling the important issues of business strategy. These issues are often shelved with the excuse that no decision can be made without reference to the Tokyo head office. The meetings are halting and inconclusive, and often leave the American manager in a fog, for which he blames the language barrier and excessive bureaucracy of the Japanese partner. But according to a Japanese employee in the same firm, when the American goes home at seven, leaving the Japanese still busy at their desks, the Japanese managers call another meeting. All the genuine strategic decisions are made at this meeting, and will eventually be filtered down to the American partner—to the extent necessary for the conduct of his business—in the guise of directives from Tokyo.

The desire to learn is by no means limited to the financial industry. For all the tremendous advances that Japan has made toward technological and commercial excellence, America still excels in many fields in the quality both of research and training. As American industries have seen their defenses battered by the onslaught of Japanese competition, the margin of leadership has become a precious commodity to many, and the sharing of technological resources has become an increasingly important political issue.

The endeavor of the Japanese to gain access to American knowledge has ranged from the individual to the mightiest corporate or governmental enterprise. At one end of the scale is the humble language student for whom English will be the key to a wider range of career opportunities. At the other is the highly controversial cross-Pacific takeover, in which billions of yen are invested in order to gain access to major technologies such as aerospace or bioengineering. Some of these acquisitions have been blocked by the U.S. government, under intense pressure from a strong protectionist lobby. Other joint ventures, such as the FSX fighter project, have been given approval only after lengthy and agonized debate, and only after having restrictions tied to them which many Japanese find intensely hurtful to their pride.

Why do American institutions allow access to the Japanese, when they can be almost sure that the knowledge gained will ultimately be used competitively against them? One reason is the increasing mutual dependence of large American and Japanese firms, as evidenced in Boeing's partnership with major would-be competitors (see Chapter 2).

At the academic level, another reason may be a tradition of openness that has generally made research available within a short time of its accomplishment.

But to make a more general case, the fundamental cause of American openness to Japanese investment is the much vaunted American capitalist system itself. Money is the lubricant of the system, and by its own internal logic, the system makes its resources available to the highest bidder. The Japanese have money, and they are ready to spend it generously to gain access to the resources that they need.

In between the extremes of individual study and giant corporate knowledge transfers are a host of disciplines which the Japanese find it worth coming to America to learn. The sum of these may be taken to define the continuing leadership role of the United States in the fields of innovation and technology. But this role may not last much longer, and Americans are now looking to Japan for reciprocal leadership in a growing range of skills.

Perhaps one reason that the public is so concerned about the Japanese thirst for American know-how is that the exchange is at the moment something of a one-way street. Japanese institutions do not have a tradition of openness. Nor does their language permit easy access to the knowledge the Japanese are willing to share. An agreement signed between the two countries in 1980 was intended to result in mutual access to government and university research. But while only a few hundred Americans have taken up studies in Japanese laboratories, thousands of Japanese researchers are now in the United States—400 of them at the National Institutes of Health alone. Of those Americans who did venture to Japan, many complain that they have been excluded from meaningful participation in Japanese research even after years spent in Japan. This concern may become even more acute in years to come, as Japanese companies make larger strides in the forefront of new technologies. But I think that the gates now being opened by the Japanese desire for American cooperation in the transfer of technology will also eventually allow a greater flow in the opposite direction.

The Herd Instinct

Greater financial returns, globalization, and the acquisition of technology are all sound reasons for Japanese companies to invest in the United States. But to say that these motivations account for all the Japanese acquisitions in recent years would not be telling the whole story.

In his excellent account of the reasons for Japanese success relative to American companies, Clyde Prestowitz mentions an old Japanese saying, *Minna watareba kowakunai*. This translates roughly as "If we all cross together, it's not frightening."[4] It is the concept of safety in numbers. In Japan's crowded, conformist society, that philosophy has a comforting ring to it. If you make a mistake, you will not be held responsible so long as everyone else has made the same mistake.

This concept has been a major underpinning of the actions of Japanese corporations. It is remarkable how often they seem to act in concert, even though they may be bitter rivals on their home ground and abroad.

For example, during the 1970s, several Japanese banks acquired or opened subsidiaries in California. In 1981, the Bank of Tokyo bought California First Bank, a medium-sized bank catering to the middle-sized business market. While the reasons for the acquisition have never been fully explained, they are thought to be connected with the fact that Bank of Tokyo was losing ground against its competitors in the domestic market and sought to strengthen its franchise in the fast-growing, Asian-oriented California economy. Following this acquisition, Mitsubishi Bank announced the purchase of First National Bank of San Diego County, Sanwa Bank acquired First City Bank of Rosemead, and Mitsui Bank acquired Manufacturers Bank of Los Angeles—all in the same year. Another wave of investments came in 1986-1988, when Sanwa Bank bought Lloyds Bank California and the Bank of Tokyo acquired Union Bank of

Los Angeles. By the end of the decade, reportedly 20% of California banking assets were owned by Japanese institutions.

What did the Japanese banks gain by their investment in California? Perhaps they have become more global, but the commitment to a single regional market hardly fits with a global growth strategy. Nor have the banks gained access to significant expertise that was unavailable before. Perhaps they have gained access to a more profitable customer base than they would otherwise have been able to lend to: the middle-market business customer. But they paid a high price for this access: Their acquisitions were at top-dollar prices in a sizzling market. If asked, executives of the Japanese banks cite all these reasons, plus one more: They had to keep up with their competitors! Perhaps the most important reason for the acquisitions was that the other banks were doing it.

We should not underestimate the importance of the herd instinct in Japanese investment decisions. After Sony acquired Columbia Pictures, its archrival, Matsushita, made a parallel purchase in MCI. When Sumitomo Bank invested in the New York investment bank Goldman Sachs, half a dozen competitor institutions followed with similar investments. When Honda decided to build a manufacturing plant in the southern Midwest, Nissan and Toyota soon followed.

Did all these buyers follow the same line of reasoning to arrive at their investment decisions? Probably not. In many cases, it was enough that their competitors were taking the plunge. They could not afford to be left behind!

Prestige

There is another factor that we should not forget in considering the willingness of the Japanese to pay high prices for prestigious properties. Forty years ago, Japan was a destitute nation under the physical occupation of a victorious America that was a symbol of wealth and power. Much has changed in the intervening time, and it is now possible for a Japanese institution to own a landmark property in the very heart of the occupying nation. Some of these properties, such as Pebble Beach or Tiffany, are household names both in the United States and the rest of the world. We should not underestimate the prestige that may accrue to the owner of one of these properties.

Strategic Implications

Is your company an attractive target for a Japanese buyer?

Here is a checklist of considerations to help analyze the question. If the answer to any of the following questions is "yes," then your property may indeed be a target.

1. Am I in a global industry?

Global industries are those in which demand for essentially similar products exists in the major markets of the world—the United States, Europe, and Japan.

Japanese companies have been increasing their local presence in major market areas in order to position themselves for effective global competition. Since buying a local company is the quickest way to achieve a local presence, Japanese companies have made a number of strategic acquisitions in the United States for this purpose.

Global industries are not necessarily high-technology industries. They include electronics, fashion design, cosmetics, automobiles, office equipment, computer hardware and software, steel, pharmaceuticals, and medical equipment, to name a few. The key test is that the demand should be worldwide, and the products sold in different markets are basically similar.

If your company competes in a global industry, it may well be an attractive target for a Japanese buyer. There are, however, some important caveats. In most cases, Japanese buyers will be market leaders in their home market, and they will be looking for a position of market leadership in their American target. At the very least, they will probably be seeking an established brand name. If they are going to invest in a U.S. presence, it makes sense for them to invest in a company that gives them a substantial presence in the U.S. market immediately.

Buying into a well-established company also gives the Japanese buyer an element of security in the acquisition. Since they are far away and have limited U.S. management skills, the Japanese tend to take a conservative approach to U.S. acquisitions, preferring established companies.

In looking at expansion in the United States to consolidate a global presence, Japanese companies may well consider building their own facility as an alternative approach to making an acquisition. For example, Japan's automobile makers have tended to adopt a "greenfield" approach, building factories in rural areas away from the traditional territory of the unionized auto industry.

For American companies in global industries, there is considerable logic in looking at potential Japanese buyers or investors. The same motives that are impelling Japanese companies to look to U.S. expansion may also make a tie-up with a Japanese company attractive. In an ideal situation, the American company will be able to market its products in Japan using the network of the Japanese affiliate.

In some cases, the goals of both sides may be met by entering into a joint venture rather than an outright sale. However, although the logic of joint venture deals has been expounded for a long time, there are few examples of successful relationships of this kind.

2. Do I have a prestige property?

The Japanese are unusually susceptible to the lure of prestigious properties, for a number of reasons:

- They are naturally conservative, and a prestige property or established brand name is perceived as a safer investment than a newer company. Japanese buyers have shown themselves willing to pay a hefty premium for this margin of safety.

- They tend to lack skills and experience in managing U.S. subsidiaries. Buying at the top end will ensure that they are purchasing a well-managed asset,

which they can safely leave in the hands of existing management.
- Because of the huge inflation in Japanese asset prices, even the most expensive American properties—especially real estate—can appear a bargain to Japanese buyers.
- The Japanese are intensely brand conscious, having been brought up admiring the glamor of Western luxury products. Owning such a product can therefore greatly enhance the prestige of a Japanese company in its home market.
- Japan was long an underdog nation, and owning a property that was an icon of American wealth and power may be a source of pride to Japanese companies and individuals.

Of course, truly prestigious properties are few and far between. In most industries, there are no more than a handful of businesses that enjoy international renown. Properties that have already found Japanese buyers or investors include real estate (Rockefeller Center), golf courses (Pebble Beach), jewelry (Tiffany), wineries (Chateau St. Jean), hotels (Intercontinental), and paintings (Van Gogh's *Inses*).

If you want to sell a penthouse on Park Avenue, or an Impressionist masterwork, or an international design house, then clearly you should be looking to the Japanese market. If you intend to stay with your business, a Japanese partner can probably provide you with unique opportunities to expand your sales in Asia. If you just want to cash out, the Japanese are still ready to pay top dollar.

Unfortunately, most of us do not fit into any of these categories, and so the opportunities created by the Japanese lust for prestige properties is of limited value.

3. Has my industry attracted Japanese buyers?

If other companies in your industry have been bought by he Japanese, chances are you will also be a target. This is because the Japanese tend to seek safety in numbers and often follow the lead of a pioneer buyer.

Industries that have attracted multiple Japanese buyers are banking (California and New York), steel, electronics, and (most recently) entertainment.

4. Do I own a technology that is attractive to the Japanese?

In their push to industrial might, the Japanese have become insatiable consumers of technology, both in the race to produce the latest and best consumer products and as a raw material for large-scale manufacturing. For example, at the time that Materials Research Corporation, profiled in Chapter 3, was sold to Sony Corporation, Sony was the largest buyer of metal coatings in the world. MRC provided for Sony not only a renowned research arm in the race to develop new products, but also a source of supply for an essential commodity.

The range of technologies that are attractive to Japanese buyers is vast. Japanese companies have made acquisitions in computers, biotechnology, pharmaceuticals, electronics, optics, software, and ceramics, to name a few.

The prerequisite to be attractive to a Japanese buyer is that your technology should be one that is not readily available in Japan. In many cases, Japanese companies have bought technologies that complement those in which they are strong. However, as Japanese companies become ever more competitive in technological development, the range of attractive American firms may narrow somewhat.

A common criticism of Japanese scientists is that they are not innovators. Although recent advances are rapidly disproving this theory, it is probably still true that the hierarchical and structured environments of the large companies that dominate Japanese high-tech industry may not be an ideal breeding ground for innovation.

For this reason, many of the American companies bought by the Japanese are smaller enterprises—often pioneers in developing and creating new technologies.

Conclusion

Every Japanese company investing in the U.S. has its own special reasons. However, analysis of investments to date does reveal some common themes. Understanding these themes or patterns can give U.S. companies an edge in identifying the right investor, and winning the best possible deal. Companies that own prestigious brand names, or that are positioned in global industries, or that are technological innovators are most likely to be attractive targets to Japanese buyers.

Endnotes

[1] Akio Morita, *Made in Japan* (New York: Dutton, 1986).
[2] Kenichi Ohmae, *Traid Power: The Coming Shape of Global Competition* (New York: Free Press, 1985).
[3] Abegglen, James C. Kaisha and Stalk, George, Jr., *The Japanese Corporation* (New York: Basic Books, 1985).
[4] Clyde V. Prestowitz, Jr., *Trading Places: How We Allowed Japan to Take the Lead* (New York: Basic Books, 1988), p. 85.

5 TALKING TURKEY, TALKING SUSHI

The most convincing way to demonstrate two opposing viewpoints is to let each speak for itself. Accordingly, two portraits follow of active participants in the Japanese acquisition game: One, a seasoned Japanese executive, buyer of more than a dozen American firms. The other, an American middleman who makes his living by representing both sides in negotiations with the Japanese.

Investing in America: A Japanese Perspective

Ryuji Kitamura has perhaps acquired more American corporations than any other Japanese manager. As president of Enprotech, a New York-based subsidiary of trading company C. Itoh (of which he is also a general manager), Kitamura has acted as principal in more than a dozen acquisitions in the manufacturing, engineering and financial sectors. Enprotech (short for Engineering, Products, and Technology) expects to continue its growth through acquisition and expansion, with a goal of $1 billion in sales.

"My policy for investment in this country is: 'Let's participate in helping America rebuild,'" says Kitamura. "Our goal is to develop companies that contribute to a healthy manufacturing base in America. This country has to go back to the basics."

Kitamura believes that foreign investment in America is "absolutely necessary." Pointing to the long neglect of core manufacturing sectors and to lagging investment in infrastructure and technology, he says: "From an economic viewpoint, the United States needs investment from Japan. But from many other viewpoints—national security, national pride, racial pride, ethical problems—Japanese investment is encountering increasingly hostile treatment."

Kitamura sees a double standard in the attitudes of politicians and the American public. "Governors and senators go to Japan and plead for Japanese investment in their states. Then they come back and criticize Japanese investment in general. Why is someone like [Sir James] Goldsmith not criticized when he buys a company, lays people off, and then sells it again, leaving less employment and huge debt? And as for so-called 'trophy' investments which have caused so much criticism (for example, Columbia Pictures or Rockefeller Center), these were not initiated by the Japanese. Americans should criticize the guy who sold it rather than the guy who responded to the plea!" However, Kitamura adds: "Japan is not free from criticism. Japan has to behave as a leader."

Kitamura explicitly distinguishes his own acquisitions from the financially motivated transactions typical in the West. "Our policy is not to engage in hoopla. We go to the basics. When we buy a company, it's to operate it, not to sell it." He adds: "A Japanese company is a family. It's employees are its babies. Usually you don't sell your babies for profit."

For Enprotech, the initial acquisition is merely the first phase in the transaction: for every $1 spent in purchasing a company, Enprotech invests another $2 in upgrading or "turning around." Using its own growing capabilities, as well as the contacts and resources of its giant parent, Enprotech's goal is to enhance and develop the technical capabilities of its subsidiaries to the point where major contracts for capital equipment and machinery (that might otherwise have gone to foreign companies) can be fulfilled using primarily American staff and sourcing.

When evaluating a potential acquisition, Kitamura's staff determine whether the company fits one of three strategic criteria: Does it qualify as a "defensive" target? a "synergistic" target? or a "proactive" target? Defensive acquisitions reinforce the position of Enprotech in areas where it lags the competition. Synergistic acquisitions contribute to making the overall operation more effective. Proactive acquisitions establish positions in new strategic businesses.

The majority of acquisitions have specifically targeted certain key assets such as equipment, facilities, process technologies, or people. The acquisition team use a checklist of desirable assets, each of which is evaluated against a list of criteria, including quality, flexibility, strategic fit, innovativeness, and cost.

The key to Enprotech's acquisition policy is to acquire strategic companies to which it can add value. But Kitamura readily admits that this does not fit the profile of the typical Japanese acquisition. "The Japanese investor to me is a fool," he says. "He does not have his own opinion. These brand-oriented purchases are crazy to me. These people don't have their own values—someone else decides the value."

The acquisition is then analyzed using conventional financial techniques. "My [American] staff are very good at that" says Kitamura. "I'm always impressed with their analytical process. But it's strange that 95% of the time I disagree with their conclusions!" Perhaps an explanation for this is that financial analysis is only one component in the final decision. "If the dilution is excessive, we have to debate again whether qualitative goals should take precedence over quantitative. Financial analysis for us is a point of reference, but it is not the master."

Similarly, although financial performance is a vital measure of success for the company [the stated objective is to achieve "excellent company" status—qualifying for issuance of noncollateralized bonds—by 1995], the approach to profits is markedly different from many U.S. companies. One-third of gross profits are allocated to future development, one-third are allocated to strengthening of the balance sheet, and one-third are reported as income.

Kitamura is clearly fond of seeing things in threes. "Our corporate culture has three components," he says: "financial targets, business targets, and our overall mission." Similarly, "I have to be loyal to three bosses: investors (in this case C. Itoh), employees, and the society in which we live. The last of these includes paying our fair share of taxes: If you don't pay taxes, society becomes poor."

Kitamura's approach to negotiations mirrors the independence of his outlook. "I'm not negotiating to squeeze the best deal out of the other party. Our approach is to debate internally and to know what we want at what price. If that's more than the seller was expecting, that's fine. But I don't budge—I don't engage in competitive negotiations. I'll determine our price, not anybody else, because we're the ones that are going to operate the company."

Kitamura is guided by another negotiating policy: "I do not fall in love when I'm lonesome. We never negotiate with only one target—we want to be always in the position that we can afford to walk away."

Nevertheless, in spite of his tough attitude, Kitamura insists that he usually makes the sellers happy. "I've made a lot of millionaires," he says.

Kitamura's approach to doing business in America is the product of a long and close relationship. "I first came to work in this country in 1962. My monthly salary of $500 was ten times what I earned in Japan! My best car ever was a 1964 Rambler Classic. When I returned to the United States in 1976 (after five years back in Japan), I bought a Buick. I owned Buicks until 1988, when I finally gave up—they were giving me so much trouble." Kitamura's wife is an American citizen, as is one of his children. "I have a lot of respect, even admiration, for this country. But perhaps partly because of that I also feel a tremendous frustration."

Perhaps Kitamura's long association with the United States is partially responsible for his forthright and sometimes controversial approach to business here. "The traditional Japanese hesitates to draw personal conclusions.

Rather, he gives you a list of options from which you can draw your own conclusions. That's not my approach!"

Japan's Overseas Investment: The View from the Middle

Few people have more experience of Japanese direct overseas investment than Paul Kelly, president of Knox & Co. in New York. Acting in a joint venture relationship with the Long Term Credit Bank of Japan, Kelly previously founded Peers & Co. and acted as intermediary in over 50 Japanese investments and acquisitions, representing both Japanese buyers and American sellers. After selling Peers & Co. to Kemper Financial Companies, Inc., Kelly has recently started a new venture, Knox & Co., in association with the Bank of Tokyo.

"The recent furor over high-profile Japanese acquisitions in the United States is more an emotional topic than a reality," says Kelly. "We do not sell secrets of a national defense nature, and American industry tends to husband and protect its proprietary technologies, whether from Japanese or American competitors." Referring to the Mitsubishi acquisition that marked the high-water mark of U.S. public indignation, Kelly says: "Rockefeller Center was never owned by you and me. It was owned by the Rockefellers, who solicited this transaction, and freed up $800 million which they then used to invest in the U.S. economy, both creating new jobs and expanding their philanthropic pursuits."

In fact, Japanese companies tend to invest in overseas assets with highly specific goals in mind. "Japanese buyers are generally looking for some proprietary asset, such as a niche or a brand-name, or a well-established dealer network" says Kelly. "They'll pay for quality, for something unique. They're the world's greatest brand-name buyers. A Japanese buyer recently paid an enormous amount for a stake in Tiffany." Investments in brand names can be rewarding to both sides, as the Japanese open distribution channels to the Far East's insatiable markets.

Generally, Japanese buyers prefer smaller, divisional-sized companies with single products rather than large conglomerates. "They are very specific in their strategic acquisitions. When you see a large company being bought, it's usually because it happens to be a single-product company, such as Firestone or Columbia Pictures."

Because the Japanese usually invest for strategic rather than financial reasons, they tend to be good owners for the management and employees of their subsidiaries. "They usually cut very good deals with the operating management because they want to keep them in place. They realize that the cultural differences between the West and Japan make them dependent on local management to maintain customer relationships, management practices and so on. Japanese buyers have kept existing management in every deal that we've been involved with," says Kelly.

"They're also good with the people on the line—they're famous of course for their participatory style of management. And perhaps most important, the Japanese are ready to invest additional capital, permitting the company to achieve things it would not otherwise have been able to."

Many of the benefits of being acquired by a Japanese company can also be realized through a joint venture. Typically, a Western company will offer its brand name, product technology, or distribution channels in exchange for access via a Japanese partner to fast-growing Asian markets. An increasingly common variant on the joint venture approach is for the Japanese partner to take a minority equity stake in the Western company (often preferred stock with special blocking rights in the event of hostile bids), thus increasing the company's protection against unwanted suitors.

Kelly sees another type of relationship evolving in the 1990s: the strategic alliance. "This entails the pooling by two large companies of substantial assets and business operations in order to reach the critical mass needed to become a major global player in a given industry." Such an alliance could have political benefits, allowing large companies to keep their domestic ownership and decision-making capabilities while building dominant positions in global markets.

It's well known that Japanese companies approach overseas investments using different criteria from those commonly employed in the West. This has sometimes resulted in astronomical prices (by Western standards) being paid by Japanese buyers. But Kelly sees the Japanese as less prone nowadays to pay top dollar. "They've become sensitive to the so-called 'Japanese premium.'" Rising capital costs and a falling stock market have also affected buyers' outlook, as has political fallout from recent high-profile acquisitions in the United States and elsewhere.

Nevertheless, the Japanese approach retains key differences. "It's hard if you're representing them sometimes," says Kelly. "They can't control their enthusiasm if they want something. They have a tendency to show all their cards, and when the other side perceives their enthusiasm, it drives a harder bargain. Our clients end up paying more." The occasional impetuousness of Japanese buyers has its reverse side. "If they're negative on a deal, even for reasons we can't fathom, then you can't sell anything to them. It doesn't matter how terrific the deal is economically: logical arguments don't have any impact. They start sucking their teeth, and you know that the deal's not going to get done."

Moreover, although financial analysis is important to the Japanese, their financial criteria may be very different from those Westerners are used to. "We were helping a Japanese client analyze an acquisition," relates Kelly, "and we couldn't understand why our return on investment calculations came out different from theirs. Finally we realized that they were not allocating any terminal value to their investment. They weren't planning to sell it!"

Using another example, Kelly relates that a Peers & Co. client paid an enormous price for a luxury hotel. "It was the most expensive hotel per room ever sold. There'll never be a return to that company. At best they may make 1 or 2%. But the deal met their two main criteria—quality and status. The buyers were willing to use a long-term return on capital concept: low, but assured over a long period of time." Conversely, Japanese investors are unlikely to be interested in companies with financial problems, even if they meet the buyers' other criteria (the exception is in industries, such as steel, where the Japanese are purchasing to circumvent quota restrictions).

Although Japanese buyers have invested billions in overseas acquisitions in recent years, their investments have mostly been channeled through a tiny network of intermediaries. Knox & Co. is a member of one the world's most exclusive financial clubs. The group is small because Japanese investors are unwilling to deal with people (or institutions) they don't know. "Candidly, I think it's a waste of time to go to Japan and try and market yourself," says Kelly. "You'll get all these cards and people will nod at you, but nothing will happen."

The key, according to Kelly, is the ability to access a network of Japanese investors effectively. Peers, Knox, and a handful of other U.S. investment banks have forged strategic alliances with Japanese institutions in order to achieve this. "The best combination is between a domestic institution that has a thorough knowledge of domestic industries and companies and a Japanese intermediary that has long-standing ties with a network of Japanese investors." Kelly adds: "Of course, if you have a terrific company, you've a good chance of selling it one way or the other."

What should Western executives be aware of when entering into negotiations with Japanese investors? "If there's a problem in your company," recommends Kelly, "don't hold it in abeyance until you think you've reeled the investor in. Confidence in management is a paramount concern for the Japanese. They don't like to be surprised." For the same reason, Kelly recommends avoiding the practice of adding last-minute provisions to agreements. "It's tempting, if you see the buyer is interested, to add a nickel or dime. But you risk blowing the whole deal if you try that. The Japanese begin to wonder about your ethics."

Kelly suggests that situations will arise that don't appear to be logical: small items that seem to become big issues no matter how much they are explained away. "If you need to be firm, be firm" he recommends. "But don't lose your patience." Kelly has a final recommendation. "I don't believe in being too much of a 'Japanophile'—constantly bowing and being oversolicitous. But nor should you give the appearance of arrogance or brashness. Extreme behavior one way or the other isn't effective. Just be natural."

How to Convince the Japanese to Pay Top Dollar

Japanese buyers have paid prices that astonished the world. In 1989, the Yasuda Fire and Marine Insurance Company paid $54 million for Vincent Van Gogh's *Irises*. The previous high price for a Van Gogh was under $20 million. When General Coast Enterprises bought the Pebble Beach golf club in 1990, it paid over $1 million per acre for the property, double the previous high price for a comparable property. And when Mitsukoshi invested $93 million in Tiffany & Co. in 1989, its offer placed a value on the company of 80 times annual earnings.

These deals were in their own way triumphs for the American sellers. By negotiating effectively with the Japanese, the sellers were able to create extraordinary value for themselves and their shareholders.

But negotiating with the Japanese is not an easy proposition. Japanese negotiators are notoriously tough and demanding.

An interesting contrast is between these sweet acquisition deals, in which the Japanese seem to have been more than willing to dig deep into their pockets, and the infamous trade negotiations that have dragged on for over a decade between the Japanese and U.S. governments. Everyone who has participated in the trade negotiations has attested to the remarkable persistence, intelligence, and skill of the Japanese trade negotiators. A candid assessment would probably have to conclude, in fact, that Japan has run rings around America in most of the negotiations.

Are we talking about the same people? Is it possible that the same group that were ready to accede to every demand of an American seller are also ready to stall for years over trivial clauses in trade treaties, dissecting minutiae with unremitting persistency?

Of course, the answer is that they are not the same group. Japan's Ministry of International Trade and Industry (MITI) is the most prestigious place that a Japanese graduate can go to work. The majority of its professional staff are culled from the elite schools. They represent the cream of Japan's talents. This in itself is a crucial difference with their American counterparts, who, with rare exceptions, are tired bureaucrats on stingy salaries whom nobody takes very seriously.

But while there are important differences between the negotiators of private enterprise and government, it is useful to focus on the similarities. Although the result may be very different, there are important similarities in their approaches that should not be ignored.

First, both groups have clear goals that underpin their negotiating tactics. In the case of the government negotiators, the goal may be to nurture an infant industry, until the point where Japanese companies can compete in the world arena. As a result of these goals, it is very much in the negotiators interest to slow talks down, because for every year that passes without concrete action, Japanese companies are able to consolidate their foothold a little more. In the case of private companies, their goal is generally to pursue a well-defined strategy, such as globalization.

Second, both groups are characterized by a high attention to detail. Japan is a disciplined society, in which attention to detail can be seen in aspects of daily life such as clean streets and trains that run on time. Even though the results may be very different, negotiators both for business and government are likely to pay close attention to points of detail. In the case of the MITI men, details may be used to score points off American negotiators or to slow proceedings down. In the case of corporate buyers, attention to detail is simply a part of the conservative approach that the Japanese generally take to business decision making.

Understand the Japanese Company's Strategies

The key to negotiating successfully with both these groups is *understanding their strategies*.

There are several benefits to achieving a good understanding of a potential Japanese buyer's strategy. First, such an understanding can help you select the right company to deal with in the first place. Since negotiations with the Japanese tend to be time consuming, it is worth talking to the right people first.

Prepare an analysis of the business strategies of potential buyers. Information on strategies can be gleaned from newspaper articles, history of recent acquisitions or initiatives, stock analysts' reports, study of annual reports, or talking to people in the company itself. On the whole, Japanese companies are not secretive about their strategies.

Once you have defined the strategies of a group of potential buyers, analyze the fit of each with your own company or asset for sale. Select the one or two companies who would further their strategies the most by an affiliation with you.

Second, understanding a buyer's strategy will help you prepare a convincing case when presenting your company or asset for sale. Japanese buyers are likely to be highly impressed if they see a presentation which hits all the "hot buttons" that are uppermost in their minds. They will be impressed not only with the attractiveness of your company, but also with your understanding of their needs.

Third, understanding a Japanese buyer's strategy will enable you to focus on fulfilling the buyer's needs, while ensuring that your own requirements are also satisfied. For example, if you are successful in convincing the buyer that your company offers exactly the strategic fit that he is looking for, the crucial question—for you—of price may be relatively unimportant for the buyer. Seek to avoid making price an issue. You may be rewarded with a ready acquiescence to the price level you want to establish.

Pay Attention to Detail

From the point of view of the American seller, it pays to anticipate requests for detailed information and to prepare such information as much as possible in advance. Information that you should be ready to provide includes

- Detailed description of all assets, including when purchased, book and appraised value, make, and model (for machinery)
- Description of customer base—numbers, profile, and names if possible
- Full resumes of senior managers, including references
- Description of staff, including numbers, job descriptions, employee contracts (where applicable), and salary and benefit levels
- Detailed business plan for next three years, including budget for coming year
- Copies of all major contracts—customer, employee, supplier, regulators, and so on
- Full description of products, including technical specifications, uses, numbers produced
- Relationships with suppliers and distributors, including names, contracts, and length of relationship

Of course, this list is not exhaustive. Additional information will depend on the nature of the business or assets for sale. But no matter how prepared you are, be ready for unexpected requests. Sometimes Japanese buyers ask for information that may seem quite irrelevant. But if they ask for it, it's important for them. It is much more sensible to provide the information rather than to argue over the need for it.

This does not mean that you have to provide proprietary information. Japanese companies are as likely as anyone else to use a due diligence exam as an excuse for "shopping" the competition. If information could be used to your competitive disadvantage, make it clear (in advance if at all possible) that the information is proprietary, and why. And don't hesitate to protect yourself with relevant confidentiality agreements.

Similarly, American sellers should be aware that long, drawn-out discussions of minutiae are not necessarily a sign of bad intentions or a desire to irritate. Answering inquiries and discussion points patiently and in sufficient detail will help convince the Japanese that you are a good and reliable manager. Sometimes it's better not to ask why the buyer is focusing on a detail item that may seem irrelevant. A patient and ready acquiescence to a desire to review or discuss detail points, no matter how irrelevant, will serve the valuable purpose of establishing your good faith and cooperativeness.

Be Patient

Do not expect to wrap up negotiations overnight. The Japanese have been known to move swiftly when the occasion warrants (the Sony acquisition of MRC, profiled in Chapter 3, is an example). But more frequently, they like to take their time. It pays to respect that desire.

You should be aware that the decision-making process tends to be far more drawn out in a Japanese company than in an American one. If your initial contacts are with a U.S. subsidiary, then chances are all discussions will have to be referred to the Tokyo head office. This means that what you had taken for acquiescence to a proposal at the meeting in Los Angeles was actually just an acknowledgment of having understood your position. The discussion will be summarized in a memo and passed on to higher authorities for eventual decision.

The Japanese process of consensus building also tends to add to the time involved in reaching a decision. Decision making in Japanese companies tends to be concentrated at the very top. To avoid bottlenecks, junior executives will painstakingly prepare a case that will enable the final decision maker to give his consent based on the understanding that the issue has been thoroughly aired at lower levels and a consensus exists that the recommended move is the right one. All of that takes time, especially given that members of top management have many other demands on their attention.

Japanese companies' relative inexperience with the world of mergers and acquisitions (M&A) will also tend to slow the process down. Although Japanese companies and financial advisors are rapidly building skills in the analysis required for successful acquisitions, there still are many Japanese managers who lack familiarity with some of the essential features of M&A. They will require more careful explanation of the various financial, legal, and sales documents inherent in the process—confidentiality agreements, letters of intent, discounted cash flow, offering memorandums, and so on.

Another factor that may slow things down is the language factor. It is probably not necessary in most cases for you or your representative to speak Japanese, or to have all documents translated into Japanese, in order to deal with a potential Japanese buyer. But it is necessary to proceed carefully, making sure at each stage that the buyers have understood the points you wanted to make. And it is likely that at some stage a good deal of the documentation will be translated into Japanese by the buyer. All of that takes time.

One investment banker recently was telling me that he had represented a company he was convinced was a good fit for a Japanese buyer. "We contacted some Japanese companies, and one of them expressed interest. Well, the first stage in providing them with information on our client was to have them sign a confidentiality agreement. That's absolutely standard practice in M&A deals." The investment banker went on: "We never got beyond that first step. By the time the Japanese had translated the confidentiality agreement, had it reviewed by their attorney, presented it to the guy with authority to sign it, and had it signed, copied, and returned to us, a month had gone by and we'd already sold the company—to an American buyer."

If, for whatever reason, you are in that sort of a hurry to conclude a deal, then you'd better forget selling to a Japanese company. The story of Sheldon Weinig and MRC is an exception—in Sony, he found an exceptionally flexible company with experience in M&A and an established U.S. presence under American management. But Sony is an unusual company by Japanese standards. Moreover, Weinig successfully sold his company even though it was in financial trouble: He had skills and technologies that were worth more to the buyer than financial stability. For the most part, though, the fact that you are in a hurry is in itself enough to put a Japanese company off. They don't generally want to buy a company that's in trouble.

That does not mean that the Japanese are interested in delaying tactics or will simply leave your proposal to gather dust. Chances are, someone will be working diligently on it for most of the time. It just has to go through a much more drawn-out process than it might if you were selling to an American company.

STRENGTHS AND WEAKNESSES OF THE JAPANESE INVESTOR

Strengths	*Weaknesses*
Abundant capital	Unfamiliarity with local markets
Low cost of funds	
Strong domestic base	Lack of U.S. management skills
Technological leadership	
Access to Asian markets	Language
Choice of targets	Long-term outlook
Long-term outlook	Lack of experience with M&A deals
Lack of shareholder accountability	Unfamiliarity with financial analysis techniques

Strengths and Weaknesses of the Japanese Investor

"Know your enemy!" says the old maxim. Well, that was devised for an earlier and more warlike era. It isn't constructive to think of the Japanese as an enemy today. They may turn out to be your best friends—or even your employers. But it still pays to know the people you are dealing with. If you understand their strengths and weaknesses, you obviously are in a stronger bargaining position.

Let's look at some of the strengths and weaknesses of the Japanese investor.

Strengths

1. **Capital**

Japanese companies have something that a lot of Americans desperately need: abundant capital. Whether it is to fund continuing research and development, to help a business owner cash out, to finance an expansion plan, or to provide liquidity to shareholders, American companies frequently find they are unable to raise sufficient capital domestically. Banks have recently curtailed lending sharply, while Wall Street is notoriously focused on the short term. In many cases, foreign companies are the only available source of capital for emerging U.S. businesses.

In spite of talk of impending capital shortage, Japanese companies remain for the time being awash in surplus liquidity. Even after funding ambitious capital programs at home, their balance sheets remain weighed down with cash. Of course, this can be construed as a weakness. Japanese companies may in turn be seen as near desperate to find productive uses for their funds. But if used smartly, the capital available to Japanese companies may offer tremendous negotiating strength.

Imagine: a house is for sale for $700,000 in a neighborhood you fancy. The purchase price is reasonable based on previous deals in the area. But times have been hard recently. No one has that sort of money. The banks are burdened with bad debt, and are unwilling to lend more than 50% loan to value. You are the only person in town who has $500,000 cash in the bank. The seller has a choice between selling to you for $500,000 or waiting for times to get better. But the seller's business has recently folded. His creditors are baying for compensation. His bank called a personal guarantee. He has no choice but to sell. Name your price.

Multiply these numbers by 1,000 or so, and you could be a Japanese buyer today in America's troubled financial marketplace. The fallout from the junk bond financing of the 1980s may well turn out to be an unparalleled opportunity for Japanese buyers to snap up good companies that got involved in inappropriate financing endeavors. And the Americans may yet be begging them to name their price.

In addition, Japanese companies have capital available for investment in the target company subsequent to acquisition. If you are a hard-pressed manager that wants to assure a future for your company, the Japanese may be the more attractive buyers.

2. Low cost of funds

Even if the Japanese company does not have cash in the bank, the extraordinarily low funding costs of recent years have enabled Japanese companies to raise money for next to nothing and, therefore, pay far higher prices for American assets than could be afforded by those companies that were forced to pay American or European costs of capital.

For example, assume an American company is for sale at an asking price of $70 million. Its earnings are $5 million a year. If an American buyer makes a bid, it will need a return on its capital invested of somewhere close to 14%— the average equity return of companies quoted on the U.S. stock market (or a loan at prime rate plus a profit factor). Assuming the target company's earnings remain static, that implies a purchase price of $35.7 million. Five million dollars is 14% of $35.7 million. On the other hand, the Japanese stock market is willing to fund companies based on a 5% return on capital. Similarly, loans are available for as low as 4 to 5%. The Japanese company can afford to pay up to $100 million for the target company. Five percent of $100 million is $5 million.

Recently, Japanese interest rates underwent a steep climb, and the stock market, which often reacts in response to interest rate moves, plunged by 50%. As a result, the cost of capital differential between Japanese and American companies has been greatly narrowed. Moreover, there is much talk of an inpending capital shortage in Japan caused by the need to repay vast amounts of bond financing. However, the economic fundamentals of Japan are healthy, and rates have recently declined. On the other hand, America's chronic borrowing needs will most likely ensure a continued higher cost of capital over the long term, in spite of recent dramatic falls in short-term rates.

3. **Strong domestic base**

Japanese buyers of American assets are usually success stories. Chances are, they will have a history of effective competition in their home territory, and an entrenched position in Japanese society. This implies, but does not prove, that management is a capable group. It also suggests that the company will have a clear-cut strategy that will give it an advantage in furthering its goals overseas. It also means that the Japanese buyer can offer unparalleled opportunities in the Japanese market for Western subsidiaries of joint venture partners.

4. **Technology**

The Japanese can translate their technological strength into financial might. An American R&D venture that might appear highly risky to a U.S. venture capitalist may represent an extension of existing research activities to a Japanese buyer. Moreover, Japanese companies may be in a position to add significantly to the technology under development by the American company. Almost certainly, the Japanese will provide unparalleled opportunities to turn research into commercially viable products. This is one of Japanese industry's greatest areas of strength. Finally, Japanese companies are major consumers of technology. A high-tech Japanese company may use dozens of inputs from smaller high-tech companies around the world. A Japanese buyer could also become a small R&D company's biggest customer.

5. Access to Asian markets

One of the most attractive features of an alliance with a Japanese company—whether through acquisition, investment, or joint venture—is the access it can provide to Asian markets. The newly-industrialized economies (NIEs) of Asia—Singapore, Korea, Taiwan, and Hong Kong—have enjoyed the fastest economic growth rates among the world's industrialized countries over the past decade. And the developing countries of the Association of South East Asian Nations (ASEAN)—Thailand, Malaysia, and Indonesia—are currently enjoying a prolonged development boom (actually even a higher growth rate than their NIE neighbors. Japanese companies tend to have long-standing ties with these countries, dating back to before World War II. Add to that the vast Japanese market, which combines strong growth with enormous purchasing power, and you have an opportunity that cannot be ignored.

Since Asian markets are among the hardest to penetrate—due to linguistic, cultural, and political barriers—an alliance with an established player may be the best, or indeed the only, opportunity to gain a foothold. Japanese companies therefore bring something very desirable indeed to the negotiating table. Given the same deal offered on the same terms by an American and a Japanese investor, you may well feel that the Japanese offer greater opportunities for future growth, and therefore that the Japanese offer has more value. Ironically, this implies that the Japanese should perhaps be paying less rather than more than average for their U.S. acquisitions.

6. Choice of targets

Japanese buyers are in a strong position in that there is a wide choice of high-quality operations available for sale in the United States. In a number of industries, good companies have gotten into trouble through unwise financial management, cyclical downturns, or dried-up lending sources.

On the other hand, for many sellers, the list of potential buyers may not be nearly so long. Depending on the industry, buyers may be limited by lack of cash and cautious capital markets. The Japanese so far remain the most resistent to these ills.

Therefore, the Japanese are generally in the position to go and find another seller if they are not satisfied with the progress of negotiations. American sellers, on the other hand, may be unusually dependent on finding a Japanese investor to help them out. This combination places the Japanese in a strong bargaining position.

7. Long-term outlook

The Japanese are in some senses playing a different game from their American competitors. While American companies are required by their shareholders to show consistent returns, usually in excess of 10% annually, Japanese shareholders, and therefore Japanese managers, are much less focused on short-term profits. This means that the Japanese may see a deal in an entirely different light from an American company reviewing the same deal.

For example, I have represented American companies that would not look at a deal if it would dilute their earnings even for *one year,* and even though the projected cash flow rate of return over ten years was as high as 40%! They simply were not prepared to face their shareholders with the news that earnings would be lower, no matter what the reason.

This can create an ideal situation for forward-looking Japanese companies. Clearly, some investments have limited prospects for short-term gains. But if the long-term return is guaranteed to be high, the initial trade-off may be more than worthwhile. On the other hand, since only the Japanese are willing to make such trade-offs, they can arguably parlay down the price for the long-term benefits on the grounds of the need for short-term sacrifice.

Some deals that are being consummated now for apparently high prices will undoubtedly seem like marvelous bargains with the hindsight of a decade or two. In the same way, when the Mitsubishi Company purchased a wasteland near the Japanese Imperial Palace, it was ridiculed for buying a useless property. But a hundred years later that land, which comprises the Marunouchi district of Tokyo in which Japan's major companies are located, is considered the most valuable real estate in the world.

8. Lack of shareholder accountability

In general, Japanese managers are less accessible to shareholders than their American counterparts. But on the whole, Japanese shareholders have had good reason to be satisfied. Although they have recently taken a steep fall, Japanese stock prices enjoyed a long and heady boom during the 1980s, and shareholders who bought in the 1970s saw the value of their holdings increase tenfold.

The Japanese stock market does not appear to be driven by earnings. Even companies with relatively low earnings enjoy strong growth in their share prices if they are perceived as high-growth companies. Rather than looking for a return on their investment in terms of dividends or retained earnings, Japanese investors have tended to look for stock appreciation based on growth. Therefore, companies have been motivated to grow more than they have to achieve high earnings.

Since acquisition is a means of rapid growth, it follows that Japanese shareholders will tend to look favorably on acquisitions, even if they reduce the overall earnings of the company. This attitude puts Japanese companies in a favorable position when they are bargaining for an American company. They can, in short, pay more and take greater risks.

Weaknesses

1. Unfamiliarity with local markets

This weakness should not be overstated. Japanese companies have been selling in the United States for decades, and the larger ones tend to have built up sophisticated operations that include competitor research. Moreover, Japanese buyers frequently hire local advisors—investment bankers and others—to assist them with acquisitions. Therefore, they can benefit from local expertise as well as their own acquired knowledge.

But 70% of acquisitions of American assets by Japanese buyers are conducted without the assistance of an intermediary. And many smaller acquisitions in recent years have been by relative newcomers to the U.S. business scene.

Unfamiliarity with the local market may be one reason for the Japanese predilection to buy well-known, well-established properties. While they are less concerned about price, the buyers do not want to make a mistake in the quality of the company they are buying.

And with any Japanese company, there is an element of unfamiliarity. The Japanese are doing deals away from their own turf, and inevitably this lends an element of caution to their dealing—and provides opportunities for American sellers.

Perhaps there is an opportunity to persuade the Japanese to pay prices that American firms would consider too high. Their investment bankers, who are usually paid a commission based on percentage of purchase price, may not try too hard to persuade their clients to lower their offers. Certainly, Japanese companies are free of local pressures that might make their American counterparts shy away from a deal that would be perceived as overpriced by financial analysts and their peers.

There is also an opportunity to create confidence in the Japanese buyer, who may have a higher regard for such factors as management competence and solidity of business rather than snapping up a business cheap or minimizing the purchase price.

2. Lack of U.S. management skills

Japanese managers are seriously handicapped by their lack of skills in running American businesses. The vast majority of buyers seek to retain existing management of the companies they acquire.

Given this need, Japanese companies are much less likely to be interested in buying badly run or loss-prone companies. They generally do not have the management skills to turn such companies around.

Clearly, there are opportunities here for American sellers. First, it is vital to gain the confidence of the Japanese buyer. He is dealing with you not just in a single deal but as a potential long-term business partner. Once you have gained his confidence, you are in a uniquely favorable bargaining position.

All the signs are that the Japanese will pay handsomely for confidence in management. This may include a higher purchase price and a generous employment package for senior managers after the deal is consummated. For an owner-manager, this can be an ideal combination.

Look at the Sony takeover of the Guber-Peters entertainment company. When Sony bought Columbia Pictures, it looked around for someone they could trust to run the company. When it decided that Guber and Peters were the men for them, Sony bought them out of their independent production company for a staggering $200 million and gave them employment packages worth tens of millions more. Guber and Peters were able to use a weakness of a Japanese buyer—even a highly sophisticated buyer—to create immense value for themselves.

3. Language

It is arguable that the language barrier creates a weakness for both sides. I have known simple linguistic muddles to ruin deals that were hitherto progressing smoothly. Either side may be responsible.

Do not be so foolish as to think you can exploit Japanese weakness in English by inserting ambiguities into agreements and subsequently using them to the disadvantage of the buyers. Most Japanese companies are sophisticated enough to take steps to protect themselves from this kind of behavior, which in any case is highly unethical.

4. Long-term outlook

This was listed as a strength earlier, but it is also a weakness in that it may substantially reduce Japanese negotiator's concern for short-term costs. In other words, items that may be a serious problem to an American buyer, such as high debt loads, one-time charges, or imminent capital requirements, may not worry the Japanese.

Astute American businesspeople may be able to take advantage of this relative disregard for short-term costs in order to increase the overall value of the deal.

5. Unfamiliarity with financial analysis techniques

Japan still does not have a tradition of formal business education. Most business executives learn their trade on the job. Although it is becoming increasingly common to send young employees to American or European business schools, these trained professionals are still in a minority.

Consequently, many of the analysis techniques that are a great strength of Western business schools are unfamiliar to Japanese managers. This unfamiliarity is compounded by the fact that Japanese managers are not frequently exposed to M&A deals. As a result, the Japanese are likely to be relatively impressed by high-quality financial analysis and may lack the tools to effectively question assumptions. However, most large Japanese companies will retain investment bankers who are likely to be thoroughly aware of analytical techniques.

6. Lack of experience with M&A deals

The Japanese are gaining experience rapidly. But a large number of first-time buyers continue to enter the market for American assets.

It is hard to say what specific advantage this inexperience may give to an American seller. Nor are mistakes limited to newcomers. But it is perhaps reasonable to assume that inexperience is a weakness, and American negotiators would do well to look for advantage in dealing with new Japanese buyers.

This does not mean that Americans should try to "pull a fast one" on the Japanese buyer. Such an action would probably come home to haunt them at a later stage, since in the majority of cases the seller stays with the company.

DO'S AND DON'TS OF NEGOTIATING WITH THE JAPANESE

Do's	*Don'ts*
Be patient	Don't be overly aggressive
Provide full information	Don't hide unpleasant facts
Explain your position clearly	Don't be argumentative
Respond in detail to inquiries	
Be courteous	
Treat the Japanese as honored guests	

The Do's and Don'ts of Negotiating with the Japanese

A few simple guidelines may help to avoid unnecessary breakdowns in otherwise fruitful negotiations. It has been my experience that miscommunication or lack of communication causes the demise of any number of deals, between American companies as well as with foreigners.

In general, the Japanese have similar motives and similar sensitivities to Westerners, and they are equally logical. So rules of good behavior that ought to be applied to all dealings are also good enough for the Japanese. But it pays to be extra sensitive. The Japanese do, after all, come from a different culture, and it would be a shame to put them off an important business deal simply because some jarring notes were struck.

Do's

1. Be patient

There may be many things that you take for granted about business analysis or mergers and acquisitions, that are quite unfamiliar to some Japanese businessmen. Moreover, they may not want to admit their ignorance or failure to understand. Communicating in a foreign language (for them) doesn't help. On top of that, due to their management structure, Japanese companies tend to take a long time to analyze material and make decisions.

A little patience can go a long way, not only in clearing up potential misunderstandings, but also in creating the goodwill that is so important for seeing a deal through to consummation.

2. Provide full information

The more information you provide at the beginning, the better. This not only helps speed up the process of analysis for the Japanese company, it also creates a good impression—the impression of preparedness.

But most important of all, providing full and accurate information up front will help avoid the suspicion that you are trying to hold something back or that you are misleading the buyer in any way.

3. Explain your position clearly

The Japanese do not like surprises. If you explain your position, they will try earnestly to understand you, and they will do their best to accommodate your needs within the scope of their authority. However, if you state your case ambiguously and then abruptly change your position at some future point, you face the danger of losing the confidence of the Japanese investor. Once lost, that confidence will be very hard to regain.

4. Respond in detail to inquiries by the Japanese

Some of the questions asked by the Japanese team may seem pointless or irrelevant. Don't let that stop you from answering fully. The other side has its reasons for asking, and it is more important for you to create goodwill by complying than to save time by dodging the questions.

Questions on some small point may seem trivial to you. But any questions asked by the Japanese are important to them. Failure to satisfy them can easily kill a deal.

5. Be courteous

This may seem a strange thing to have to recommend, but it is worth remembering that the Japanese standard of courtesy is higher than that prevailing in the West. While we may find it rather flattering to be treated familiarly as an old friend by someone we don't know well, a Japanese would be more likely to find such familiarity insulting.

A classic example is the famous "Ron-Yasu" relationship between President Reagan and Prime Minister Nakasone. Ronald Reagan attempted to underline his regard for Yasuhiro Nakasone by publicly calling him "Yasu." Nakasone had little choice but to respond in the same spirit. Although this was countenanced by the Japanese for the sake of the desperately important political relationship it implied, most Japanese actually found it profoundly shocking that a foreigner, indeed, anyone but a family member, should treat their prime minister with such familiarity. Mr. Nakasone was invariably referred to in Japan, by newspapers, business associates, and fellow politicians, as Prime Minister Nakasone, or The Prime Minister.

On the whole, the Japanese are ready to make plenty of allowances for American informality. They are used, after all, to being the underdog nation, the one that has to adapt. But it pays to be sensitive to the unusually formal culture in which they grew up, and to err if anything on the side of courtesy.

6. Treat the Japanese as honored guests

The Japanese are accustomed to a very high standard of business entertainment. Japanese companies, encouraged by liberal tax laws, spend vast sums on entertaining. In addition, they have a tradition of treating a visiting business associate with a very high degree of respect and courtesy. A Japanese securities company gave instructions to its British employees that they were not to conclude any deals with customers until they had entertained those customers at least twice.

You don't have to go out and spend a fortune on providing your Japanese counterparts with ultraluxury commodities. But they will certainly appreciate being treated with respect, and one way to show respect is through small gestures of hospitality. They are after all, probably away from home and on your turf.

Flowers or a bottle of champagne delivered to their hotel room, or a thoughtful gift that represents your company in some way are appropriate gestures. If you take the Japanese out to dinner, make sure you take them to the best restaurant available—and don't stint on the wine!

Don'ts

1. Don't be overly aggressive

As you will have been told countless times, the Japanese like to reach decisions through the building of consensus. Consensus building requires relatively harmonious relationships, and showing aggression is a sure way to kill that harmony.

Of course, you should not try and hide your personality, and if your style is naturally aggressive, you may not be doing the right thing by negotiating with the Japanese. If you are going to stay and work for them, your aggressive style will be a problem time and again.

Avoiding aggression means avoiding overt displays of aggressive behavior to others. It does not mean reverting to passive behavior when it comes to business strategy or combating competitors. The Japanese have amply proved that they understand the usefulness of aggression in business competition.

2. Don't hide unpleasant facts

If your company has some undesirable features that you feel may deter a buyer, you are much better off coming clean with these at the outset or soon after negotiations begin. It does not pay to wait until the fish has bitten and then to spring an unpleasant surprise on them. Again, the danger is that you will lose the buyer's confidence—something that is vital to win and, once lost, hard to win back.

That does not mean that you have to paint the flaw in all its hideous colors. These may anyway seem worse to you than they would to a buyer who may be interested in your company or property for reasons unaffected by the problem. Give them the information along with all the rest of the data, and let them decide if it's a problem.

3. Don't be argumentative

The Japanese seek on the whole to avoid confrontation. Even if all sides understand that serious differences exist, the Japanese tend to act as though nothing marred the harmony between the sides. This is basically a matter of courtesy: It is considered disrespectful to argue or contradict—it implies that someone does not know what he or she is talking about.

Westerners have had all sorts of problems with this propensity to avoid contradiction. They may conclude a negotiation under the impression that they have reached full agreement with their Japanese counterparts only to discover later that the Japanese didn't agree with a word they said, but were too polite to admit it.

It isn't necessary to become an inscrutable Oriental yourself. The Japanese are ready to hear your point of view and would probably welcome having it honestly presented. If you ask them, they will probably be as honest in presenting theirs. But these views are basically impersonal and relate to negotiating positions. What you must try to avoid is contradicting or arguing on the personal level. That is considered both unnecessary and insulting.

6 CAPITAL CONCEPTS

There is more to saying "yes" to Japan than just selling out your business or property. The Japanese have a number of immensely valuable resources that American businessmen can benefit from, including cash, technology, and access to important markets. These do not necessarily involve selling the whole company. Access to these resources may be achieved through minority stakes, joint ventures, strategic alliances, or issues of debt or stock.

In short, there are many ways in which an American business can structure a relationship with a Japanese firm. American businessmen should study all of these before going out and soliciting a relationship. In particular, American businessmen should carefully examine their own goals and motivations and select from a range of options the one that gives them the best opportunity to achieve those goals.

SEVEN WAYS THAT JAPANESE CAPITAL CAN HELP YOUR COMPANY

1. By maximizing value to your shareholders
2. By providing funding for expansion or R&D
3. By enabling you to restructure financially
4. By saving you from closure
5. By helping you expand in Asian markets
6. By acting as a "White Squire" to ward off takeover attempts
7. By providing access to new technologies

Motives for Seeking Japanese Investors

Motives That Might Drive an American Business to Look to Japanese Sources

1. *Maximizing Value to Shareholders*

This is perhaps the traditional motive for looking to the Japanese. If the shareholders want to cash out of their investment with the maximum gain, a Japanese buyer may be the Santa Claus they're looking for.

Historically, the Japanese have paid high premiums for "trophy" investments—those in properties of unusual quality or prestige. Examples are prestigious San Francisco retailers Gump's; investment bankers Goldman, Sachs and Co., and the Bel Air Hotel in Los Angeles.

2. *Seeking Additional Capital*

For companies requiring additional capital for expansion, research and development, or enhancing financial clout, the Japanese may be an excellent source.

First, the Japanese have traditionally had access to very-low-cost sources of financing, and the larger companies enjoy surplus liquidity. They may therefore be ready to invest at a lower return than an American investor.

Second, the Japanese may have their own strategic reasons for wishing to invest in an American company. This motivation may encourage the Japanese to offer favorable terms to the American company. An example is Sumitomo Bank's $500 million capital infusion in the New York investment bank, Goldman, Sachs and Co. Sumitomo was very anxious to develop a presence in the global investment banking arena; consequently, it was ready to make the investment in Goldman Sachs on favorable terms.

Third, using the Japanese as a source of capital may also open the door to additional marketing opportunities. For example, the Mitsukoshi department store's $100 million capital infusion in Tiffany & Co, although on very favorable terms in itself, also created opportunities to market Tiffany products in Japan.

3. *Seeking Financial Restructuring*

A company may seek Japanese capital for a variety of internal restructuring needs, ranging from refinancing of debt to leveraged buyout.

Typically, Japanese banks will be the source for this financing, and they will be competing for this kind of business on similar terms to American bank competitors. The large Japanese banks compete actively for lending relationships with the *Fortune* 500 group of large American companies. Japanese banks have also participated in important leveraged buyout deals, such as the acquisition of RJR Nabisco by Kohlberg, Kravis, Roberts in 1989 for a record $25 billion purchase price.

Normally, Japanese banks will not offer this kind of financing on significantly better terms than their American competitors. Because they remain quite risk averse relative to the American market, Japanese banks have more or less abandoned leveraged buyout financings in recent years, and for the most part they limit their lending activities to large customers.

4. *Avoiding Closure*

A desperate person will try anything, and a company on the brink of closure may well seek assistance from the Japanese as well as other sources.

On the whole, the Japanese are unlikely to invest in companies that are in trouble. The Japanese lack the management skills to turn companies around, and therefore they prefer investing in companies that are well managed and profitable.

But there are exceptions, as is evidenced by the Sony acquisition of Materials Research Corporation (MRC), profiled in Chapter 3. In another unusual example, Salem College, an institution in West Virginia that was offering declining enrollment and threatened with closure merged with wealthy Teikyo University of Japan. The student body will be enlarged by an influx of up to 500 students from Japan.

5. *Expanding in Asian Markets*

Breaking into the Japanese market is notoriously difficult and costly. Other overseas markets are similarly costly to penetrate. It is widely acknowledged that the most effective way to penetrate overseas markets—for any but an industrial giant—is through alliance or joint venture with a local company.

As American companies continue to adjust their vision toward a more global perspective, and as they recognize the importance of Asia, which is growing at twice the rate of Europe and the United States, the interest in developing ties with Japanese companies is vastly increasing.

An example of a deal which gave a company access to the Japanese market is the acquisition of the Mentholatum Co., Inc., by Rohto Pharmaceutical Co. in 1988. Mentholatum, a private company based in Buffalo, New York, makes antiseptics, laxatives, and other over-the-counter health care products. Rohto introduced an extended lineup of Mentholatum lip balm products through its Japanese distribution network. The lip balm became a best-seller among Japanese school girls, who are forbidden to use lipstick. Mentholatum's Japanese sales now reportedly exceed U.S. sales.

6. *Seeking "White Squire"*

Japanese investors are increasingly being looked to as a source of protection against hostile takeover.

A "white squire" is an investor who takes a minority position in a company that is threatened with hostile takeover. The name derives from the traditional "white knight" buyer who would buy a company in a friendly acquisition deal when the company is threatened by a hostile suitor. The difference is that the squire only takes a passive, minority position. The squire's position is usually large enough to deter a corporate raider from pursuing a hostile takeover attempt.

In a sense, the entire Japanese corporate ownership system is based on extensions of the white squire concept.

Most larger Japanese companies belong to fellowships of affiliated companies (known as *keiretsu*) which own sizable chunks of stock in each other. These stockholdings, which are usually accompanied by more or less captive business relationships, effectively prevent interference by outsiders (or by disgruntled individual shareholders).

Japanese investors make attractive candidates for white squire investments, because they have a tradition of making long-term, passive investments. They are unlikely to interfere in the management of the company once the investment is made. They may provide useful business relationships. And, most important, they are unlikely to use their stockholding to mount their own hostile takeover in future.

In a few cases, Japanese companies have also acted as white knights, taking majority positions in companies threatened with hostile takeover attempts. Examples are Bridgestone's acquisition of Firestone, which was under threat from Pirelli, and Onoda Cement's acquisition of Cal-Mat, which was fending off a takeover attempt by New Zealand financier Sir Ron Brierley.

7. *Gaining Access to Technologies*

Japanese companies are currently taking a leading role in developing many leading-edge technologies. As Japanese companies pull away from American competitors and capture large shares of new markets, such as optical laser discs, they tend to build commanding leads in a range of related technologies, further distancing themselves from the competition.

Increasingly, American companies are looking to the Japanese to provide them with essential technologies—either to enable the American company to further its own research and development or to manufacture essential parts.

Japanese companies may similarly be interested in allying with American companies to benefit from their technology development. Technology has become a two-way street.

> **SEVEN WAYS TO GAIN ACCESS TO JAPANESE CAPITAL**
> 1. Direct equity investment—minority position
> 2. Direct equity investment—100% acquisition
> 3. Debt financing—Japanese bank
> 4. Debt financing—Japanese corporation
> 5. Japanese bond issue
> 6. Japanese equity issue
> 7. Joint venture/strategic alliance

A successful relationship with a Japanese company or investor will be achieved by matching the goals of the American business with the most appropriate means of creating a tie with the Japanese.

Alternative Vehicles for Accessing Japanese Investment

Vehicles for Accessing Japanese Capital or Creating Relationships with Japanese Companies

1. *Direct Equity Investment—Minority Position*

The majority of equity investments made by Japanese investors are not in fact outright takeovers; they are minority stakes, usually in companies with which some business relationship (i.e. distributorship) already exists or as a part of inaugurating a relationship. (In the case of real estate assets, the investment may be purely for financial reasons.)

The Japanese are strong proponents of minority stakeholdings, as is evidenced by the extensive system of share cross-ownership that exists in Japan. Buying a stake in a company is seen as a tangible gesture of long-term commitment.

Benefits to the American Side

- *Can provide additional capital.* If the investment is

through a new issue of equity stock, the issuing company can benefit from a capital infusion on favorable terms. Indeed, the pricing of the stake may be as generous as it would in the event of a buyout. An example is Nikko Securities investment in The Blackstone Group.

- *Can provide liquidity/capital gains to existing shareholders.* In the event that one or more existing shareholders wish to cash out of the company (especially if the company is unlisted), sale of a stake to a Japanese company can provide a generous medium.

- *Can provide access to future source of capital.* The Japanese tend to look on equity stakes as symbols of a long-term relationship. This means that if circumstances dictate a further need for additional capital in future, the Japanese stakeholder may be a ready source.

- *Represents no loss of control.* For business owners who are jealous of their control position, the minority stake is the ideal medium to generate equity capital without losing control.

- *Provides protection from hostile takeover.* A minority stakeholder can be a powerful ally, particularly when it comes to deterring corporate raiders.

- *Cements long-term business relationship.* Minority stakes are frequently accompanied by some form of tangible business relationship, such as mutual distribution of the other company's products or major sales contracts. The equity stake tends to assure the long-term stability of a valuable relationship.

Benefits to the Japanese Side

- *Creates special relationship.* If a Japanese company is concerned to secure a long-term business relationship—either sales outlet, distributorship, or technology collaboration—an equity stake may be an ideal way to cement the relationship.

- *May provide long-term financial gain.* Depending on the pricing of the deal and subsequent performance, a minority equity stake, whether of common or preferred stock, may also be a sound financial investment for a Japanese company particularly when compared to high-priced domestic investment opportunities.

- *Allows for ownership stake without excessive commitment of capital.* Japanese companies have been extremely successful at creating far-flung empires with a minimum commitment of capital, thanks to the practice of making strategic minority investments. A 10% stake in a company can create substantial influence, even a special business relationship, without requiring the larger amounts of capital needed for an outright takeover.

2. *Direct Equity Investment—100% Acquisition*

This is the closest that American companies come to "selling out." It is the deals that involve outright acquisition that usually capture the news headlines. Selling your company or property outright to the Japanese is often the way to secure maximum value to your shareholders: The Japanese are sometimes ready to pay prices that no conceivable near-term earnings of the company could match.

Benefits to the American Side

- *Maximizes dollar value to shareholders.* If shareholders want to claim the maximum gain today and walk away from the company, a sale to the Japanese may be the best way to achieve this goal. Usually there are few more significant ways of creating value than sale of a company. Even to American buyers, such sales usually command high premiums to the traded market value of the firm. Japanese buyers often add a "Japanese premium" to that.

- *Ensures future supply of capital.* For managers who are concerned to ensure a future supply of capital for their firm—especially a fast-growth or high-tech firm—a major Japanese parent ensures an ample supply of capital for future investment. Ryuji Kitamura, a frequent buyer of American companies, comments that he expects to invest an additional $2 for every $1 of purchase price. This attitude is extreme, but not atypical.

- *Creates link with market leader/Asian network.* Japanese buyers of U.S. companies tend to be leaders in their own country. They are therefore able to create substantial added value for their new U.S. subsidiaries, by providing Asian market opportunities.

- *Provides benefits to managers while eliminating ownership risk.* Managers are often given substantial employment packages by Japanese buyers, who are concerned to ensure continuity of management. The benefits included in these packages, including stock options and bonuses, can equal the type of reward that a business owner might expect—without the risk of ownership.

Benefits to the Japanese Side

- *Creates rapid growth.* Through outright purchase, a Japanese company can double its sales virtually overnight.

- *Ensures control.* Especially for Japanese companies attempting to create a global network, outright purchase means unequivocal ownership. Because Japanese management methods may differ markedly from those in the United States, and because the Japanese owner may be making a substantial investment in upgraded facilities and technology, control is important to protect the investment.

- *Allows future integration into global network.* A 100%

owned subsidiary can eventually be absorbed into the brand and culture of the parent corporation. An overseas acquisition therefore creates the possibility for rapid expansion of the parent company.
- *Provides full access to proprietary technologies, markets, and so on.* In anything short of an outright purchase, the Japanese investor must always provide something in exchange for benefits such as technology or market access. If the American company feels that sharing certain technologies would be a threat, it may withhold them. A 100% subsidiary, on the other hand, shares all of its secrets—and its competitive advantages—with its owner.

3. *Debt Financing—Bank*

Debt financing from a Japanese bank is similar to arranging debt financing from any other bank. Be aware, though, that the majority of Japanese banks limit their lending activity to *Fortune* 500 companies. The exceptions are Bank of Tokyo's Union Bank subsidiary, which has traditionally been active in the "middle market," and Mitsubishi Bank's California subsidiaries.

Benefits to the American Side

- *Offers virtually unlimited financing source.* Japanese banks are the largest in the world. Of the ten biggest banks, eight are Japanese. Due to their massive size, no loan is too large for a major Japanese bank—as they proved when they were able to absorb some $6 billion in loans to RJR Nabisco during the course of a week.
- *Retains complete control.* A loan agreement allows American business owners to keep complete control of revenues, markets, and proprietary technologies. For managers looking for financing for growth without sacrificing control, this is the ideal medium.
- *Increases shareholder returns.* Because the cost of debt

is fixed, any additional returns that the company earns on debt-financed capital will accrue to shareholders. That applies to any debt, not just Japanese. And the corollary is increased risk to shareholders—in the event of an earnings shortfall, debtholders have first claim in earnings.

Benefits to the Japanese Side

- *Invests in world's largest economy.* For all its problems, the American economy remains an immensely attractive investment opportunity, due to its size and stability. Japanese financial institutions cannot afford to miss out on these opportunities.
- *Permits portfolio diversification.* Overseas investment will diversify a bank's portfolio, thus reducing overall risk.
- *Represents an opportunity for global expansion.* The majority of major Japanese banks seek to be global players. Lending in the U.S. market is a relatively secure method of global expansion.
- *Permits higher yields.* Although the gap has recently narrowed, yields on dollar-denominated debt have typically been several percentage points higher than those on domestic yen debt. Although this higher rate is accompanied by a high level of currency risk, Japanese banks have nevertheless found it an attractive way to enhance earnings.

4. *Debt Financing—Corporate*

In addition to traditional bank debt, many larger Japanese corporations are in a position to offer substantial amounts of financing from their own cash-laden balance sheets.

Debt financing directly from corporations is likely to occur if there is a significant business relationship between two companies. For example, a supplier of machinery to a distributor or end user may well finance the acquisitions.

Benefits to the American Side

- *Injects capital without sacrificing control.* A similar benefit to borrowing from Japanese banks.
- *Tightens links with Japanese partner.* A borrowing relationship with a Japanese corporation can lead to closer ties and eventually to mutually advantageous business opportunities.

Benefits to the Japanese Side

- *Offers attractive yield.* As with Japanese banks, corporations may be attracted by the higher yields in the U.S. market. Note that several Japanese companies are so loaded with cash that their balance sheets actually resemble those of banks.
- *Tightens links with American partner.* As for the American side, financial links may be a precursor to important business affiliations.

5. *Japanese Bond Issue*

Capital markets are becoming increasingly globalized, and companies find it more advantageous to place their debt issues overseas. An overseas offering may offer some combination of lower rates, untapped buyer demand, and increased profile in the country of issuance.

Benefits to the American Side

- *Accesses world's second largest capital market.* Japan is a vast source of capital. For many American companies, it remains virtually untapped.
- *Results in potentially lower funding cost (yen bond).* For debt denominated in yen, interest rates may be several percentage points lower than the equivalent in dollars. However, unless the American company is using the yen directly to fund Japanese purchases, borrowing in yen will create currency risk. (Note, however, that an element of currency diversifica-

tion may also be an integral part of an international Treasury strategy.)

- *Increases awareness of company in Japanese market.* A public offering can, if handled well, be a form of public relations, increasing awareness of the company and its products.
- *Paves the way for future equity issue.* By managing your bond issue, Tokyo-based securities houses will come to know your company better and will be better equipped to help you find buyers when you decide to list your stock in Japan.

Benefit to the Japanese Side

- *Represents an opportunity to invest in strong U.S. market.* Japanese investors may welcome the opportunity to invest domestically in the U.S. market. By investing in a local issue, institutional investors may bypass regulations limiting foreign investment.

6. *Japanese Equity Issue*

Another feature of the globalization of capital markets is the opportunity to raise equity capital on overseas markets. Most of the non-Japanese companies listed on the Tokyo Stock Exchange are major multinationals, but smaller companies have also ventured into the field of Japanese public offerings. If your product has high consumer awareness in Japan, or if your company would benefit from a higher profile in Japan, a Japanese stock offering may well be appropriate. In addition, your company may benefit from the high multiples placed on stocks by the Japanese market.

Benefits to the American Side

- *Provides access to world's second largest capital market.* A similar benefit to tapping the Japanese bond market.
- *Increases awareness of company in Japanese market.* The

benefit is also held in common with a Japanese bond issue.

- *Represents an opportunity to share in high multiples.* The Japanese stock market tends to place much higher values on companies than the U.S. market. Although foreign companies tend to reflect their U.S. valuations when listed as depository receipts on the Tokyo exchange, if the company has a substantial Japanese presence, the market may add a substantial premium when a subsidiary is listed.

- *Involves market where behavior differs from the American market.* The Japanese stock market tends to react differently from the U.S. market. For example, Japanese stocks are notoriously fad driven, pushing up some categories of stock sharply as they come into fashion (an example is AIDS-related stocks, which were pushed to incredible heights in 1986). Sometimes what is fashionable in Japan may not be in the United States. If your company happens to be in a fashionable industry, it may well benefit from the unique behavior of the Japanese market.

Benefits to the Japanese Side

- *Increases globalization of Japanese capital market.* U.S. equities may present an attractive alternative to Japanese investors, especially since they are generally more attractively priced than those of competing Japanese firms.

- *Represents an opportunity to invest in overseas ventures.* In an age in which international investing is becoming the norm, accessing investment opportunities in foreign companies through domestically issued stock is one of the cheapest and most efficient methods. The opportunity to invest in foreign companies is made available to a much wider public.

7. Joint Venture/Strategic Alliance

The joint venture or strategic alliance is aimed primarily at gaining greater penetration of Japanese markets. It may also provide access to proprietary technology.

The logic behind these relationships is that in an increasingly globalizing economy, local companies have much greater knowledge of the tastes of their consumers, as well as more effective distribution channels. This is particularly valuable in Japan, where domestic markets are notoriously tough to crack. A joint venture or strategic alliance can marry the benefits of a saleable product with on-the-spot market expertise. In a truly bilateral relationship, each partner in the venture may provide marketing on its home territory and feed products to its partner's territory. The cost of becoming a global player is thus greatly reduced.

Joint ventures are fraught with risks and difficulties, as any number of war stories from scarred ex-partners will attest to. Since neither party usually has outright control, there are frequent occasions for dispute or disagreement. In these situations, the substantial cultural differences between Japanese and American business practices will be sharply exposed.

Nevertheless, there have been notably successful ventures. An example is that between Fuji Photo Film and Xerox Corporation's Rank Xerox division. Fuji-Xerox, as the joint venture is known, was initiated in the 1960s and has become a well-established player in Japan's office technology marketplace. Although the relationship was initially formed to provide distribution channels in the Japanese and Asian marketplace, Fuji-Xerox is now actively involved in major R&D projects and serves as a technology resource for the Xerox group.

While a joint venture usually involves a separately capitalized, jointly owned subsidiary, a strategic alliance may involve anything from simple sharing of information to substantial sharing of assets and joint marketing programs.

Benefits to the American Side

- *Accesses Japanese markets/technology.* A joint venture with a well-established Japanese player may well be the most effective way to penetrate the Japanese market. Strategic alliances may also lead to the sharing of crucial Japanese technology (usually on a quid pro quo basis). Japan is rapidly building an enviable technology base, and joint venture or strategic alliance may be the only means of access other than expensive licensing arrangements—if these are available.

- *Provides source of capital.* If the American partner's main motivation is to access new capital, a joint venture with a Japanese company may well be an appropriate method, especially if the American side owns technology or a brand name that it can offer in exchange.

- *Constitutes a method of spreading risk.* A joint venture or strategic alliance can spread the cost of a venture and therefore the risk of loss. This is especially important in large projects, such as aerospace development, which could otherwise stretch the resources of an American company beyond the limit.

Benefit to the Japanese Side

- *Accesses U.S. markets/technology.* American technology remains highly attractive to Japanese firms, and a joint venture or strategic alliance may be the most effective way to access this technology: effective, because the full cooperation of the original designer is assured. Because the Japanese company is offering useful benefits, the financial cost of acquiring technology through joint venture is often minimized (although joint ventures can also be extremely expensive).

Choosing the Right Vehicle

For each of the goals described at the beginning of this chapter, there are one or more appropriate relationship structures with Japanese companies or investors. These may be summarized as follows:

Goal: *Maximize value to shareholder*
    Vehicle: Equity sale—100%
                 Equity sale—minority stake

Goal: *Seek additional capital*
    Vehicle: Equity sale—minority stake
                 Debt—bank or corporate
                 Issue of Japanese bonds or stocks
                 Joint venture

Goal: *Seek financial restructuring*
    Vehicle: Bank debt
                 Bond issue

Goal: *Avoid closure*
    Vehicle: Equity sale—100%
                 Equity sale—minority

Goal: *Expansion in Asian market*
    Vehicle: Joint venture/strategic alliance
                 Equity sale—100% or minority stake
                 Public offering—stock

Goal: *Seek "White Squire"*
    Vehicle: Equity sale—minority stake

Goal: *Access to technologies*
    Vehicle: Joint venture/strategic alliance
                 Equity sale—100% or minority stake

How to Gain Access to Japanese Equity Capital

Should You Use an Intermediary?

According to a report by investment bankers Ulmer Brothers, Inc., about 70% of equity investments involving Japanese companies are completed without the aid of any intermediary. One reason for this high level of unassisted deals is the high number of transactions involving companies that already know each other. If you already have a business relationship with one or more Japanese companies, these may be your first candidates to offer an equity stake in your company.

If, on the other hand, you have no existing relationships with Japanese companies, and you are simply seeking an investor or buyer, then you will probably find it worthwhile to engage the services of a specialized intermediary—an investment bank or financial advisor with contracts in the Japanese business world.

To this point, it has been customary on the whole for U.S. companies to appoint American advisors, while Japanese buyers may use an American or a Japanese advisor, or both (since most Japanese investment banks have joint ventures with U.S. firms, it is possible to hire an American and a Japanese advisor within the same firm).

But Japanese institutions are also anxious to serve the American sellers' market, and if you are primarily looking for a contact network with Japanese companies, a Japanese investment advisor may be appropriate. Japanese investment banks tend to have less experience in mergers and acquisitions than their U.S. counterparts. But most have by now established a solid expertise, and Japanese companies are generally eager to build their business. Consequently, they may be willing to work for a lower fee or to represent a smaller company than the major U.S. investment banks. For example, Nikko Securities' mergers and acquisitions department is housed in the same building as its U.S. partner, the Blackstone Group. But while Blackstone is reputed to prefer large deals involving major corporations, Mr. Masakatsu Sakamoto, head of Nikko's M&A practice, says he welcomes smaller transactions.

Selecting an Intermediary.

Your choice of financial advisor will be dictated by your specific needs: Do you require comprehensive financial advice, including valuation, fairness opinion, negotiating tactics, and so on? If so, select an advisor with a strong reputation as a negotiator. Are you mainly interested in a contact network of Japanese companies and an understanding of their inner workings? If so, focus on an advisor with a reputation as an "insider" in Japan. In this case, you may wish to restrict the scope (and cost) of your contract to a "finder's fee."

Be warned that there are a large number of so-called "investment banks" specializing in Japan that are trying to cash in on the recent boom in Japanese investment. While some of these boutique operations are highly reputable, others may lack some of the basic expertise needed for the M&A process. Look carefully at the credentials of the principals. Have they been associated with major investment banks in the past? Do they have a verifiable list of prior customers? Make sure that you follow up carefully on their references, taking note of the credibility of the referees as well as of the principals.

Another general rule in selecting an investment advisor is to establish in detail the services that are to be performed, prior to signing a contract with the advisor. Services may include analysis of the decision to sell; development of buyer profile criteria; search for companies conforming to the criteria; evaluation of choices and development of a short list; valuation of the selling company; preparation and distribution of a Descriptive Memorandum; translation services; presentations to potential buyers; management of negotiations with the buyer; management of public releases, regulatory filings, and so on; fairness opinion (may require valuation of the seller in the case of a stock transaction); oversight of closing documents; and management of the closing. Most contracts used by financial advisors are quite vague in their description of the duties to be performed. If there is a particular service that you need, make sure that it is specified in the contract.

Following is a list of U.S. and Japanese financial advisors that offer M&A services focusing on Japanese acquisitions:

Morgan, Stanley & Co
The Blackstone Group
Goldman, Sachs and Co.
Merrill Lynch Pierce Fenner & Smith
Ulmer Bros, Inc.
Peers & Co.
Kidder, Peabody & Co.
IBJ/Schroder
Nikko Securities
Nomura Securities
Daiwa Securities
Dai Ichi Kangyo Bank
The Bank of Tokyo

Select a Target List.

It is helpful to prepare a buyer profile sheet, detailing the range of companies that may be buyers for your company's equity. The sheet may include the industry, size, and financial standing of potential buyers. Once you have defined your criteria, you will be able to expedite your search for companies that fit the criteria. Some databases (such as Compustat, Disclosure, and Dunsprint) allow on-line searches using defined criteria. But these do not generally cover Japanese companies. A good source of information of Japanese companies is the *Japan Companies Handbook* (published quarterly by Toyo Keisai, Inc.), which organizes Japan's largest companies by industry and which includes financial data as well as contact names.

Prepare a Descriptive Memorandum.

The behavior of Japanese companies is in most respects similar to that of corporate buyers in the United States. To analyze the merits of an acquisition, they will want to see a detailed information package about the company. In the case of public companies, much of this information will be available from publicly filed returns such as annual reports and 10-Ks, but buyers will look for additional information such as lists of assets, and management projections of future earnings. Japanese buyers should be offered a detailed Descriptive Memorandum, to include

- *Strategic analysis.* Analysis of the current competitive position of the company and its future prospects. Discussion of management's recent and current competitive strategies.
- *Financial information.* Summary and detailed financial data, including balance sheets, income statements, and statements of cash flow. Analysis of financial data, including discussion of appropriate financial ratios.
- *Industry analysis.* Analysis of the current state of the industry, and its future prospects. This section may be especially important to Japanese buyers, since they may be unfamiliar with the prospects for the industry in the United States. This is likely to be a vital consideration in their purchase decision.
- *List of assets.* Japanese buyers have been noted for their conservative approach to acquisitions in the United States: they are said to have a predilection for companies with identifiable assets, such as real estate, plant and equipment, or a well-known brand name. They are reportedly least comfortable when negotiating for intangible assets such as intellectual property. If you can justify your asking price in terms of underlying asset values, that is likely to strengthen your case in the eyes of the Japanese buyer.
- *Financial projections.* Like any buyer, Japanese companies like to see management's projections of future prospects for the company. You will find that they question your assumptions as rigorously as any other prospective buyer.

The Descriptive Memorandum does not need to be in Japanese. Most Japanese companies—or their financial advisors—are accustomed to reviewing such documents in English. But once a Memorandum is prepared, it may be advisable to produce a summary sheet in Japanese—a single sheet of paper that summarizes the acquisition opportunity (usually without naming your company) that can be quickly sent or faxed to companies that show initial interest, without the need of securing signed confidentiality agreements. Summary sheets can be readily translated and typed into Japanese by a professional translator. Generally, the Descriptive Memorandum will require execution of a confidentiality agreement by the Japanese buyer. This can be something of an obstacle, as some companies have to refer back to Japan to obtain authorization to sign such a document.

Letter of Intent.

Generally, by the time you reach the stage of signing a Letter of Intent, the Japanese buyer will have a U.S. attorney working on the case, and detailed negotiations relating to the Letter of Intent can be routed directly to the buyer or through the attorneys. From this point, the transaction will be very similar to a transaction between two U.S. companies. The Japanese will assemble a due diligence team (very likely including their U.S. accountants), and the Japanese company's attorneys will work toward producing a definitive agreement and other closing documents.

Exon-Florio Act.

In the case of acquisitions that may potentially compromise the defensive capabilities of the United States, approval of the transaction must be granted by the Committee on Foreign Investment. Bearing in mind the increasing lead of Japanese companies in some strategic industries, as well as the high level of public resentment of Japanese takeovers, the Committee is likely to question seriously deals in which the purchased company plays a significant role in any defense-related industry or in technologies that are considered crucial to U.S. defensive capabilities.

How to Gain Access to Japanese Debt Capital

The majority of major Japanese banks have offices in the United States, and for those that make loans to U.S. companies, the relevant departments are generally staffed by at least some Americans with corporate lending experience. Consequently, applying for a loan from a Japanese bank need be no different from applying to a U.S. bank. Be warned, though, that the majority of Japanese banks to this point have restricted their corporate lending to *Fortune* 500 companies.

In preparing a loan request, compile a Confidential Memorandum similar to what you would produce for an American lender. It should include

- *Historical financial data.* Data provided should encompass the past five years and include balance sheet, income statement, and cash flow statement. Analysis of financial data should contain key ratios and full explanation of any losses, extraordinary charges, or gains.
- *Term sheet.* This consists of summaries of the amount, purpose, and provisional terms of the debt requested.
- *Strategic summary.* Discussion of management strategy, focusing on the uses of the debt being requested, is required along with justification of the loan request in terms of the strategic advantage that will be gained by the investment.
- *Financial forecasts.* Forecasts should clearly demonstrate the ability of the company to repay the loan being requested.

How to Raise Capital in the Japanese Market

Is an Issue Appropriate for Your Company?

A capital issue in Japan offers significant benefits, but it's not appropriate for all companies. Daniel Schwartz, president of Ulmer Brothers, Inc., in New York, gives an example of an inappropriate candidate:

"A Californian businessman came to us to ask if we could help with a Japanese equity issue. He planned to buy a number of properties in the United States, and he felt that Japanese investors might be willing to pay a premium to participate in these investments. He wanted to establish a 'shell' company in Japan and then take it public in an equity offering."

Although the Japanese may indeed be interested in U.S. real estate investment opportunities, the idea was not appropriate for a Japanese stock offering.

"In order to raise equity in a Japanese public offering, you must have a subsidiary in Japan with a substantial operating record," says Schwartz. This is not only in order to attract the interest of the investment community; it is a requirement of the Tokyo Stock Exchange.

There are several alternative methods of accessing Japanese capital in Japan. Each is appropriate for a limited range of companies. The major methods are

1. *Public stock offering*. This is appropriate for established Japanese subsidiaries of foreign corporations that have significant business in Japan.
2. *Private stock placement*. While available to most companies, the firm must be in appropriate business and size range to interest Japanese investors.
3. *Public debt offering*. This approach is generally limited to major multinational corporations with internationally recognized credit ratings.
4. *Private debt offering*. This alternative available to most companies. But in practice offerings are likely to be limited to well-known companies. An example is Kohlberg, Kravis, Roberts' placement of several billion dollars in debt to finance the RJR Nabisco buyout.
5. *Depositary receipt listing*. Similar to American Depositary Receipts (ADRs) in the United States, depository receipts are issued for major foreign companies who

wish to have their shares traded in Japan. Depository receipts generally trade at their home country prices converted into yen. They do not benefit from the high premiums prevailing in the Japanese stock markets. They are primarily available to major multinational companies.

Hiring a Financial Advisor.

To complete a public offering in Japan, it is virtually essential to have a Japanese financial advisor. However, a number of U.S. institutions have ties with Japanese counterparts that would enable you to hire a U.S. advisor who would in turn bring in a Japanese agent to perform those tasks that require a Japanese institution. "The advantage of using U.S. advisors," says Daniel Schwartz, "is that they will tend to understand your needs better. They will make sure that you do not give away more competitive information than you absolutely need to, and they will help present the required information in a way that puts the best possible light on your company." Japanese advisors are essential for managing the filing process and for underwriting and placing the issue with investors.

Process of a Public Offering.

Public offerings in Japan are regulated by the relevant exchanges on which securities will be traded. There is no Japanese equivalent to the Securities Exchange Commission (SEC) in the United States. However, regulations and procedures are extremely similar to those set by the SEC. Disclosure requirements and required offering documents follow a similar format to those mandated by the SEC.

According to Daniel Schwartz, a company should allow from one to three years to complete an initial stock offering in Japan: "At least a year is required to build up a record of financial performance, in accordance with the requirements of the Japanese authorities. In addition, time is needed to prepare the ground for the offering: enlisting institutional support, answering questions from regulators, and promoting the offering."

A test that subsidiaries must meet in order to qualify for initial public offerings (IPOs) in Japan is that of independence. The subsidiary has to demonstrate that its operations are independent from those of its parent. "That turned out to be a big issue for Kentucky Fried Chicken in their IPO," says Schwartz. To be considered independent, a subsidiary must be locally managed and must have independent access to relevant sources of raw materials, as well as process technologies.

Once the decision is made to issue equity in Japan, a similar process applies as to an IPO in the United States: A prospectus must be prepared, giving potential investors access to wide-ranging information about the subsidiary's management and financial performance, as well as alerting investors to the risks of investment in the subsidiary. The prospectus will, of course, be in Japanese. Schwartz cautions that companies are required to make substantial disclosures about their operations in the prospectus and that they may be forced to divulge information that could be used against them by their competitors. "A company should carefully weigh the time and risks involved in going the IPO route in Japan," says Schwartz. "On the plus side, though, is the opportunity to raise equity capital at a very attractive price. The Japanese market still pays a much higher price for stocks than does the U.S. market." Schwartz points out that the majority of IPOs by foreign companies in Japan have been extremely successful, showing substantial price appreciation and finding widespread public recognition.

Entering Joint Ventures

Most joint ventures are between two companies that already know each other reasonably well, either as competitors or as trading partners. Consequently, if you are looking for a joint venture with a Japanese company, the chances are that you already know the best prospects. Your analysis should focus on those companies with which you have developed a working relationship within your own industry.

Joint ventures can have outstanding benefits, but they are also notoriously difficult to make a success. Often conflicting management styles, or more fundamental conflicts of interest, mar the harmony and capabilities of the joint venture. All too many joint ventures have ended in acrimony and mutual recrimination. This applies to joint ventures between U.S. companies as well as between U.S. and Japanese companies, but given the physical and cultural distance separating the United States and Japan, the potential for misunderstandings and conflicts is all the greater between U.S. and Japanese companies.

The key to success in a joint venture is the clear definition at the outset of the function, responsibilities, and limitations of the venture. In particular, lines of authority should be very clearly defined and understood. Since American and Japanese management styles are very different, it is unwise to try to combine them. Generally, joint ventures in Japan are likely to rely on Japanese management, whereas those based in the United States will have American managers.

Make sure also that your initial agreement covers mutually acceptable means of exiting the joint venture in the event it does not work out. Divorce in the world of joint ventures can be a very messy business.

Here are some additional recommendations for entering joint ventures with partners who you do not know well or who come from a significantly different culture:

1. *Identify specific benefits for both partners.* A successful joint venture will create a "win-win" situation in which both sides reap tangible, identifiable benefits. Ideally, these benefits will be specified and targeted at the outset of the joint venture. Benefits should be significant enough to ensure long-term cooperation. A seven- to ten-year time horizon is appropriate.

2. *Settle issues in advance.* Before signing the joint venture agreement, make every possible effort to identify po-

tential areas of misunderstanding or contention and resolve them through discussion in advance. The less surprises the joint venture produces for each partner, the better. Of course, identification of potential problems must be made diplomatically, since there is some danger of precipitating the very disputes you hope to avoid. Stick to significant issues: it's better to air differences on these up front, rather than be taken by surprise after investing significant effort and capital.

3. *Identify roles and responsibilities in advance.* Each side should know clearly what is expected of them. Especially between partners who do not know each other well, this kind of focused approach will help safeguard the operational smoothness and cooperative spirit of the joint venture. Of course, you should still remain flexible if the future opportunities arise which require modification of the rules.

4. *Walk before you try to run.* The Fuji-Xerox case study that follows indicates how far a successful joint venture can go. But, however high your hopes, it is better to start with modest, clear-cut, and achievable goals. Success in reaching these will provide the firmest basis for future expansion of the endeavor.

More specifically, as you go through the negotiating process to create a joint venture, bear in mind the following recommended steps:

1. *Define a negotiating timetable.* Outline the timeframe for negotiation, location of meetings, and procedures for resolving issues as they arise and, crucially, identify the people on each side that are to be involved in the negotiation, and clarify the extent of their authority.

2. *Cover key negotiating issues.* These include:
    - *Technology:* Who will provide key technologies? How will the technology be transferred? How will use be restricted, by the joint venture and the parent companies?

- *Construction of facilities:* What size of investment is required? What type of facilities/equipment are required? Where will plant and equipment be located? What will the sources be for procurement?
- *Employment practices:* Will employees be transferred or hired? Which parent company's practices, benefits, salary scale, etc. will apply, if either? What protection will transferred employees be given from management abuses, lay-offs, and so on? This can be a crucial question for the motivation of employees, especially when differences between U.S. and Japanese management practices are so great.
- *Financing:* what will sources be? How much is required? Schedule of repayment? Expected return on investment? (Again, there may be wide divergence between Japanese and U.S. expectations)
- *Management structure:* To whom will the joint venture's management report? What will be the limitations of their authority? How will the interests of each partner be represented in the joint venture's management?
- *Distribution of profits:* What is the time scale? What is the percentage to be distributed?

3. *Approvals and licenses.* Allow time and resources for securing all necessary government approvals and licenses, *prior* to commencing operations. Neither the U.S. nor the Japanese government is overly bureaucratic compared to governments in many developing countries. But some industries require special licenses—finance and pharmaceuticals are examples—and the joint venture cannot be considered underway until these are secured.

Fuji-Xerox: A Joint Venture Success Story

In the 1950s the Xerox Corporation formed its first joint venture designed to expand overseas sales. The joint venture was with Britain's Rank Organization and was 51% owned by Xerox. The joint venture, known as Rank Xerox, had responsibility for worldwide sales outside the United States. To penetrate the Japanese market, which at the time was heavily protected, Rank Xerox, in turn, formed a joint venture with Fuji Photo Film. The 50/50 joint venture, known as Fuji-Xerox, is widely credited as being the most successful joint venture between a Japanese and a foreign company.

Fuji-Xerox is now a major company in Japan. The company is fully integrated, with functions from research through manufacturing, customer delivery, and service. Fuji-Xerox is responsible for marketing products to Japan, Korea, Vietnam, the Philippines, Thailand, Taiwan, Indonesia, Australia, and New Zealand.

Fuji Photo Film is a relatively passive partner. Business management input comes from Xerox Corp. "But since we own only 50%, we don't have the authority to tell them exactly what we want them to do," says Dr. Roger Levien, Xerox Corp.'s corporate vice president of strategy. "Rather, we, and they, have to rely on moral suasion and logical reasoning."

"One of the critical issues for us as a multinational company without necessarily a single control point," adds Levien, "is to achieve coordination, particularly between Fuji Xerox and Xerox Corp., to make sure that the products developed by both companies become global products wherever appropriate."

Levien adds: "Even though one can conceive of such a straightforward product as a copier being inherently global, there are regional differences, and we have to design for them." For example, one successful

U.S. product failed in Japan because it was designed to work with the Latin alphabet and U.S./European paper as opposed to Japanese/Chinese characters, which require very precise delineation of fine lines and lighter weight Japanese paper. "Consequently," says Levien, "we have developed means to work across organizational boundaries to try to develop the capacity for global products—those that require only modest change in each marketplace."

The group has recently announced a product called the 5100, which was designed by Xerox with strong participation from Fuji-Xerox and is intended to be sold worldwide without substantial change.

Dr. Levien says that he works closely with the planning department of Fuji-Xerox. "Their internal organization is different from ours. In contrast to our approach, they have their own planning department at the corporate level. But the head of the corporate planning department and myself are in close contact." For example, Fuji-Xerox played a major role in the development of several key parts of Xerox Corp.'s "Xerox 2000" long-term plan.

In 1990 there was a six-month exercise known as Co-destiny III, between Xerox Corp and Fuji-Xerox. Its purpose was to improve the strategic cooperation between the joint venture partners as well as to develop a series of relationship management mechanisms that would result in effective coordination at the operating level.

According to Levien, "The exercise addressed the question of what was the intended goal for cooperation between our development and manufacturing groups. For example, should we have no overlap at all in our development programs? Should we have modest overlap? Should there be mutual dependence? The same questions were asked about manufacturing. We asked about geographic responsibilities for marketing:

Should they be diversified or not? We agreed that we should aim for a degree of coordination in our development and manufacturing functions, with some appropriate degree of overlap. We have a close working coordination at the research level, but we basically decided that we should retain the geographic separation of responsibilities.

Another result of the Co-destiny exercise was the "Presidential Summit," a semiannual meeting between the president of Fuji-Xerox and the chief executive officer of Xerox Corp. The purpose of these meetings is to agree on strategic direction and vision, as well as to resolve functional issues that may have arisen. In addition to the strategy meetings, the heads of Xerox Corp. and Fuji-Xerox see each other at Xerox Corp board meetings because Yotaro Kobayashi, president of Fuji Xerox, is a member of the board.

Note: Portions of this case study were previously published in Business International *and are reproduced by kind permission of Business International Corporation.*

7 WORKING FOR JAPAN INC.

For a growing body of workers, already numbering over 500,000, the influence of Japanese management style is felt directly: They work for Japanese companies in the United States. What is it like to have a Japanese boss? Experiences have differed greatly among different industries and among different companies in the same industry.

One study of U.S. workers at a Japanese-owned auto plant revealed an enormously heightened level of stress compared to the workers' peers in the American auto industry. This plant, which has very high productivity levels, exerts irresistible pressure on its workers to contribute long overtime hours: The average working week is close to 60 hours. Workers feel that there is an unwarrantably high level of personal supervision in their lives: The company takes an interest in their private activities as well as their associations at work. Any tendencies toward coalescing into unauthorized groups are strongly discouraged. On the other hand, workers are expected to contribute fully to group activities supported by the company. According to the survey, the word that best expressed the workers' prevailing mood was *fear*. They were terrified of failing to meet deadlines, failing to maintain quality, failing to please their employers. But, ironically, they were afraid above all of losing their jobs and being forced to return to the mediocrity of the opportunities outside the Japanese plant.

Other manufacturing employees have reported being

blissfully happy under Japanese management. They have been sent to Japan for training and for workers' exchanges, and they have been "treated as responsible adults for the first time in their working lives."

Japanese factories also have a more widespread influence on the communities in which they are located. In Smyrna, Tennessee, where the Nissan plant is located, the Japanese language has become an optional subject in the local schools. Japanese corporations are also increasingly active in the patronage of the arts and in humanitarian projects throughout the United States.

While many manufacturing installations run by Japanese managers in the United States have succeeded in achieving very high levels of profitability, American workers in Japanese service organizations often report that their employers are ill managed, bureaucratic, indecisive, and lacking in focused business strategies. This would tend to reemphasize the theory that the Japanese are leaders mainly in manufacturing and that they are followers in many other fields of endeavor. As I have discussed, in the service industries the relationship between Japanese and Americans seems truly to be one of mutual dependence: the Japanese on American know-how and creativity in developing new products and the Americans on the financial strength of the Japanese.

One comment that a number of my friends in Japanese firms have made is that, while American employees may be needed for their technical expertise, their opportunities to join the ranks of top management are in practice severely restricted. However, because of the desire of Japanese managers to avoid confrontation and to give the appearance of consensus, elaborate formalities have been developed in some companies to hide the real decision-making process.

Working for the Japanese: Profiles from Each Side

The following profiles illustrate some of the opportunities and difficulties seen by a Japanese manager and two American executives in Japanese-owned companies.

A Japanese Manager in New York.

Mr Yoshida is a midlevel manager at one of the major Japanese banks. He has been stationed in New York for the past three years. In his middle thirties, he sees himself as stuck uncomfortably between a deeply conservative older generation of Japanese and a younger group who, as Yoshida sees it, have lost the values essential to Japan's continuing prosperity.

A graduate of prestigious Waseda University, Yoshida is representative of an elite cadre who are groomed by leading Japanese companies for senior management positions (80% of his bank's "home" staff [i.e., staff members based in Japan on temporary overseas assignment] are graduates of four top Japanese universities). Perhaps because his education was a general one, centered on the humanities, Yoshida's interests extend far beyond his work. An avid reader, he has his parents send him regular shipments of newly released books. He is also a music fanatic. On the train back to his suburban New Jersey home, he is more likely to be seen reading *Billboard* magazine than the latest banking report. Yoshida runs a trading desk which daily wagers hundreds of millions of dollars in the currency, bond, and futures markets. A single mistake could cost the bank literally millions.

Yoshida has a staff of 25, of whom 5 are Japanese expatriates and the remainder local. All his staff are young—none over age 30. "I used to prefer having Japanese working for me. Although they generally have less specialized experience, they tend to learn more quickly. But," adds Yoshida, "the way Japan's younger generation is turning out, I think I'm happier with Americans now." This may also have something to do with Yoshida himself adjusting to American working culture. "My American staff are very good," he says, showing obvious pride. "I really think of them as my family." Another reason for his growing fondness of his American employees: Yoshida has little control over the Japanese staff who pass through his department—they are selected and evaluated elsewhere, and they often pay scant attention to their department head. Yoshida has no power to dismiss them or even to discipline them. American staff, on the other hand, Yoshida personally selects, and he has full responsibility for their training, management, and evaluation. It is a responsibility that he clearly enjoys.

Yoshida admits that the quality of Japanese staff is generally higher than that of the Americans who work for him. This is partly a factor of the selection process. Japanese staff are recruited from the top universities—the equivalent of an elite American business school. "We haven't in general hired American staff from the top rank. We felt that we would invest a lot of time and money in training these people, and then they would leave us. The problem is that Americans do not have the same ethic of loyalty to the company that we Japanese have."

When pressed a little, Yoshida admits that there is a good reason for this absence of loyalty. American staff have virtually no chance of reaching a top management position within the bank. "Our bank has been in New York for decades. We were one of the first Japanese companies to establish an office in the United States. Some of our American staff have over 30 years' service with us. We have more than a thousand American employees. Yet in spite of all those factors, we remain essentially a Japanese bank." All decisions of any significance must be approved by Tokyo, with the result that the Japanese language and a contact network within the home office become virtually essential for effective senior management. The bank does have some American senior vice presidents, but they tend to be in functions such as audit or operations that lie outside the major decision-making areas. "Our planning department, where the real decisions are analyzed and finalized in close consultation with Tokyo—that department is entirely Japanese."

What sort of a career does Yoshida's bank offer an American employee? "When I hire a new member of my department, I tell them honestly that I cannot guarantee them a successful career within our bank." Not only does the bank limit top management positions to Japanese "home staff," but Yoshida like other Japanese managers is in the U.S. on a limited assignment. Within a year, he will be back in Japan. Yoshida feels that he cannot guarantee the continuing support of his successor. "I have a very open attitude to my staff. But the person who comes after me—I have no idea what his views will be. I cannot promise something that I won't be here to deliver."

Yoshida says that he offers American employees two things. "Money. Our salary range is very competitive for the type of people we are hiring. So that is one important attraction. Second, I offer my staff some experience in trading that will make them attractive candidates for positions with other banks. When the time comes, I'll do everything in my power to help them get a job with another bank." This seems an ironic commentary from a representative of a culture famed for valuing loyalty.

Yoshida is the first to admit that recruiting Americans on the assumption that they will leave before long (most do—few stay beyond five years) is an unsatisfactory arrangement. He believes—and hopes—that it will change. "We have to do two things before we can offer attractive careers to top-flight American professionals. First, we have to transform ourselves into a more American bank. It shouldn't be necessary for all decisions to be approved by Tokyo. Second, we have to improve our operating environment so that a professional coming into the company will be able to understand and use it effectively. At the moment, our infrastructure is very weak."

What does Yoshida look for when evaluating American candidates? "First, I want them to be smart. Perhaps that goes without saying. But I am looking for a particular kind of smartness. I need my staff to be extremely steady-going." Because Yoshida's department invests vast sums daily, and because a single mistake could be enormously costly, Yoshida explains that he would rather have a "steady-going hard worker than a temperamental genius."

"Then, I would like them to be logical. I would rather have someone contradict me with a logical argument, than have that person quietly agree to everything I say." Yoshida says he welcomes aggressive types, but "aggression in words is one thing, aggressive action is another. I want the latter."

In general, Yoshida comments that a weakness of American candidates is their tendency to specialize too much. "Japanese managers are rotated every two or three years. The more they are targeted for a top management position, the more they will be rotated. Thus, they have a good overall picture of how a bank operates. Americans I meet tend to be focused in one small area. Even if they've been successful in that area, they don't understand well how it fits into the overall running of the company. That's another reason why our managers don't trust Americans for top positions." Another weakness that Yoshida mentions is a lack of commitment to self-improvement. "If I give them a book and tell them that they really should read it to improve their understanding of a work-related subject, in most cases they won't read it. They prefer spending their leisure hours in a bar or in front of the TV."

Yoshida is aware that Japanese companies are frequently the targets of bias-related lawsuits. His company's personnel department seek to impress the issue forcefully on Japanese managers. But he insists that a candidate's sex would in no way impair her prospects for hiring or promotion if she had the required qualities. This attitude is in spite of the fact that in Japan, women would not expect to be given important jobs. "I think our attitude is much more open here than in Japan."

Two Americans Working for Japanese Banks in New York.

Frank Brewster is a vice president at one of the top Japanese banks in New York. Frank's skills are highly specialized: He is a trader of sophisticated "swap" and "option" contracts. He was recently hired away by his present employer from a large American securities company.

"I went into this firm with somewhat limited expectations," he says. "I never expected that my career path in this company would include a shot at a top management position."

The firm has an entirely Japanese senior management group—with the exception of the personnel head, who Frank points out is not involved in vital strategic decisions made by the management team. "This company is investing huge amounts of money in American markets," he says. "It's not surprising to me that the bank's central management in Tokyo should want to keep a very close eye on what's going on. And given the language and cultural differences, the most logical way to do that is to have people they know, Japanese people, managing the shop."

Frank's own boss is American. "I had known him for several years through the marketplace, and he eventually hired me here." Frank comments that working in his specialized field is little different in his current situation from his previous experience in an American company. There are about two Americans for every one Japanese on the trading floor. Frank notes that the Americans tend to be specialized professionals like himself, while the Japanese are generally less specialized, rotating every two years or so to a different function within the bank. "That's probably an excellent way of training all-round senior managers. But it means they have less expertise in the highly complex markets in which we operate."

During the interview stage, Frank notes that he was interviewed primarily by Americans—particularly his current boss, whom he had known for some years on a professional basis. "After two or three interviews, a Japanese manager came in to meet me. He asked me some very general questions—nothing very challenging. I think he was really acting on the recommendation of my boss. It was more or less a rubber-stamp meeting."

Frank recalls that he asked the Japanese manager what opportunities there might be for eventual relocation to Japan or Europe. "He didn't exactly say there wasn't an opportunity. But he quietly dropped the subject in a way that led me to believe that was the case."

There were absolutely no questions about corporate loyalty. Frank agrees that it is paradoxical that in spite of their much vaunted culture of loyalty, Japanese firms don't seem to expect or even want long-term loyalty from their American employees, because they cannot offer them a career path into senior management. "There are Americans who have been in the bank for ten or more years. But I would say that they are the people who are the most disappointed with the opportunities offered by this company—and I would add they are perhaps the least likely people to succeed elsewhere—or they would have left."

Why did Frank join a company when he recognized that it would offer him limited career opportunities? "It was primarily a matter of compensation. They offered me an attractive salary and bonus scheme." Frank adds that although he hopes eventually to be a top manager, for the present he is content to focus on income. "Some of the oil traders at Salomon Brothers made more than the chairman of the firm last year," he says. "Trading offers the opportunity for substantial compensation without the need to take on management responsibility."

The salary offered by his Japanese employers was not substantially higher than what might be offered by an American company. "But," explains Frank, "another important motivator for me was the high credit standing of this bank—it has a triple-A rating. I can use that rating to make investments at a higher spread, which means in the end more profits and more bonus for me."

Frank says he is very comfortable with his decision to work for a Japanese company. "Actually it doesn't make much difference to me whether I work for a Japanese or an American company. But the salary is right, the bonus formula's right, and the credit standing of this bank helps me maximize income."

His major criticism of his working conditions is that

his Japanese colleagues—including managers—talk in Japanese, cutting the Americans out of any participation. "I don't know if they're making decisions behind our backs or just discussing last night's sushi," says Frank. "But it makes me uncomfortable."

When he needs a decision approved, he generally has to fax the request to Tokyo. "It usually gets approved within twenty-four hours. But the people in Tokyo like to know what's going on." The correspondence is always in English, and Frank has not found any serious communication foul-ups to this point. "Tokyo is like a black box to me," he says. "I feed faxes and telexes in, and get responses out. I've no idea what's really going on over there."

Frank praises his company's attitude to hiring and treatment of women and minorities. "Of course, they should realize that like all Americans their opportunities for upward mobility are limited in this company. But," he adds, "there are a surprising number of women and minority people in the company, and the company's treatment of them seems in every way honorable."

Michael is a vice president in a large Japanese bank. In his early forties, Michael is a Chinese-American, a highly specialized trader who develops complex models to predict market movements. Prior to joining his company, Michael worked for a major U.S. bank and spent two years on a posting in Tokyo.

Like Frank, Michael feels that working in a Japanese company is appropriate for a specialist. "I decided a while ago that I wasn't going to be Chairman of the bank—any bank. Working for a Japanese company allows me to pursue my interests without getting mired in the office politics of American companies."

Michael comments that opportunities for advancement within his company are extremely limited. "Yes, there are a couple of Americans in Senior Vice President positions, but let's face it, they're in highly specialized areas. If I was looking for a career progression leading to top management, I'd be very disappointed. But on the positive side, my employers here give me a great deal of freedom and respect to develop my ideas. Because the top managers all come from Japan, I don't have to worry about palace coups, power politics, or sudden changes in direction."

Michael's greatest criticism of his Japanese employers is their rigid attitude to employees. "They treat you as an investment," he comments. "The Japanese are the world's greatest investors, and they bring the same attitude to their American employees as they would to buying a piece of New York real estate. They hire you for a particular set of specialized skills, and they're really not interested in helping you develop beyond that level. To an American company, an employee is a human asset, to be developed as far as he or she can go. Japanese companies hire you for a specific function, and that's it."

Rigidity extends also to attitudes and behavior in the workplace. "There's a real tendency to think inside boxes," says Michael. He adds: "There's a tendency to focus on form more than substance.

"For example, there's a rule in my company that employees may not leave work before 5 P.M. Now a lot of companies have that kind of rule, but they're generally applied to junior and clerical staff. Here, a Vice President with a six-figure income is treated in just the same way: He has to fill out a request form and get it signed by his boss if he wants to leave work fifteen minutes early to go to the dentist. Now I call that excessively rigid. The bank is trusting me with millions of dollars of its money, but it can't trust me not to play hooky!"

Michael adds: "The President of the company told me a story recently. We have a loan officer on our staff, who's kind of a flamboyant character. He likes to get out of the office and onto the golf course, and he knows all the best restaurants in town. Well, this guy's colleagues, who are mainly Japanese, used to complain all the time about his work behavior. He wasn't punctual, he left work early, he stretched the expense account rules. But one day, a real crisis blew up. The bank was faced with the possibility of losing millions of dollars. None of the Japanese had a solution to the problem—it was outside the boxes that they think in. The American loan officer came up with a highly creative solution that saved the bank millions. Now which was more valuable: The form or the substance?"

However, says Michael, the unfortunate thing is that only the president of his bank would see the lesson in this story. "The Japanese middle managers, they don't have the maturity to see that kind of a thing. They're where the problem is."

Michael notes that the Japanese distaste for creativity and the inability to promote have affected the bank's hiring practices. "For the most part, this bank hires mediocre people," he says. "Salaries are low compared to the industry; and of course there's virtually no opportunity for career development. No ambitious, bright high-flyer would want to work in this environment." But Michael suggests that it suits the Japanese to hire relatively unimaginative people. "They don't want people who'll rock the boat." He adds that since Japanese companies tend not to have the same focus on profitability as American companies, they are more ready to accept mediocre performance by employees, so long as it is accompanied by a "conformist" attitude.

"In my opinion, you can divide the people who work for Japanese companies into three types," says Michael. "First, there are those who come for a short time and then move on. They may be motivated by the opportunity to get to know Japanese culture, or it may just be a job at the right time. But these people realize the opportunities are limited and soon go elsewhere to put their skills to work.

"Second, there are the deadbeats. Unfortunately, these are the most numerous type. By deadbeats, I mean people who don't have the ambition or abilities to get ahead in an American firm. For these people, working for a Japanese company is a cozy way to while away a career.

"And third, there are a few highly qualified, senior people, probably close to retirement age, who take largely symbolic jobs with Japanese companies, acting mainly in an advisory capacity. But this group is obviously very few in number."

Michael comments that working for a Japanese company is definitely not for everyone. "If you have a very specialized skill—as in my case—then a Japanese company may give you the freedom and respect to develop that skill." He adds: "A bright young person can certainly benefit from a year or two with a Japanese company. They say there's a great increase in people studying Japanese in college. If you want to get to know Japanese culture or broaden your horizons, certainly a Japanese company can be a good experience. But for most other people with any ambition to get to the top, I wouldn't recommend it."

Michael adds one more observation. "I'm an Asian-American. And although I couldn't prove it, I felt certain that in the American companies I worked for, there was an invisible barrier that would have prevented me from getting to the top. I noticed it more as I became more senior. Now I happen not to want to be Chairman of the Board, and I certainly wouldn't be able to reach that level in this company either. But at least here I don't feel I'm being discriminated against as an Asian-American. If anything, I think the Japanese managers here looked more favorably on me because of my Asian descent. They have a preconception that Asians work harder."

Michael and Frank have both decided that for them, the advantages of working for a Japanese company outweigh the disadvantages. Although they see the limitations of their companies as employers, they accept the situation because they are able to pursue their individual goals. But not all American employees of Japanese companies are so accepting. There have been numerous complaints of discrimination and unfair treatment both by minority groups and by American managers who feel they have been denied opportunities or unfairly dismissed. Several of the biggest Japanese employers in the United States—including Matsushita, Sumitomo, and NEC—are reported to have settled lawsuits recently that complained of discrimination against American managers. In 1990, a federal court awarded $2.5 million damages against a Matsushita subsidiary for discrimination on grounds of national origin. The suit asserted that the company had dismissed 66 American managers in a cost-cutting move but had retained all its Japanese managers. *The New York Times* recently reported that the Labor Department's Office of Federal Contract Compliance Programs in San Francisco (covering California, Arizona, Nevada, and Hawaii) has negotiated agreements with at least eight Japanese companies in the past three years, which it accused of hiring too few female, Black, and Hispanic workers.

Summary: The Pluses and Minuses of Working for the Japanese

PLUS

1. Successful, well-capitalized, growing employer
2. International orientation
3. Harmonious working environment
4. (For assembly workers) Greater on-the-job responsibility
5. Lack of power politics

MINUS

1. Limited room at the top—top jobs generally filled by Japanese
2. Bureaucratic working environment
3. Slow decision making
4. The encouragement of initiative/creative behavior
5. Poor record with women, minorities
6. Limited opportunities for international career

How to Sell Yourself to a Japanese Employer

It's important to remember that if you interview with a Japanese company, the first person you meet is quite likely to be American. Japanese companies often staff their personnel departments with locals, on the assumption that

American personnel professionals will be best able to manage local staff issues, including hiring.

Nevertheless, the personnel staff will be sensitive to their corporate culture, and to the requirements of the senior managers, who in the vast majority of Japanese companies operating in the United States are Japanese. If you are applying for a senior-level position, you are likely to be interviewed by a Japanese manager at some stage.

DO'S AND DON'TS OF INTERVIEWING FOR A JOB IN A JAPANESE COMPANY

Do's	*Don'ts*
1. Be modest	1. Don't be argumentative
2. Emphasize technical qualifications	2. Don't sound overly-ambitious

---

Here are some tips on how best to present yourself to a Japanese manager.

1. *Be modest.*

In your resume, stick to facts about your background as much as possible. In Japan, resumes are purely factual. Following a set format, they list education and employment history in bare note form. They do not contain lists of "strengths," or "accomplishments," or evidence of "leadership."

Japanese managers are not expecting you to turn in a Japanese-style resume. And, frankly, the average American resume looks a whole lot more appealing in its layout than its Japanese equivalent. But several Japanese managers have told me that they are suspicious of people who include long lists of personal qualities in their resumes. If possible, stick to the facts about your background. If you feel your resume looks a little thin, fill in some details about the jobs you undertook in your prior job.

The Japanese are often described as the world's most brand-conscious nation. Japanese managers tend to be impressed by attendance at prestigious institutions or prior employment by leading companies. If you can display this type of background, you may well have an advantage.

In an interview, be very careful not to talk yourself up too much. The Japanese have a horror of bragging. If you can, follow the resume policy of sticking to the facts. Of course, you want the interviewer to be aware of your achievements. But it's much better to introduce them in the context of the relevant facts about your career to date.

2. *Don't be argumentative.*

The Japanese love discussion. They spend endless hours discussing everything under the sun. But they do not consider it polite to argue or contradict. Although close friends in Japan may argue as much as anyone else, the tradition of courtesy and harmony dictates that it is extremely impolite to get into an argument with someone you don't know.

If an interviewer asks for your opinion, of course you should give it. Don't forget that in Japan, when someone gives his opinion to a superior, he usually prefaces it with some deprecating remark such as "Of course, I'm not an expert in this area, but. . . ." In fact, if he can present the opinion as belonging to someone else more qualified, he will probably do so: "Mr. Tanaka explained that . . . ." You don't have to follow these dictates, but remember that the interviewer is unaccustomed to forceful statements of personal opinion, especially from someone much younger than himself.

If the interviewer states his own opinion, don't argue with it or contradict it. If you disagree, you may want to make some noncommittal comment such as "I see." At a later point, you may want to bring out your own view on the subject, preferably giving the impression that you are simply adding to the conversation.

Some American interviewers like to place interviewees in confrontational situations, to see how they react or how aggressive they are. It is highly unlikely that a Japanese interviewer will do this (although some senior Japanese managers can be very blunt). But the correct way to react is with courtesy and tact.

3. *Don't sound overly-ambitious.*

In most larger Japanese companies, promotion comes regularly with age and length of service. At least until a manager reaches near the top of the pyramid, promotion—and salary—are not dictated by merit or achievement.

The Japanese find that this system, which seems so strange and demotivating to Western ears, works for them. For a start, everyone working in the company (at the management level) has been rigorously screened at the outset. Being admitted to the club is the major battle of your career. Then, the Japanese tend to value the security and stability of their organization, and the sense of belonging more than hefty salaries or rapid promotions.

So in Japanese companies, it is on the whole unnecessary—and in rather bad taste—to appear too ambitious. Of course, ambition exists in Japan as it does anywhere. Indeed, Japan as a nation has displayed quite breathtaking ambition ever since the opening of the country in 1860. But to show too much ambition would give the undesirable appearance of pushing yourself forward, at the expense of others with whom you work.

When interviewing an American candidate, Japanese managers will naturally look for evidence that the candidate is hardworking and bright. They value these qualities as much as anyone else. But if the candidate displays too much ambition or desire to excel, they may be a little put off. There are additional reasons for this, on top of the basic cultural predilection.

Japanese companies are usually unable to offer development of an employee beyond a middle-management level. That's because the senior-management jobs tend to be filled by Japanese. If they feel that an American employee is constantly chafing to reach a top job, that employee may end up rocking the boat and causing disharmony—and the employee will probably end up disappointed. An overly ambitious employee will probably either cause friction before too long, or quit.

Also, Japanese companies, although they generally pay reasonably well, do not on the whole like to be too lavish in their remuneration policies. They tend, for example, to avoid lavish bonus schemes. An interviewee who seems to be looking to make large amounts of money in the future will probably be disappointed. Japanese managers will be aware of these limitations and will try and avoid hiring people whose expectations are too high.

4. *Emphasize technical qualifications.*

Japanese companies in the United States seldom hire people into general management programs. That's because a cadre of Japanese managers is being prepared for the senior management posts. The company is more likely to be interested in hiring people with specific technical skills—for example, engineering experience, auditing, accounting, research and development, or marketing.

If you have technical qualifications that may match the needs of a Japanese employer, emphasize them. And be prepared to have a Japanese colleague sitting at your shoulder, learning these skills from you!

How to Present Your Name Card

Many Americans who visit Japan are impressed by the somewhat elaborate ceremony that seems to accompany the exchange of name cards. Impressed, and at times somewhat embarrassed. After all, most Americans are accustomed to flinging their cards down on the table, rather like a challenge.

The Japanese insist that there are no firm rules for the exchange of name cards. The appearance of a ritual simply stems from a tradition of courtesy. But here are some guidelines on a polite way to offer your card, in case you would like to practice!

1. *Make sure you have your card with you!* If you are introduced to a Japanese businessman, you can be almost sure that a card will be produced. The first rule is to have one handy to return.

2. *Have your card ready in advance.* I have not discovered any rule as to who should produce his or her card first. But it doesn't hurt to be ready promptly with your card rather than having to fumble at the bottom of your briefcase. Take a few out before you go into your meeting, and have them handy in a case or in your pocket.

3. *Offer and receive your card standing up.* A good rule is to fish out your card immediately after shaking hands. You will still be standing, and that position will show the requisite amount of courtesy. Some Japanese have rather elaborate ceremonies of handing over cards, using both hands and bowing as they present it to you. You don't have to reciprocate. When you receive a card, take it in your right hand, say "thank you," and look at it.

4. *Say something polite as you give your card.* Hand over your card with your right hand. Some Japanese use a two-handed approach, but I don't recommend this—it looks a bit strained in a Westerner. So does bowing.

   As you give your card, smile and say something polite, such as "Here's my card." Actually, it doesn't matter what you say. It's the politeness that counts.

5. *Read the card, then put it away carefully.* If you are being introduced to several people, wait till you have met them all, then examine their cards, and put them away. Put them into an inside pocket or into a wallet or some place where it doesn't look as though you're

being casual. If you are unsure about the names of the people you are dealing with, place the cards on the table in front of you and refer to them as needed. Of course, it's much better to memorize the names in advance.

Incidentally, never call a Japanese businessman by his first name, even though it's printed on the card. They don't call each other by first names, even if they've known each other for 30 years. It's always Tanaka-san or Mr. Tanaka. You're safest with Mr. or Dr., if appropriate. The only exception is if a Japanese (probably having lived in the United States) has adopted a Western-style name, which he states to you at the beginning of the meeting: for example, "I'm Matt."

Information on Recruitment by Japanese Companies

Some placement companies specialize in serving the needs of Japanese companies. Examples are Interlangue (phone 212-949-0170) and Fanning (212-349-3800). Note, however, that these companies primarily seek candidates with fluency in Japanese.

For graduating students with knowledge of Japanese, DISCO International Career Resources, Inc. organizes an annual Career Forum attended by 120 Japanese and American companies. Call 617-695-1366.

8 SELLING TO THE JAPANESE

The Services that the Japanese Need

"Every day for the coming year and more *you* could be receiving *arigato*s (thanks) from a huge number of your potential customers. It could include the 70,000 Japanese living in the New York City Metropolitan Area, plus the more than 2,000 Japanese-affiliated companies and their employees. . . ."

This is the sales pitch of the *Japanese-American Yellow Pages*, a publication that is mailed annually to the Japanese community in the New York area. For $25, a local company can be listed in the directory—larger advertisements are also available for a higher price.

The *Japanese-American Yellow Pages* provides a fascinating insight into the range of services that the Japanese community wants. There are over 300 different categories of service listed by Japanese and American providers in the book.

Let's look at some of the categories listed.

Accountants

The Japanese in America must pay their taxes like everyone else. Indeed, since they tend to be well paid, and since they often like to make investments in homes or other assets while in the United States, it would be a reasonable bet that their taxes are more complicated than the average.

Even for literate Americans, understanding the ever-changing U.S. tax laws is a Herculean task. Imagine how an overworked Japanese with limited English must feel when confronted with the instructions to tax form schedules A through Z! That's in addition to the obvious need by Japanese companies for expert tax and accounting advice.

So it's not surprising that there are accountants who see opportunity in the Japanese community. After all, socioeconomically they probably represent an ideal target.

Obviously, the primary consideration in offering accounting services to the Japanese community is that you should offer a Japanese language service. Ideally, you will have a Japanese professional on your staff. For example, Coopers & Lybrand advertises under its own name, as well as under the name of one of its Japanese members. By printing its ad in Japanese, Coopers & Lybrand indicates its ability to provide native Japanese language services.

Other accounting firms do not specifically indicate their expertise in Japanese, but we can assume that since they are targeting the Japanese market, they have made arrangements to deal with their clients in their native language.

An understanding of Japanese accounting and tax rules would also be very useful—that way, you can explain the differences between the Japanese and American tax codes.

Note that some companies retain accountants to advise their Japanese staff on tax matters. This may narrow the market a little—but it also offers an opportunity!

Art Galleries

Of the 20 or so galleries listed in the *Japanese-American Yellow Pages*, perhaps half specialize in oriental works of art. This may indeed be interesting to Japanese buyers, who have a natural interest in the art of their own region and who may be able to pick up Japanese art at lower prices here than in the astronomically expensive Tokyo galleries.

But perhaps more interesting are the sellers of American and European art that have taken out Japanese language ads in the Yellow Pages. They have recognized that the Japanese now represent a major market for Western art. In the last two years, Japanese buyers have broken a dozen world records on the international art market, including the staggering $54 million purchase of Van Gogh's *Irises*.

Even at a more modest level, Japanese executives in the United States are flush with cash and are immune to much of the recessionary cycle that art dealers live in such fear of.

Again, those galleries that can afford it have hired Japanese-speaking salespeople. But speaking Japanese may not be as important as understanding the tastes and buying propensities of the Japanese market.

Note that many Japanese art buyers are not living in the United States; they may merely be jetting over for a shopping spree. Direct advertising through the right channels in Japan may also be a productive move.

Bakers

That's a surprising entry! But the Japanese are renowned for their love of fresh bread and cakes, Japanese-style or French-style. Some enterprising bakers have probably doubled the quality of their products—and their margins!

Beauty Salons

While some salons cater exclusively to Japanese customers (some indeed are branches of Japanese chains), there's no reason why Japanese customers won't use a local service—so long as they're convinced they can get the level of attention, care, and understanding of the unique characteristics of Japanese hair that they expect. For example, Keiko, a woman with straight hair and bangs, tells me that she cannot find an American hairdresser who can cut her hair in the exact straight line that it needs.

Business Consultants

As with accounting, business consulting is a service required by Japanese companies establishing themselves in U.S. markets. Consultants can be of particular value in providing information about local markets, government and regulations, and competition, as well as training and advice in American business practice, personnel management, and so on.

Childbirth Education

The typical profile of the Japanese "salaryman" employee in the United States is a younger male with a wife and growing family. Often the wives have a much harder time adapting than their husbands: Wives often speak little English and are left to handle the practical aspects of family life. Services to ease their transition into American society are therefore enormously valuable to Japanese wives and children. These include social groups, medical advice (the U.S. medical system can be utterly intimidating to a non-English-speaking newcomer), language classes, and many others. The single ad under this category is a Japanese language service providing full training in handling giving birth in America.

Clothing

In 1991, *The New York Times* carried a story on a fashion show in New York City, intended mainly for Asian women. Fashion designer Akira Maki had created a line specifically tailored to the generally smaller outlines of many Asian women. According to the *Times*, Japanese women living in the New York area typically return to Japan to buy clothes, since American-designed clothes usually don't fit. Clearly, their is opportunity for those willing to cater to the special needs of Japanese men and women.

Computer Equipment & Services

Although the Japanese are leaders in the manufacture of computer hardware, companies establishing in the United States have to adapt to American systems and software configurations. Additionally, the Japanese have become so important in fields like finance that it is essential for software providers to tailor service to the needs of Japanese companies. Those that are successful selling locally may enhance their prospects for entering the enormous and lucrative Japanese market.

Curtains & Draperies

Japanese nationals typically rotate their overseas positions every three to five years. As a result, there's an enormous turnover of furniture and furnishings. Some wily local stores have recognized this huge potential demand and hired Japanese-speaking salespeople to make their Japanese clients as comfortable as possible. The reward is a loyal clientele with a low propensity to shop around and often with generous allowances.

Dentists

How would you feel stepping into a Japanese dentist's office, unable to communicate a word about your teeth or medical history, or to understand the dentist's explanation about his proposed course of treatment? Nothing is more alarming than giving up one's body to an unknown medical system. So the need for dentists and doctors who are equipped to understand the needs of their Japanese patients, and communicate reassuringly their treatments, is clear. Offering a Japanese language medical service is an enormous benefit to the Japanese community, as well as a large potential enhancement to your practice.

Employment Agencies

Whatever the employment situation may be in the labor market at large, there's a persistent shortage of Japanese-speaking job candidates in the United States. Japanese companies have a variety of specialized needs in their U.S. subsidiaries. These may be for Japanese-speaking staff or for some specialized functions such as currency management, accounting, or law. A number of specialized agencies have grown up to cater to the needs of Japanese companies. Obviously, a Japanese-speaking employment consultant is a virtual requirement for this activity.

In addition, there's another need that employment agencies can fulfill. Often the spouses of Japanese expatriates are highly qualified and educated. They may well be lonely on arriving in the United States, and a job can be the ideal outlet for them to develop their own life-style in the United States. Their skills may be of value to Japanese companies (who are constantly on the lookout for Japanese-speaking staff) or to American companies eager to do business with the Japanese. This market has special needs, as often these women have virtually no knowledge of the U.S. job market, and they usually will need special visas before they can start work.

Food Markets

Food markets that cater to Japanese tastes have sprung up in areas with a concentration of Japanese residents. The Japanese are generally ready to pay high prices for good-quality food—they are used to that from their home country. On the whole, these shops are managed and staffed by Japanese, who understand the special wants and service requirements of their Japanese customers.

But it's noteworthy that these shops are increasingly frequented also by non-Japanese. Other Asians, such as Koreans and Chinese, find many familiar products there, and with Japanese food experiencing a boom, Americans also are shopping at such specialized shops in increasing numbers.

One noteworthy example of the Japanese specialty food store is the Yaohan Mall in Edgewater, New Jersey. Opened by the Yaohan chain of Japan, the mall is a sparkling clean cluster of modernistic buildings looking out across the Hudson River toward the glittering towers of Manhattan. The mall includes a full-sized supermarket, its shelves crammed with Japanese imported food—rice cakes, soy sauce, pickles, dried fish, and a host of other delicacies and everyday items. On a typical Saturday, the aisles are packed with Oriental families piling groceries high on their carts. The average sale at Yaohan is said to be in excess of $90.

Yaohan is owned by a Japanese grocery store chain that had the vision to invest in a giant facility in the United States. The company's maverick owners believe passionately in the globalization of their business, so much so that they recently moved their headquarters from Japan to Hong Kong. But although the expertise and flavor of the store are Japanese, Yaohan entered into a partnership with American property developers to get them through the hurdles of local real estate development. These developers in turn had the foresight to devote their resources to this enormously successful development.

Health & Exercise

For every Japanese executive who comes to work in the United States—and there are approximately 400,000 of them here at present—there is usually a wife left alone in a strange new country, often lonely and lacking confidence. Exercise classes are a good way not only to stay trim, but also to meet other people in the community. A class may provide support in many ways beyond care of the body. While the Japanese community may not support an exercise facility on its own, it is well worth promoting your club or school among the Japanese community. In addition to increasing your membership, you would be offering a valuable service.

Hotels

Many hotels on both east and west coasts have developed special services for Japanese guests. The majority of Japanese visiting the U.S. do, after all, stay in hotels.

There are two types of Japanese visitors—tourists and businesspeople—each with somewhat different needs. While business visitors may gravitate towards large, established hotels with conference and other facilities, tourists look for well-located, reasonably priced hotels that provide good service and can help them enjoy their vacation.

Even smaller hotels or guest-houses can carve out a niche servicing Japanese tourists. Aim to provide a high standard of cleanliness, personal service, and information.

Insurance

The Japanese need insurance just like everyone else. While many of their personal insurance needs may be taken care of by their companies, or in Japan, there is a wide variety of special needs that must be met in the United States. These include

- Automobile insurance
- Home owners' insurance, for those Japanese families who buy property in the United States
- Group health insurance, generally through the company
- Corporate liability insurance

While selling insurance to a Japanese company may be like any other sale—the purchasing manager is as likely as not to be an American—Japanese companies and individuals appreciate, as in other things, a high level of personal service and an understanding of their special needs.

Lawyers

In Japan, the Japanese are not great users of lawyers. Japan has only one tenth the number of lawyers relative to the population as the United States. They tend to be used as a last resort in the event that all normal channels of mediation break down.

But when in Rome, one must do as the Romans do. Japanese companies and families use lawyers in the United States for the same reasons that everyone else does, plus a few more. A number of law firms, both big and small, provide special services to the Japanese community and to Japanese corporations.

At the family level, the greatest need of Japanese families is for assistance with immigration law. Although companies will generally arrange temporary visas for their staff coming from Japan, such visas are very restrictive. They do not generally allow a wife to work, and they do not permit permanent residence in the United States. Many families seek to arrange work permits for wives, or to change the family's status from temporary to permanent resident, outside the scope of the husband's company. In addition, many Japanese individuals and families arrive independently in the United States seeking permanent residence.

Japanese families are significant buyers of U.S. real estate, and hence also need real estate attorneys.

At the corporate level, Japanese subsidiary corporations naturally need the support of a full range of corporate legal services. However, they may have a special requirement for

- Corporate acquisition-related services, in the event they are acquiring existing U.S. corporations
- Immigration services, to assure smooth entry for their expatriate staff
- Labor law services, to deal with the special demands and threats posed by operating in a foreign environment

It goes without saying that having Japanese-speaking attorneys on a company's staff will maximize access to the Japanese market. Several large law firms have staffs of Japanese-speaking attorneys with highly specialized skills in acquisitions or corporation law. These firms compete in a high-stakes market for lucrative relationships with major Japanese corporations. However, in the case of smaller law firms in areas with a large Japanese population, a bilingual legal assistant—and a few well-placed recommendations—may be enough to attract the business of Japanese families and small companies.

All of us are confused and frightened by the law. But law firms dealing with Japanese communities should not forget that dealings with U.S. law are even stranger for the Japanese, unaccustomed as they are to using attorneys, unfamiliar as they are with specialized legal terminology, and threatened as they may feel by uncertain immigrant status and an Immigration and Naturalization Services (INS) often perceived as hostile.

Limousines

In the New York area, there are no fewer than five limousine services that specialize in the Japanese community. Most of these are subsidiaries of large Japanese limousine service companies.

This may be a hard market to break into—established players have made large investments to establish themselves. But the rewards are also great. Japanese companies—as well as visiting and resident individuals—enjoy the privacy, comfort, and safety afforded by limousine services. They travel a lot—and they can afford to pay!

Moving Companies

The Japanese represent an ideal market for moving specialists. A typical Japanese multinational company may have as many as two moves a week by employee families into and out of major U.S. cities such as New York and Los Angeles.

Sales are best made to the companies, which tend to handle moving on behalf of their employees. A good relationship with a sizable Japanese company can keep a moving company busy year-round.

Physicians

In communities with substantial Japanese populations, there tend to be large numbers of medical practices specializing in the Japanese community. For example, in the New York area there is a Japanese Medical Society of New York, an Asian American Health Service with a Japanese Section, a Nippon Medical Clinic, as well as dozens of Japanese-born practitioners.

The specialized services are in response to a real need: Nothing could be more intimidating to a sick foreigner than an American doctor's office, with its unfamiliar practices, differing approaches to medicine, and strange vocabulary.

Medical services offered to the Japanese community vary from family practice to such luxury services as plastic and cosmetic surgery.

Real Estate

As many as 100,000 Japanese come to live each year in the United States. All of them need housing.

In many cases, corporations provide housing for their employees, either directly or by suggesting they take over the residences of returning colleagues.

At one time, most Japanese corporations rented or purchased houses and apartments on behalf of their employees. But recently, the trend has been to give employees greater freedom by supplying them with a housing allowance and letting them find their own accommodation.

Although most Japanese nationals coming to the United States on limited assignments initially rent, the relative cheapness of American real estate (compared with Japan's sky-high prices) often prompts them to buy later. In addition, many Japanese who do not live in the United States buy property in the United States as an investment or as a base for frequent visits.

Although the Japanese are well known for their interest in property at the top end of the market—many luxury condominium developers establish sales offices in Tokyo—they do in fact rent and purchase at all levels of the market. Young Japanese nationals often live in quite humble accommodations, while senior executives or wealthy individuals vie with the millionaires for exclusive addresses.

A large number of real estate companies have targeted the Japanese market. At the corporate level, the market is, of course, dominated by the major international players in the business, including the great investment banks of New York and Tokyo. But for smaller commercial deals, and for residential real estate, services are provided by a mixture of local companies with hired Japanese associates and some companies started by Japanese nationals specifically to target the Japanese market.

Restaurants

The Japanese have a great tradition of dining out, particularly when entertaining, and with corporate expense accounts run up staggering bills at exclusive restaurants and clubs. The average Japanese company is known to spend as much as five times as much as its American counterpart on entertaining. The reasons for this are various: liberal Japanese tax rules, poor housing conditions which encourage eating out, and a culture of generous gift-giving.

To provide corporate executives with the kind of dining experience they have become accustomed to in Japan, many Tokyo restaurants have opened branches in New York and Los Angeles. In addition, the top-ranking restaurants in all major American cities cater to large numbers of Japanese.

But the Japanese are not interested only in luxury food. Well known for their innate curiosity, the Japanese enjoy exploring all sorts of ethnic cuisines as well as down-to-earth American fare. It is well worth advertising and offering services to attract a Japanese clientele, no matter what the type of restaurant. Because the Japanese tend to be faddish, once they start eating in a particular restaurant, they tend to flock in increasing numbers to the same place.

Some restaurants have established enormous reputations with the Japanese through special services they offer. Examples are the Village Vanguard and Blue Note jazz clubs in New York. Others become fashionable among the Japanese for no apparent reason.

In general, the Japanese—like anyone else—expect cleanliness and good service in a restaurant. But they are not notably more fussy than anyone else, and they are a customer group clearly worth having.

Schools

A number of schools have grown up in areas with Japanese populations to cater to the special needs of the Japanese community. Among these are Japanese language schools that Japanese children attend to supplement their attendance at

American public schools. These Japanese schools usually meet on Saturdays. They are needed to ensure the children do not fall too far behind the Japanese school curriculum in such areas as reading and writing Japanese.

But in addition to these Japanese-run schools, the Japanese also look to other schools to help them integrate into American life. Most popular are English language schools.

The Japanese consider it important to speak English when living in the United States. In spite of the fact that most of them have had at least ten years of English at school, many think they can improve their skills by enrolling in language schools once they are in the United States. While improving their English is the outward motivation, an important additional impetus is the opportunity offered by language schools to meet other people new to the community, and to fill the empty hours that often follow transfer to a strange and friendless land. This is of course especially true for wives.

Other popular schools with the Japanese community include driving schools—most Japanese in the United States have to pass driving tests under very different conditions from those they were accustomed to in Japan (where many people do not drive at all); music schools; and schools in various art forms such as calligraphy, flower arranging, or dance.

Sporting Areas and Goods

The world knows that the Japanese love golf. In addition, they are avid users of tennis equipment and facilities, ski resorts and equipment, and country clubs—both for the golf and the socializing.

Travel Agencies

A Japanese travel account, especially a corporate one, can be a rewarding piece of business. The Japanese are prodigious travelers. In addition to trips to and from Japan, they have a taste for resort vacations, generally of an upmarket variety. There are a large number of Japanese travel services in U.S. cities, mainly specializing in travel to and from Japan. It may be hard to compete with these suppliers, who have the advantage of Japanese staff both in the United States and often in Japan.

But for domestic business travel and for vacation travel, the field is relatively open, and the Japanese respond as always to reliable, courteous service and an understanding of their tastes.

WINNING JAPANESE BUSINESS

Advertise in Japanese language media.
Join/support Japanese social groups.
Locate in Japanese neighborhoods.
Research the market.
Involve the Japanese in your business.
Emphasize services.
Create special/differentiated products.
Provide Japanese-speaking support.

How to Win Japanese Business

Winning the business of the Japanese community requires much the same attributes as winning anyone else's business: good service and high quality. Half the battle is understanding that a Japanese market exists for your services, and actively positioning yourself to target the Japanese market.

Here are some ideas on how you might win Japanese business.

Target the Japanese.

1. *Advertise in Japanese language media.* In addition to the *Japanese-American Yellow Pages*, there are a number of Japanese language publications available in most larger cities. These include U.S. supplements to major Japanese newspapers, such as Asahi Shinbun's *Asahi Weekly*. There are also local papers published by some communities. And the *Beikoku Mainichi* has been publishing a daily for the Japanese-American community for the last 30 years.

2. *Join/support Japanese social groups.* The Japanese communities in the United States have many social and support groups, both formal and informal. At the formal level, there are several national Japan-oriented organizations, including the Japan America Society and the Japan Society.

You can probably find out what societies exist locally by contacting the Japanese consulate nearest you. Once you start to meet the Japanese community, you'll soon learn more. One good place to start is the local golf or country club.

3. *Locate in Japanese areas.* If you have something that the Japanese really want to buy, then they'll travel to you to buy it—once they know it's there. But you will make it much easier for them to purchase your services—and demonstrate your own commitment to the Japanese community—by setting up locally in a Japanese-oriented community. In Fort Lee, New Jersey, for example, whole streets have shop fronts decked out with Korean and Japanese writing, reflecting the two dominant communities on the area. Midtown Manhattan, where many major Japanese businesses are located, is another area that has a high concentration of Japanese-oriented stores and restaurants.

3. *Research the Market.* There are a number of ways in which you can get good information on the local Japanese community. One is through local societies. A membership list could make an extremely promising mailing list. Another is through the Japanese consulate, which collects some data on local communities.

If you are looking for sales leads, another good approach is the telephone book: Scanning a local directory can quickly yield a comprehensive customer list of the local Japanese community.

5. *Involve Japanese in your business.* If you hire a Japanese worker to assist you in your business, you have the potential to benefit in several ways. First, you may gain a

good worker (look for unemployed wives of Japanese businessmen—they tend to be well educated, intelligent, and hardworking). Second, you will have the ability to communicate directly to potential Japanese clients in their own language. Although they may speak good English, still they often appreciate the chance to express those subtle extra wishes in Japanese. Third, your Japanese employee will be a source of referrals: If, for example, she is the wife of an executive in a Japanese firm, you can be sure that the wives of her husband's colleagues will come and support her in her enterprise. And finally, you will be demonstrating to the Japanese community that you have a commitment to serve their needs. That kind of commitment inspires confidence, which in turn can lead to business.

Hiring a Japanese national can be tricky. Some companies discourage—or prohibit—the wives of their native Japanese staff from seeking employment. It is almost always because of the husbands' jobs that Japanese couples are living in the States. The wives are often bored and would welcome useful employment, especially the younger ones. If they have their husband's company's consent, there's still the problem of work permits. Most temporary residents in the United States are not permitted to work by the U.S. government, unless you apply for a special temporary visa on their behalf, generally at a cost in legal fees of at least $2,000. Some Japanese children of expatriates have American citizenship (anyone does who is born in the United States), and opt to live permanently in the United States. Such people, if they speak perfect Japanese, are generally in high demand and can command above-average salaries.

Win the Business.

1. *Emphasize service.* The Japanese are accustomed—in Japan—to an extraordinarily high level of service. If you have visited Japan, you will have seen this standard at work in all sorts of big and small ways. I was astonished the first time I walked into a bank and heard the entire staff of tellers and clerks call out, "Welcome!" When Jap-

anese consumers have a problem or a particular need, they don't hesitate to spell it out in detail to the service supplier, who will generally listen carefully and do his best to provide for it.

The Japanese in America often comment on the lack of service, particularly in public services such as buses, trains, or government agencies. They are quite good at adapting to American standards, and as a result, their expectations are probably much lower here than they were in Japan. But if they know where they can get a really high standard of service, they probably won't hesitate to use that service, and they may not mind paying a premium price.

2. *Create special/differentiated products.* Whether you are planning to sell to the Japanese community, or to Japanese companies located in your area, it helps to let the Japanese know that you have targeted them and are tailoring products especially to their needs. Don't hesitate to ask them what they look for in your product or service. You'll find that they're finicky customers. But if you can meet their standards, then promote your product as one that makes the grade. The very fact that you're tailoring products especially for the Japanese community is an indication of your commitment—though it's not a guarantee of sales.

3. *Provide Japanese-speaking support.* Even though many Japanese speak excellent English (they've all been learning it in school for at least ten years), it's easier for them to explain the subtleties and finer points of their needs in their own language. In addition, they appreciate the evidence of your commitment to provide them with a high quality of service.

Should You Sell Your House or Business to a Japanese Buyer?

Here are some guidelines to determine whether it might be appropriate for you to sell your home or business to a Japanese buyer. Note that members of the Japanese community have somewhat specialized needs and represent a small market compared with other ethnic or social groupings. So you should learn, if possible, that you do in fact have an appropriate property before investing a lot of effort in marketing it to the Japanese.

Do I Have a Well-established Brand/Product?

When it comes to buying businesses, the Japanese tend to be extremely conservative. They are, after all, on foreign ground.

If you have a well-established product or brand that is familiar to the Japanese community, even if it's something local like a movie theater or restaurant, then you may well be able to attract a Japanese buyer. On the whole, the Japanese are likely to be more attracted by a brand name or established reputation than by balance sheets showing pages of healthy statistics—numbers that the Japanese, who have some differing accounting standards, may not fully understand or trust.

Does the Business Require Active Management?

The Japanese are far more likely to want to play the role of investor than manager. The typical investor may be a successful businessman or company executive, who has lived for some time in the United States, but still regards his permanent home as Japan. Consequently, such a person will be much more comfortable knowing that his investment will be well managed as he goes about his other affairs. The best guarantee of good management is, of course, that you will stay on with the business, if you're currently an owner-manager. In compensation, you may be given an attractive buyout price as well as incentives for future performance. Look at what would be attractive for you, and ask for it.

Is My House in a Japanese Area?

When it comes to selling your home to the Japanese, you need to be sure that it is the sort of place that a Japanese family can live in.

If you own a luxury condo in midtown Manhattan, then your market may be wider than just the Japanese community. Such properties are marketed as investments by brokers in Japan and are even purchased sight unseen. But as you can imagine, your property would need to have cast-iron credentials to attract that sort of confidence.

For expatriates, a good indicator as to whether your house is attractive would be whether other Japanese families have moved into similar houses in the area. Ask the local real estate brokers—they have a good feel for who's buying and renting what.

Are There Other Japanese Living on the Street?

If there are, that's a sure sign that you're in the right area.

Is the House Low Maintenance?

The Japanese are usually inexperienced in the practicalities of home ownership, and they are probably not in the market for fixer-uppers and "TLC" specials. On the whole, they prefer something newer, cleaner, and maintenance free.

Is It Convenient for Commuting?

This is extremely important if you are to sell to an expatriate executive.

The Japanese are great users of public transportation, and they may be most attracted to properties that are within easy reach of train or buslines.

They are also very concerned about the frequency and reliability of transportation. One executive-style community in New Jersey wanted to attract more Japanese residents, but discovered that the Japanese were put off by the fact that the last train to the community left Manhattan at 9.00 P.M.—too early for many Japanese businessmen.

In another instance, a Japanese bank in Atlanta insisted that its manager rent an apartment close to the subway line, even though he commuted by car, on the grounds that if there should be an unexpected snowstorm, they wanted to be sure that their manager would still be able to turn up to work!

How to Find a Japanese Buyer for Your House or Business

The most important step you can take to sell your business or property to a Japanese buyer is to recognize that your property is an appropriate offering and to target Japanese buyers actively.

Here are some guidelines as to practical steps you can take to offer your property to the Japanese market.

Use Japanese Brokers.

In areas with a heavy concentration of Japanese residents or businesses, there are generally one or more brokers specializing in finding properties on behalf of the Japanese community.

In addition, many of the local real estate companies have added Japanese-speaking brokers to their staffs in order to attract Japanese buyers. Hori and Bunker, a real estate company, offers a listing service in Japan for U.S. properties. Call 1-800-872-2111.

Entering into an exclusive contract with a Japanese broker may be more of a commitment to the Japanese market than you are willing to take on. Ask for a semiexclusive or shared contract, with a regular local broker. Or sign with a company that offers to both Japanese and local buyers.

Advertise in Japanese Media.

This will help you reach a highly focused market segment.

Prepare Japanese Brochure, Offering Documents.

This can be expensive—it requires a translator and a specialized printer. But if you are serious in your search for a Japanese buyer, a Japanese language brochure will both underline the link between your property and the

Japanese market and be much more accessible to Japanese buyers.

You may be able to persuade a real estate or business broker or specialized investment bank to prepare the brochure.

At the least, a single photocopied sheet describing your property will make a useful flyer.

Conclusion

Japanese families hiring in the United States represent an affluent market segment with some needs in common with other Americans and others unique to their special circumstances. Throughout this book, the theme has been opportunity. The Japanese in America represent yet another opportunity for smart U.S. businesses to benefit from the growing Japanese presence in the United States.

9 MENUS AND SOURCES

Although the Japanese in general are known for their willingness to invest in U.S. assets, it is often hard to locate the right company—or individual—to turn to. Not all Japanese companies have a readily accessible presence, and language barriers may also prevent ready communication. In the event that you do not know whom to contact, I suggest that you write to the president, either of the firm's U.S. subsidiary or of the Japanese headquarters. Your letter will probably be transferred to the relevant department (these vary), but it doesn't hurt to start at the top. Table 9.1 lists the top 50 Japanese investors in the United States from 1985-1990, and Table 9.2 lists the largest Japanese companies by selected industries.

TABLE 9.1 50 TOP JAPANESE INVESTORS IN THE UNITED STATES, 1985-1990

Name of Acquirer	No. of Transactions	Combined Value ($ Million)
Matsushita Electric Industrial	2	6,125
Sony	9	5,810
Bridgestone	1	2,600
Saison Group	1	2,150
Aoki Corp	1	1,530
Dai-Ichi Kangyo Bank	3	1,450
Dainippon Ink and Chemicals	7	1,318

Mitsubishi Corp.	10	1,189
Nippon Mining	4	1,119
Nippon Life Insurance	4	1,033
Fujisawa Pharmaceutical	6	967
Kyocera	4	870
Bank of Tokyo	2	860
Paloma Industries	1	850
Mitsubishi Estate	1	846
Sumitomo Bank	2	550
Ito-Yokado	2	505
Settsu	4	481
Ryobi	4	401
Hitachi Ltd.	1	398
Yamanouchi Pharmaceutical	2	395
Sanwa Bank	5	383
Kawasaki Steel	5	376
Onoda Cement	3	367
NKK	4	345
Shiseido	2	345
Industrial Bank of Japan	3	344
Dai-Ichi Mutual Life Insurance	2	332
Daiwa Bank	1	330
Jusco	1	325
Kao	2	314
Mitsubishi Mining and Cement	5	305
Yasuda Mutual Life Insurance	2	300
Kubota	10	285
Orix	5	272
Secom	3	265
Pioneer Electric	2	260
Mitsui & Co.	14	256
Sumitomo Rubber Industries	2	251
Nippon Sheet Glass	2	235
Nikko Securities	2	225
Tokio Marine and Fire Insurance	4	219

Mitsubishi Kasei	3	216
Fuji Heavy Industries	1	208
TDK	2	205
Long-Term Credit Bank of Japan	3	201
Nippon Steel	4	193
Anritsu	1	180
Toshiba Corp.	4	175
Nippon Sanso	4	175

Source: Ulmer Brothers, Inc

TABLE 9.2 LARGEST JAPANESE COMPANIES IN SELECTED INDUSTRIES

Note: All phone numbers are listed as you would dial from within Japan. From the United States add the country code 81 and delete the first zero of the city code.

Banks

1. **Dai-Ichi Kangyo Bank**
   Assets: $413 billion
   1-1-5, Uchi-Saiwaicho, Chiyoda-ku, Tokyo 100
   Tel: 03-3596-1111
   Fax: 03-3596-2585
   President: Kuniji Miyazaki
   U.S. Office:
   One World Trade Center, Suite 4911, New York, NY 10048
   Tel: 212-466-5200

2. **Sumitomo Bank**
   Assets: $407 billion
   5-22, Kitahama, Higashi-ku, Osaka 541
   Tel: 06-227-2111
   Fax: 06-229-1083
   President: Soto Tatsumi
   U.S. Office:
   One World Trade Center, Suite 9651, New York, NY 10048
   Tel: 212-553-1011

3. **Fuji Bank**
   Assets: $398 billion
   1-5-5, Ohtemachi, Chiyoda-ku, Tokyo 100

Tel: 03-3216-2211
Fax: 03-3214-4150
President: Toru Hashimoto
U.S. Office:
One World Trade Center, Suite 6011, New York, NY 10048
Tel: 212-839-5600

4. **Mitsubishi Bank**
   Assets: $381 billion
   2-7-1, Marunouchi, Chiyoda-ku, Tokyo 100
   Tel: 03-3240-4274
   Fax: 03-3240-1111
   President: Tsuneo Wakai
   U.S. Office:
   One World Trade Center, Suite 8527, New York, NY 10048
   Tel: 212-524-7000

5. **Sanwa Bank**
   Assets: $373 billion
   4-10, Fushimi-machi, Higashi-ku, Osaka 541
   Tel: 06-202-2281
   Fax: 06-229-1064
   President: Hiroshi Watanabe
   U.S. Office:
   200 Park Avenue, New York, NY 10166
   Tel: 212-949-0222

6. **Industrial Bank of Japan**
   Assets: $292 billion
   1-3-3, Marunouchi, Chiyoda-ku, Tokyo 100
   Tel: 03-3214-1111
   Fax: 03-3201-7643
   President: Yo Kurosawa
   U.S. Office:
   245 Park Avenue, New York, NY 10167
   Tel: 212-557-3500

7. **Tokai Bank**
   Assets: $239 billion
   3-21-24, Nishiki, Naka-ku, Nagoya 460
   Tel: 052-211-1111
   Fax: 052-203-1207
   President: Kiichiro Ito

U.S. Office:
One World Trade Center, Suite 8763, New York NY 10048
Tel: 212-432-2600

8. **Bank of Tokyo**
   Assets: $222 billion
   1-3-2, Nihonbashi-Hongokucho, Chuo-ku, Tokyo 103
   Tel: 03-3245-1211
   Fax: 03-3279-3926
   President: Tasuku Takagaki
   U.S. Office:
   100 Broadway, New York, NY 10005
   Tel: 212-766-3400

9. **Mitsubishi Trust & Banking**
   Assets: $222 billion
   1-4-5, Marunouchi, Chiyoda-ku, Tokyo 100
   Tel: 03-3212-1211
   Fax: 03-3284-0934
   President: Hiroshi Hayashi
   U.S. Office:
   One World Financial Center, 200 Liberty Street, New York, NY 10281
   Tel: 212-341-0300

10. **Mitsui Taiyo Kobe Bank**
    Assets: $411 billion
    1-1-2, Yuraku-cho, Chiyoda-ku, Tokyo 100
    Tel: 03-3501-1111
    Fax: 03-3580-6647
    President: Kenichi Suematsu
    U.S. Office:
    277 Park Avenue, New York, NY 10172-0121
    Tel: 212-644-3131

11. **Sumitomo Trust & Banking**
    Assets: $208 billion
    5-15, Kitahama, Higashi-ku, Osaka 541
    Tel: 06-220-2121
    Fax: 06-220-2043
    President: Hiroshi Hayaski
    U.S. Office:
    527 Madison Avenue, 3rd Floor, New York, NY 10022
    Tel: 212-326-0600

12. **Long-Term Credit Bank of Japan**
    Assets: $197 billion
    1-2-4, Ohtemachi, Chiyoda-kui, Tokyo 100
    Tel: 03-3211-5111
    Fax: 03-3214-4372
    President: Tetsuya Horie
    U.S. Office:
    140 Broadway, New York, NY 10005
    Tel: 212-248-2000

13. **Mitsui Trust & Banking**
    Assets: $192 billion
    2-1-1, Nihonbashi-Muromachi, Chuo-ku, Tokyo 103
    Tel: 03-3270-9511
    Fax: 03-3246-1541
    President: Ken Fujii
    U.S. Office:
    One World Financial Center, 200 Liberty Street, New York, NY 10281
    Tel: 212-341-0300

14. **Daiwa Bank**
    Assets: $162 billion
    2-5-6, Bingo-machi, Higashi-ku, Osaka 541
    Tel: 06-271-1221
    Fax: 06-222-1880
    President: Akira Fujita
    U.S. Office:
    75 Rockefeller Plaza, New York, NY 10019
    Tel: 212-399-2710

15. **Yasuda Trust & Banking**
    Assets: $160 billion
    1-21-1, Yaesu, Chuo-ku, Tokyo 103
    Tel: 03-3278-8111
    Fax: 03-3278-0309
    President: Fujio Takayama
    U.S. Office:
    One World Trade Center, Suite 8871, New York, NY 10048
    Tel: 212-432-2300

16. **Toyo Trust & Banking**
    Assets: $125 billion

1-4-3, Marunouchi, Chiyoda-ku, Tokyo 100
Tel: 03-3287-2211
Fax: 03-3201-1448
President: Mitsuo Imose
U.S. Office:
437 Madison Avenue, New York, NY 10022
Tel: 212-371-3535

17. **Nippon Credit Bank**
    Assets: $124 billion
    1-13-10, Kudan-Kita, Chiyoda-ku, Tokyo 100
    Tel: 03-3263-1111
    Fax: 03-3265-7022
    President: Seishi Matsuoka
    U.S. Office:
    245 Park Avenue, 50th Floor, New York, NY 10167
    Tel: 212-984-1200

18. **Kyowa Saitama Bank**
    Assets: $110 billion
    1-1-2, Ohtemachi, Chiyoda-ku, Tokyo 100
    Tel: 03-3287-2111
    Fax: 03-3287-2556
    President: Shigehiko Yoshino
    U.S. Office:
    One World Trade Center, Suite 4673, New York, NY 10048
    Tel: 212-432-6400

Beverages

1. **Kirin Brewery**
   Sales: $4.9 billion
   6-26-1, Jingumae, Shibuya-ku, Tokyo 150
   Tel: 03-3499-6111
   Fax: 03-3499-6151
   President: Hideo Motoyama
   U.S. Office:
   Kirin USA, Inc.
   600 Third Avenue, New York, NY 10016
   Tel: 212-687-1865
   Fax: 212-286-8065

2. **Asahi Breweries**
   Sales: $3.7 billion

3-7-1, Kyobashi, Chuo-ku, Tokyo 104
Tel: 03-3567-5111
Fax: 03-3563-0326
President: Hirotaro Higuchi
U.S. Office:
Asahi Breweries, Ltd.
200 Park Avenue, Suite 4114-1, New York, NY 10166
Tel: 212-878-6775
Fax: 212-878-0975

Building Materials

1. **Ube Industries**
   Sales: $4.6 billion
   1-12-32, Nishihonmachi, Ube City, Yamaguchi Pref.
   Tel: 0836-31-1111
   Fax: 0836-22-1271
   President: Motoo Nakahigashi
   U.S. Office:
   Ube Industries (America), Inc.
   666 Fifth Avenue, New York, NY 10103
   Tel: 212-765-5865
   Fax: 212-765-5263

2. **Onoda Cement**
   Sales: $3.1 billion
   6276 Onoda, Onoda City, Yamaguchi Pref. 756
   Tel: 08368-3-3331
   Fax: 08268-3-2011
   President: Kazusuke Imamura
   U.S. Office:
   Onoda USA, Inc.
   901 Mariner's Island Boulevard, Suite 505, San Mateo, CA 90013
   Tel: 415-570-2270
   Fax: 415-570-2279

Chemicals

1. **Mitsubishi Kasei**
   Sales: $8.6 billion
   2-5-2, Marunouchi, Chiyoda-ku, Tokyo 100
   Tel: 03-3283-6111
   Fax: 03-3213-4094

President: Masahiko Furukawa
   U.S. Office:
   Mitsubishi Kasei America, Inc.
   81 Main Street, White Plains, NY 10601
   Tel: 914-761-9450
   Fax: 914-681-0760

2. **Asahi Glass**
   Sales: $8.1 billion
   2-1-2, Marunouchi, Chiyoda-ku, Tokyo 100
   Tel: 03-3218-5555
   Fax: 03-3212-4026
   President: Jiro Furumato
   U.S. Office:
   Asahi Glass America, Inc.
   1185 Avenue of the Americas, 20th Floor, New York, NY 10036
   Tel: 212-764-3155
   Fax: 212-764-3384

3. **Sumitomo Chemical**
   Sales: $6.9 billion
   4-5-3, 3 Kitahama, Chuo-ku, Osaka 541
   Tel: 06-220-3891
   Fax: 06-220-3347
   President: Hideo Mori
   U.S. Office:
   Sumitomo Chemical America, Inc.
   345 Park Avenue, New York, NY 10154
   Tel: 212-207-0600
   Fax: 212-207-0607

4. **Dainippon Ink & Chemicals**
   Sales: $5.6 billion
   3-7-20, Ninonbas, Chuo-ku, Tokyo 103
   Tel: 03-3272-4511
   Fax: 03-3278-8558
   President: Shigekuni Kawanura

5. **Sekisui Chemical**
   Sales: $5.1 billion
   2-4-4, Nishi-Tenma, Kita-ku, Osaka 530
   Tel: 06-365-4122
   Fax: 06-365-4370

President: Kaoru Hirota
U.S. Office:
Sekisui American Corp
780 Third Avenue, Suite 3102, New York, NY 10017
Tel: 212-308-7800
Fax: 212-759-0077

6. **Showa Denko**
   Sales: $4.2 billion
   1-13-9, Shiba-Daimon, Minato-ku, Tokyo 105
   Tel: 03-5470-3111
   Fax: 03-3431-6442
   President: Makoto Murata
   U.S. Office:
   Showa Denko America, Inc.
   West Building, 27th Floor, 280 Park Avenue, New York, NY 10538
   Tel: 212-687-0773
   Fax: 212-573-9007

7. **Mitsui Toatsu Chemicals**
   Sales: $3.7 billion
   3-2-5, Kasumigaseki, Chiyoda-ku, Tokyo 100
   Tel: 03-3592-4111
   Fax: 03-3592-4267
   President: Haruo Sawamura
   U.S. Office:
   Mitsui Toatsu Chemicals, Inc.
   140 East 45th Street, New York, NY 10017
   Tel: 212-867-6330
   Fax: 212-867-6315

8. **Mitsubishi Petrochemical**
   Sales: $3.2 billion
   2-5-2, Marunouchi, Chiyoda-ku, Tokyo 100
   Tel: 03-3283-5700
   Fax: 03-3283-5472
   President: Masaki Yoshida

9. **Shin-Etsu Chemical**
   Sales: $3.2 billion
   2-6-1, Ohtemachi, Chiyoda-ku, Tokyo 100
   Tel: 03-3246-5011

Fax: 03-3246-5358
President: Chihiro Kanagawa
U.S. Office:
Shin-Etsu Silicones of America, Inc.
431 Amapola Avenue, Torrance, CA 90501
Tel: 213-533-1101
Fax: 213-533-8936

Computers/Electronics

1. **Hitachi**
   Sales: $50.9 billion
   4-6, Kanda-Surugadai, Chiyoda-ku, Tokyo 101
   Tel: 03-3258-1111
   Fax: 03-3258-5480
   President: Katsushige Mita
   U.S. Office:
   Hitachi Denshi America
   3610 Clearview PArkway, Doraville, GA 31340
   Tel: 404-451-9453
   Fax: 404-458-8356

2. **Matsushita Electric Industrial**
   Sales: $43.1 billion
   1006, Kadoma, Kadoma City, Osaka 571
   Tel: 06-908-1121
   Fax: 06-908-2351
   President: Akio Tanii
   U.S. Office:
   375 Park Avenue, New York, NY 10020
   Tel: 212-371-4848
   Fax: 212-371-5675

3. **Toshiba**
   Sales: $29.5 billion
   1-1-1, Shibaura, Minato-ku, Tokyo 105-01
   Tel: 03-3457-4511
   Fax: 03-3456-4776
   President: Joichi Aoi
   U.S. Office:
   Toshiba America, Inc.
   375 Park Avenue, Suite 1705, New York, NY 10152
   Tel: 212-308-2040
   Fax: 212-838-1179

4. **NEC**
   Sales: $24.6 billion
   5-7-1, Shiba, Minato-ku, Tokyo 108-01
   Tel: 03-3454-1111
   Fax: 03-3457-7249
   President: Tadahiro Sekimoto
   U.S. Office:
   NEC America, Inc.
   8 Old Sod Farm Road, Melville, NY 11747
   Tel: 516-753-7000
   Fax: 516-753-7041

5. **Mitsubishi Electric**
   Sales: $21.2 billion
   2-2-3, Marunouchi, Chiyoda-ku, Tokyo 100
   Tel: 03-3218-2111
   Fax: 03-3218-2431
   President: Moriya Shiki
   U.S. Office:
   Mitsubishi Electric Sales America, Inc.
   645 Fifth Avenue, Suite 505, New York, NY 10022
   Tel: 212-223-2250
   Fax: 212-223-2265

6. **Fujitsu**
   Sales: $18.7 billion
   1-6-1, Marunouchi, Chiyoda-ku, Tokyo 100
   Tel: 03-3216-3211
   Fax: 03-3216-9365
   President: Tadashi Sekizawa
   U.S. Office:
   Fujitsu America, Inc.
   680 Fifth Avenue, New York, NY 10019
   Tel: 212-265-5360
   Fax: 212-541-9071

7. **Sony**
   Sales: $16.7 billion
   6-7-35, Kita-Shinagawa, Shinagawa-ku, Tokyo 141
   Tel: 03-3448-2111
   Fax: 03-3448-2183
   President: Norio Ohga
   U.S. Office:
   Sony Corp. of America

9 West 57th Street, 43rd Floor, New York, NY 10018
Tel: 212-371-5800
Fax: 212-421-1674

8. **Sanyo Electric**
   Sales: $10.5 billion
   2-18, Keihan-Hondori, Moriguchi City, Osaka 570
   Tel: 06-991-1181
   Fax: 06-992-0009
   President: Satoshi Iue
   U.S. Office:
   Sanyo Corp. of America
   522 Fifth Avenue, New York, NY 10036
   Tel: 212-819-1910
   Fax: 212-921-8229

9. **Canon**
   Sales: $10.0 billion
   2-7-1, Nishi-Shinjuku, Shinjuku-ku, Tokyo 163
   Tel: 03-3348-2121
   Fax: 03-3349-8519
   President: Keizo Yamaji
   U.S. Office:
   Canon USA
   One Canon Plaza, Lake Success, NY 11042
   Tel: 516-488-6700
   Fax: 516-488-1648

10. **Sharp**
    Sales: $9.9 billion
    22-22, Nagaike-cho, Abeno-ku, Osaka 545
    Tel: 06-621-1221
    Fax: 06-628-1653
    President: Haruo Tsuji
    U.S. Office:
    Sharp Electronics Corp.
    725 Old Norcross Road, Lawrenceville, GA 30245
    Tel: 404-995-0717
    Fax: 404-995-0620

11. **Ricoh**
    Sales: $5.7 billion
    1-15-5, Minami Aoyama, Minato-ku, Tokyo 107
    Tel: 03-3479-3111

Fax: 03-3403-1578
President: Hiroshi Hamada
U.S. Office:
Ricoh Corp.
5 Dedrick Place, West Caldwell, NJ 07006
Tel: 201-882-2000
Fax: 201-882-5840

12. **Fuji Electric**
    Sales: $5.4 billion
    1-12-1, Yuraku-cho, Chiyoda-ku, Tokyo 100
    Tel: 03-3211-7111
    Fax: 03-3211-7971
    President: Takeshi Nakao
    U.S. Office:
    Fuji Electric Corp. of America
    6-A Frassetto Way, Lincoln Park, NJ 07035
    Tel: 201-633-9000
    Fax: 201-790-0765

13. **Oki Electric Industry**
    Sales: $4.4 billion
    1-7-12, Toraemon, Minato-ku, Tokyo 105
    Tel: 03-3501-3111
    Fax: 03-3581-5522
    President: Nobumitsu Kosugi
    U.S. Office:
    Oki America, Inc.
    650 North Mary Avenue, Sunnyvale, CA 94086
    Tel: 408-720-1900
    Fax: 408-720-1918

14. **Pioneer Electric**
    Sales: $3.3 billion
    1-4-1, Meguro, Meguro-ku, Tokyo 153
    Tel: 03-3494-1111
    Fax: 03-3779-2163
    President: Seiya Matsumoto
    U.S. Office:
    Pioneer Electronics USA, Inc.
    2265 East 220th Street, Long Beach, CA 90810
    Tel: 213-835-6177
    Fax: 213-816-0402

15. **TDK**
    Sales: $3.3 billion
    1-13-1, Nihonbashi, Chuo-ku, Tokyo 103
    Tel: 03-3278-5111
    Fax: 03-3278-5358
    President: Hiroshi Sato
    U.S. Office:
    TDK Corp. of America
    12 Harbor Park Drive, Port Washington, NY 11050
    Tel: 516-625-0100
    Fax: 516-625-0653

16. **Alps Electric**
    Sales: $3.0 billion
    1-7, Yukigaya-Ohtsukacho, Ohta-ku, Tokyo 145
    Tel: 03-3726-1211
    Fax: 03-3726-9797
    President: Masataka Kataoka
    U.S. Office:
    Alps Electric (USA), Inc.
    3553 North First Street, San Jose, CA 95134
    Tel: 408-432-6000
    Fax: 408-432-6035

17. **Omron**
    Sales: $2.9 billion
    Nanajo-Sagaru, Karasuma-dori, Shimogoyo-ku, Kyoto 600
    Tel: 075-344-7000
    Fax: 075-344-7131
    President: Yoshio Tateishi

18. **Kyocera**
    Sales: $2.7 billion
    5-22, Kita-Inouecho, Higashino, Yamashina-ku, Kyoto 607
    Tel: 075-592-3851
    Fax: 075-501-6536
    President: Kensuke Ito
    U.S. Office:
    Kyocera International, Inc
    8611 Balboa Avenue, San Diego, CA 92123
    Tel: 619-576-2600
    Fax: 619-492-1456

Food

1. **Taiyo Fishery**
   Sales: $8.3 billion
   1-1-2, Ohtemachi, Chiyoda-ku, Tokyo 100
   Tel: 03-3216-0821
   President: Keijiro Nakabe
   U.S. Office:
   Taiyo Fishery Co. Ltd.
   c/o Reefer Express Lines
   Becker Farm Road, Roseland, NJ 07068
   Tel: 201-740-0470

2. **Snow Brand Milk Products**
   Sales: $7.2 billion
   13, Honsho-cho, Shinjuku-ku, Tokyo 160
   Tel: 03-3226-2111
   Fax: 03-3226-2109
   President: Katsuya Shono
   U.S. Office:
   One Executive Drive, Fort Lee, NJ 07024
   Tel: 201-592-9299
   Fax: 201-592-7357

3. **Nippon Meat Packers**
   Sales: $4.6 billion
   3-6-14, Minami Honmachi, Chuo-ku, Osaka 541
   Tel: 06-282-3031
   Fax: 06-282-1056
   President: Yoshinori Ohkoso

4. **Nippon Suisan Kaisha**
   Sales: $4.2 billion
   2-6-2, Ohtemachi, Chiyoda-ku, Tokyo 100
   Tel: 03-3240-6211
   Fax: 03-3244-7287
   President: Seigo Urano
   U.S. Office:
   900 Fourth Avenue, Suite 3001, WA 98164
   Tel: 206-624-7720
   Fax: 206-587-6248

5. **Ajinomoto**
   Sales: $4.1 billion

1-5-8, Kyobashi, Chuo-ku, Tokyo 104
Tel: 03-3272-1111
Fax: 03-3297-8704
President: Tadasu Toba
U.S. Office:
1001 Connecticut Avenue, Suite 704, Washington, DC 20036
Tel: 202-457-0284
Fax: 202-457-0107

6. **Itohan Foods**
   Sales: $3.2 billion
   4-27, Takahata-cho, Nishinomiya City, Hyogo Pref. 663
   Tel: 0798-66-1231
   President: Kenichi Ito

7. **Meiji Milk Products**
   Sales: $3.1 billion
   2-3-6, Kyobashi, Chuo-ku, Tokyo 104
   Tel: 03-3281-6118
   Fax: 03-3275-1466
   President: Hisashi Nakayama
   U.S. Office:
   520 Madison Avenue, New York, NY 10022
   Tel: 212-980-3059
   Fax: 212-308-3059

8. **Yamazaki Baking**
   Sales: $3.1 billion
   3-2-4, Iwamoto-cho, Chiyoda-ku, Tokyo 101
   Tel: 03-3864-3111
   President: Nobuhiro Iijima

9. **Nisshin Flour Milling**
   Sales: $2.8 billion
   19-12, Nihonbashi-Koamicho, Chuo-ku, Tokyo 103
   Tel: 03-3660-3111
   Fax: 03-3660-3844
   President: Osamu Shoda

10. **Morinaga Milk Industry**
    Sales: $2.6 billion
    5-33-1, Shiba, Minato-ku, Tokyo 108
    Tel: 03-3798-0111

Fax: 03-3798-0101
President: Akira Ohno
U.S. Office:
c/o Beechnut California Corp.
1661 Senter Road, San Jose, CA 95112
Tel: 408-295-8118
Fax: 408-295-8118

Forest Products

1. **Oji Paper**
   Sales: $4.7 billion
   2-1-1, Nishi-Shinjuku, Shinjuku-ku, Tokyo 163
   Tel: 033-347-1111
   Fax: 033-347-1140
   President: Kazuo Chiba
   U.S. Office:
   First Interstate Center, 999 Third Avenue, Suite 3710, Seattle, WA 98104
   Tel: 206-622-2820
   Fax: 206-292-7978

2. **Jujo Paper**
   Sales: $3.9 billion
   1-12-1, Yuraku-cho, Chiyoda-ku, Tokyo 100
   Tel: 03-3211-7311
   Fax: N/A
   President: Takeshiro Miyashita
   U.S. Office:
   One Union Square, 600 University Street, Suite 3320, Seattle, WA 98101
   Tel: 206-622-8724
   Fax: 206-223-0723

3. **Sanyo-Kokusaku Pulp**
   Sales: $3.5 billion
   1-4-5, Marunouchi, Chiyoda-ku, Tokyo 100
   Tel: 03-3211-3411
   Fax: 03-3287-6481
   President: Choji Kuramochi
   U.S. Office:
   208 Norton Building, Seattle, WA 98104
   Tel: 206-682-4698
   Fax: 206-624-4610

4. **Honshu Paper**
   Sales: $3.4 billion
   5-12-8, Ginza, Chuo-ku, Tokyo 104
   Tel: 033-3543-1862
   Fax: N/A
   President: Yoshinobu Yonezawa
   U.S. Office:
   One Union Square, 600 University Street, Suite 2300, Seattle, WA 98101
   Tel: 206-624-5145
   Fax: 206-625-1362

5. **Daishowa Paper Manufacturing**
   Sales: $2.9 billion
   4-1-1, Imai, Fuji City, Shizuoka Pref. 417
   Tel: 0545-30-3000
   Fax: 0545-32-0005
   President: Kiminori Saito
   U.S. Office:
   Daishowa America Co.
   7200 Columbia Center, Seattle, WA 98154
   Tel: 206-623-1772
   Fax: 206-382-9130

Industrial/Agricultural Equipment

1. **Mitsubishi Heavy Industries**
   Sales: $15.0 billion
   2-5-1, Marunouchi, Chiyoda-ku, Tokyo 100
   Tel: 03-3212-3111
   Fax: 03-3201-4517
   President: Kentaro Aikawa
   U.S. Office:
   630 Fifth Avenue, Suite 3450, New York, NY 10111
   Tel: 212-969-9000
   Fax: 212-262-3301

2. **Matsushita Electric Works**
   Sales: $6.7 billion
   1048, Kadoma, Kadoma City, Osaka Pref. 571
   Tel: 06-908-1131
   Fax: 06-906-1860
   President: Toshio Miyoshi

U.S. Office:
10400 North Tantau Avenue, Cupertino, CA 95014
Tel: 408-446-5010
Fax: 408-446-2108

3. **Komatsu**
   Sales: $6.3 billion
   2-3-6, Akasaka, Minato-ku, Tokyo 107
   Tel: 03-3584-7111
   Fax: 03-3605-9662
   President: Tetsuya Katada
   U.S. Office:
   Komatsu America Corp.
   31145 San Antonio Street, Hayward, CA 94554
   Tel: 415-489-3490
   Fax: 415-489-4544

4. **Ishikawajima-Harima Heavy Industries**
   Sales: $6.3 billion
   2-2-1, Ohtemachi, Chiyoda-ku, Tokyo 100
   Tel: 03-3244-5111
   Fax: 03-3244-5139
   President: Kosaku Inaba

5. **Kubota**
   Sales: $5.6 billion
   1-2-47, Shikitsu-Higashi, Naniwa-ku, Osaka 556-91
   Tel: 06-648-2111
   Fax: 06-648-2398
   President: Shigekazu Mino
   U.S. Office:
   Kubota America Corp.
   523 West Artesia Boulevard, Compton, CA 90220
   Tel: 213-537-2531

6. **Sumitomo Heavy Industries**
   Sales: $2.9 billion
   2-2-1, Ohtemachi, Chiyuda-ku, Tokyo 100
   Tel: 03-3245-4321
   Fax: 03-3245-4337
   President: Masataka Kubo
   U.S. Office:
   Park Avenue Tower, 65 East 55th Street, Suite 2303,
     New York, NY 10022

Tel: 212-888-1212
Fax: 212-688-0068

Metals

1. **Nippon Steel**
   Sales: $20.8 billion
   2-6-3, Ohtemachi, Chiyoda-ku, Tokyo 100-71
   Tel: 03-3242-4111
   Fax: 03-3275-5611
   President: Hiroshi Saito
   U.S. Office:
   Nippon Steel USA, Inc.
   345 Park Avenue, 41st Floor, New York, NY 10154
   Tel: 212-486-7150
   Fax: 212-486-7044

2. **NKK**
   Sales: $10.9 billion
   1-1-2, Marunouchi, Chiyoda-ku, Tokyo 100
   Tel: 03-3212-7111
   Fax: 03-3214-8428
   President: Yoshinari Yamashiro
   U.S. Office:
   NKK America, Inc.
   450 Park Avenue, New York, NY 10022
   Tel: 212-826-6250
   Fax: 212-826-6358

3. **Kobe Steel**
   Sales: $9.9 billion
   1-3-18, Wakinohama-cho, Chuo-ku, Kobe 651
   Tel: 078-261-5111
   Fax: 03-5252-7961
   President: Sokichi Kametaka
   U.S. Office:
   Kobe Steel America, Inc.
   299 Park Avenue, New York, NY 10171
   Tel: 212-751-9400
   Fax: 212-355-5564

4. **Sumitomo Metal Industries**
   Sales: $9.6 billion
   4-5-33, Kitahama, Chuo-ku, Osaka 541

Tel: 06-220-5111
Fax: 06-223-0305
President: Yasuo Shingu
U.S. Office:
Sumitomo Metal America, Inc.
420 Lexington Avenue, Suite 1800, New York, NY 10170
Tel: 212-949-4760
Fax: 212-490-3949

5. **Kawasaki Steel**
   Sales: $9.1 billion
   2-2-3, Uchi-Saiwaicho, Chiyoda-ku, Tokyo 100
   Tel: 03-3597-3111
   Fax: 03-3597-3160
   President: Shinobu Tosaki
   U.S. Office:
   Kawasaki Steel America, Inc.
   55 East 52nd Street, New York, NY 10055
   Tel: 212-935-8710
   Fax: 212-308-9292

6. **Mitsubishi Materials**
   Sales: $6.7 billion
   1-6-1, Ohtemachi, Chiyoda-ku, Tokyo 100
   Tel: 03-5252-5200
   Fax: 03-5252-5280
   President: Masaya Fujimura
   U.S. Office:
   Mitsubishi Metal America Corp.
   520 Madison Avenue, New York, NY 10022
   Tel: 212-688-9550
   Fax: 212-758-7273

7. **Furukawa Electric**
   Sales: $5.7 billion
   2-6-1, Marunouchi, Chiyoda-ku, Tokyo 100
   Tel: 03-3286-3001
   Fax: 03-3286-3694
   President: Kengo Tomomatsu
   U.S. Office:
   500 Fifth Avenue, Suite 1435, New York, NY 10110
   Tel: 212-719-4433
   Fax: 212-719-4738

8. **Toyo Seikan**
    Sales: $5.2 billion
    1-3-1, Uchi-Saiwaicho, Chiyoda-ku, Tokyo 100
    Tel: 03-3508-2113
    President: Yoshiro Takasaki

9. **Nippon Light Metal**
    Sales: $4.1 billion
    3-13-12, Mita, Minato-ku, Tokyo 108
    Tel: 03-3456-9211
    Fax: 03-3769-2451
    President: Shigeki Mukoyama

10. **Nisshin Steel**
    Sales: $3.5 billion
    3-4-1, Marunouchi, Chiyoda-ku, Tokyo 100
    Tel: 03-3216-5511
    Fax: N/A
    President: Tsuyoshi Kai
    U.S. Office:
    375 Park Avenue, New York, NY 10152
    Tel: 212-980-0580
    Fax: 212-421-0496

11. **Daido Steel**
    Sales: $3.3 billion
    1-11-18, Nishiki, Naka-ku, Nagoya 460
    Tel: 052-201-5111
    Fax: 052-221-9268
    President: Toshio Kishida
    U.S. Office:
    2200 East Devon Avenue, Des Plaines, IL 60195
    Tel: 312-699-9066
    Fax: 312-699-9067

12. **Toyo Sash**
    Sales: $3.0 billion
    2-1-1, Ohshima, Koto-ku, Tokyo 136
    Tel: 03-3638-8111
    Fax: 03-3638-8254
    President: Kenjiro Ushioda
    U.S. Office: Not available

Motor Vehicles/Parts

1. **Toyota Motor**
   Sales: $60.4 billion
   1, Toyota-cho, Toyota City, Aichi Pref. 471
   Tel: 0565-28-2121
   Fax: 0565-23-5721
   President: Shoichiro Toyoda
   U.S. Office:
   9 West 57th Street, Suite 4550, New York, NY 10019
   Tel: 212-223-0303
   Fax: 212-759-7670

2. **Nissan Motor**
   Sales: $36.1 billion
   6-17-1, Ginza, Chuo-ku, Tokyo 104-23
   Tel: 03-3543-5523
   Fax: 03-3546-0109
   President: Yutaka Kume
   U.S. Office:
   1683 Sunflower Avenue, Costa Mesa, CA 90247
   Tel: 714-549-1277
   Fax: 714-433-3746

3. **Honda Motor**
   Sales: $26.5 billion
   2-1-1, Minami-Aoyama, Minato-ku, Tokyo 107
   Tel: 03-3423-1111
   Fax: 03-3423-8947
   President: Nobuhiko Kawamoto
   U.S. Office:
   Honda North America, Inc.
   700 Van Ness Avenue, P.O. Box 2206, Torrance, CA 90509
   Tel: 213-781-4655

4. **Mitsubishi Motors**
   Sales: $16.8 billion
   5-33-8, Shiba, Minato-ku, Tokyo 108
   Tel: 03-3456-1111
   Fax: N/A
   President: Hirokazu Nakamura
   U.S. Office:
   Mitsubishi Motor Sales of America, Inc.

10540 Talbert Avenue, Fountain Valley, CA 92728
Tel: 714-963-7677
Fax: 714-964-3741

5. **Mazda Motor**
   Sales: $15.6 billion
   3-1, Shinchi, Fuchu-cho, Akigun, Hiroshima Pref. 730-91
   Tel: 082-282-1111
   Fax: 082-287-5237
   President: Norimasa Furuta
   U.S. Office:
   Mazda (North America), Inc.
   1444 McGraw Avenue, Irvine, CA 92714
   Tel: 714-261-9429
   Fax: 714-250-3155

6. **Isuzu Motors**
   Sales: $9.9 billion
   6-22-10, Minami-O8i, Shinagawa-ku, Tokyo 140
   Tel: 03-3762-1111
   Fax: 03-3762-1156
   President: Kazuo Tobiyama
   U.S. Office:
   Isuzu Motors America, Inc.
   205 Hembree Park Drive, Roswell, GA 30076
   Tel: 404-475-1995
   Fax: 404-442-8473

7. **Nippondenso**
   Sales: $9.7 billion
   1-1, Showa-sho, Kariya City, Aichi Pref. 448
   Tel: 0566-25-5511
   Fax: 0566-25-4509
   President: Tsuneo Ishimaru
   U.S. Office:
   Nippondenso Sales, Inc.
   3900 Via Oro Avenue, Long Beach, CA 90810
   Tel: 213-834-6352
   Fax: 213-513-5319

8. **Suzuki Motor**
   Sales: $7.4 billion
   300, Takakatsu, Kamimura, Hamana-gun, Shizuoka

Pref. 432-91
Tel: 053-440-2111
Fax: 053-456-0002
President: Osamu Suzuki
U.S. Office:
Suzuki of America Automotive Corp.
3251 East Imperial Highway, Brea, CA 92621
Tel: 714-996-7040
Fax: 714-970-6005

9. **Daihatsu Motor**
   Sales: $5.7 billion
   1-1, Daihatsu-cho, Ikeda City, Osaka Pref. 563
   Tel: 0727-54-3047
   Fax: 0727-53-6880
   President: Jiro Ohsuga
   U.S. Office:
   Daihatsu America, Inc.
   4422 Corporate Center Drive, Los Alamitos, CA 90720
   Tel: 714-761-7000
   Fax: 714-952-3197

10. **Fuji Heavy Industries**
    Sales: $5.2 billion
    1-7-2, Nishi-Shinjuku, Shinjuku-ku, Tokyo 160
    Tel: 03-3347-2111
    Fax: N/A
    President: Isamu Kawai
    U.S. Office:
    Subaru Plaza, 2235 Route 70 West, Cherry Hill, NJ 08002
    Tel: 609-488-3310
    Fax: 609-488-9279

11. **Aisin Seiki**
    Sales: $4.6 billion
    2-1, Asahi-machi, Kariya City, Aichi Pref. 448
    Tel: 0566-24-8239
    Fax: 0566-24-8848
    President: Shigeo Aiki
    U.S. Office:
    14109 Farmington Road, Livonia, MI 48154

Tel: 313-523-1800
Fax: 313-522-8519

12. **Hino Motors**
    Sales: $4.2 billion
    3-1-1, Hinodai, Hino City, Tokyo 191
    Tel: 0425-86-5011
    Fax: 03-3281-0013
    President: Tomio Futani
    U.S. Office:
    Hino Diesel Trucks (USA), Inc.
    31 Amlajack Boulevard, Shenandoah, GA 30265
    Tel: 404-251-9644
    Fax: N/A

13. **Yamaha Motor**
    Sales: $4.1 billion
    2500, Shingai, Iwata City, Shizuoka Pref. 438
    Tel: 0538-32-1115
    Fax: 0538-37-4252
    President: Hideo Eguchi
    U.S. Office:
    Yamaha Motor Manufacturing Corp. of America
    1000 Highway 34, Newnan, GA 30265
    Tel: 404-254-4000
    Fax: 404-254-4321

14. **Toyoda Automatic Loom Works**
    Sales: $5.5 billion
    2-1, Toyoda-cho, Kariya City, Aichi Pref. 448
    Tel: 0566-22-2511
    Fax: 0566-23-3255
    President: Yoshitoshi Toyoda
    U.S. Office: Not available

15. **Nissan Shatai**
    Sales: $2.8 billion
    10-1, Amanuma, Hiratsuka City, Kanagawa Pref. 254
    Tel: 0463-21-8001
    Fax: 0463-21-8155
    President: Satoshi Uemura
    U.S. Office: Not available

16. **Kanto Auto Works**
    Sales: $2.6 billion

Taura-Minatomachi, Yokosuka City, Kanagawa Pref. 237
Tel: 0468-61-5111
Fax: 0468-61-2329
President: Takatoshi Ando
U.S. Office: Not available

17. **Nippon Seiko**
    Sales: $2.5 billion
    1-6-3, Ohsaki, Shinagawa-ku, Tokyo 141
    Tel: 03-3779-7111
    Fax: N/A
    President: Toshio Arata
    U.S. Office: Not available

18. **Nissan Diesel Motor**
    Sales: $2.5 billion
    1-1, Oaza, Ageo City, Saitama Pref. 362
    Tel: 048-781-2301
    Fax: 03-3294-9198
    President: Takuro Endo
    U.S. Office:
    Nissan Diesel America, Inc.
    5930 West Campus Circle, Irving, TX 75063
    Tel: 214-550-8400
    Fax: 214-550-8685

Petroleum Refining

1. **Nippon Oil**
   Sales: $14.6 billion
   1-3-12, Nishi-Shinbashi, Minato-ku, Tokyo 105
   Tel: 03-3502-1111
   Fax: 03-3502-9352
   President: Kentaro Iwamoto
   U.S. Office:
   380 Madison Avenue, New York, NY 10017
   Tel: 212-986-7385
   Fax: 212-599-2628

2. **Idemitsu Kosan**
   Sales: $11.2 billion
   3-1-1, Marunouchi, Chiyoda-ku, Tokyo 100
   Tel: 03-3213-3111
   Fax: N/A
   President: Shosuke Idemitsu

U.S. Office:
Idemitsu Oil Development Co.
5051 Westheimer Road, Suite 500, Houston, TX 77056
Tel: 713-850-0781
Fax: 713-850-1937

3. **Cosmo Oil**
   Sales: $9.5 billion
   1-1-1, Shibaura, Minato-ku, Tokyo 105
   Tel: 03-3798-3211
   Fax: 03-3798-3211
   President: Hiroto Sumiyoshi
   U.S. Office:
   Cosmo Oil of USA, Inc.
   280 Park Avenue, 22nd Floor, New York, NY 10017
   Tel: 212-949-9710
   Fax: 212-949-8136

4. **Showa Shell Sekiyu**
   Sales: $8.2 billion
   3-2-5, Kasumigaseki, Chiyoda-ku, Tokyo 100
   Tel: 03-3580-0132
   Fax: 03-3581-9347
   President: Takeshi Henmi

5. **Nippon Mining**
   Sales: $6.3 billion
   2-10-1, Toranomon, Minato-ku, Tokyo 105
   Tel: 03-3505-8111
   Fax: 03-3582-1813
   President: Tatsuo Nakamura
   U.S. Office:
   6 East 43rd Street, New York, NY 10017
   Tel: 212-682-5060
   Fax: 212-949-0722

6. **Tonen**
   Sales: $4.9 billion
   1-1-1, Hitotsubashi, Chiyoda-ku, Tokyo 100
   Tel: 03-3286-5115
   Fax: 03-3286-5120
   President: Nobuyuki Nakahara
   U.S. Office:
   Tonen Energy Int'l Corp.

630 Fifth Avenue, New York, NY 10111
Tel: 212-765-5780
Fax: 212-246-7626

7. **Mitsubishi Oil**
   Sales: $3.9 billion
   1-2-4, Toranomon, Minato-ku, Tokyo 105
   Tel: 03-3595-7663
   Fax: 03-3508-2521
   President: Kikuo Yamada
   U.S. Office:
   520 Madison Avenue, New York, NY 10022
   Tel: 212-832-8838
   Fax: 212-308-9279

Pharmaceuticals

1. **Takeda Chemical Industries**
   Sales: $5.5 billion
   2-3-6, Dosho-machi, Chuo-ku, Osaka 541
   Tel: 06-204-2111
   Fax: 06-204-2035
   President: Yoshimasa Umemoto
   U.S. Office:
   Takeda Chemical Products USA, Inc.
   P.O. Box 2577, Wilmington, NC 28402
   Tel: 919-762-8666
   Fax: 919-762-8646

2. **Sankyo**
   Sales: $3.4 billion
   2-7-12, Ginza, Chuo-ku, Tokyo 104
   Tel: 03-3562-0411
   Fax: N/A
   President: Yoshibumi Kawamura
   U.S. Office:
   780 Third Avenue, Suite 2301, New York, NY 10017
   Tel: 212-753-3172
   Fax: 212-308-2491

Printing

1. **Dai Nippon Printing**
   Sales: $7.9 billion

1-1-1, Ichigaya-Kagacho, Shinjuku-ku, Tokyo 162-01
Tel: 03-3266-2111
Fax: 03-3266-2129
President: Yoshitoshi Kitajima
U.S. Office:
5 Third Street, San Francisco, CA 94103
Tel: 415-392-5320
Fax: 415-495-4481

2. **Toppan Printing**
   Sales: $7.2 billion
   1, Kanda-Izumicho, Chiyoda-ku, Tokyo 101
   Tel: 03-3835-5111
   Fax: 03-3837-7675
   President: Kazuo Suzuki
   U.S. Office:
   680 Fifth Avenue, New York, NY 10019
   Tel: 212-489-7740
   Fax: 212-969-9349

Rubber/Plastics

1. **Bridgestone**
   Sales: $12.4 billion
   1-10-1, Kyobashi, Chuo-ku, Tokyo 104
   Tel: 03-3567-0111
   Fax: 03-3567-4615
   President: Akira Ieiri
   U.S. Office:
   100 Briley Corners, Nashville, TN 37214
   Tel: 615-391-0088
   Fax: 615-391-3760

2. **Sumitomo Rubber**
   Sales: $3.5 billion
   1-1-1, Tsutsui-cho, Kobe 651
   Tel: 078-231-4141
   Fax: 078-232-0264
   President: Tasuku Yokoi
   U.S. Office:
   832 Nancy Way, Westfield, NJ 07090
   Tel: 201-332-5872
   Fax: 201-522-0402

3. **Yokohama Rubber**
   Sales: $2.6 billion
   5-36-11, Shinbashi, Minato-ku, Tokyo 105
   Tel: 03-3432-7111
   Fax: 03-3432-5616
   President: Kazuo Motoyama
   U.S. Office:
   1325 Remington Road, Suite Q, Schaumburg, IL 60195
   Tel: 312-882-6818
   Fax: 312-882-5196

Photographic

1. **Fuji Photo Film**
   Sales: $7.4 billion
   2-26-30, Nishi-Azabu, Minato-ku, Tokyo 106
   Tel: 03-3406-2111
   Fax: 03-3406-2193
   President: Minoru Ohnishi
   U.S. Office:
   Fuji Photo Film USA, Inc.
   555 Taxter Rd., Elmsford, NY 10523
   Tel: 914-789-8100
   Fax: 914-789-8540

2. **Konica**
   Sales: $3.7 billion
   1-26-2, Nishi-Shinjuku, Shinjuku-ku, Tokyo 163
   Tel: 03-3349-5251
   Fax: 03-3349-5290
   President: Takanori Yoneyama
   U.S. Office:
   Konica USA
   440 Sylvan Avenue, Englewood Cliffs, NJ 07632
   Tel: 201-568-3100
   Fax: 201-569-2167

Soaps/Cosmetics

1. **Kao**
   Sales: $4.5 billion
   1-14-10, Nihonbashi-Kayabacho, Chuo-ku, Tokyo 103
   Tel: 03-3660-7111
   Fax: 03-3660-7981

President: Fumikatsu Tokiwa
U.S. Office: Not available

2. **Shiseido**
   Sales: $3.2 billion
   7-5-5, Ginza, Chuo-ku, Tokyo 104-10
   Tel: 03-3572-5111
   Fax: 03-3572-6973
   President: Yoshiharu Fukuhara
   U.S. Office:
   Shiseido Cosmetics (America) Ltd.
   900 Third Avenue, 15th Floor, New York, NY 10022
   Tel: 212-752-2644
   Fax: 212-688-0109

Textiles

1. **Asahi Chemical Industry**
   Sales: $8.0 billion
   1-1-2, Yuraku-cho, Chiyoda-ku, Tokyo 100
   Tel: 03-3507-2730
   Fax: 03-3507-2495
   President: Reiichi Yumikura
   U.S. Office:
   Asahi Chemical Industry America, Inc.
   350 Fifth Avenue, Suite 7412, New York, NY 10018
   Tel: 212-695-6720
   Fax: 212-239-4165

2. **Toray Industries**
   Sales: $6.3 billion
   2-2-1, Nihonbashi-Muromachi, Chuo-ku, Tokyo 103
   Tel: 03-3245-5111
   Fax: 03-3245-5459
   President: Katsunosuke Maeda
   U.S. Office:
   Toray Industries America, Inc.
   280 Park Avenue, New York, NY 10017
   Tel: 212-697-8150
   Fax: 212-972-4279

3. **Kanebo**
   Sales: $5.0 billion
   1-5-90, Tomobuchi-cho, Miyakojima-ku, Osaka 534

Tel: 06-922-8151
Fax: 06-922-8160
President: Kazutomo Ishizawa
U.S. Office:
Kanebo USA, Inc.
20th Fl., Empire State Building, 350 5th Ave. New York, NY 10118
Tel: 212-244-1506
Fax: 212-563-4064

4. **Teijin**
   Sales: $4.4 billion
   1-6-7, Minami-Honmachi, Chuo-ku, Osaka 541
   Tel: 06-268-2132
   Fax: 06-268-3205
   President: Hiroshi Itagaki
   U.S. Office: Not available

5. **Toyobo**
   Sales: $4.0 billion
   2-2-8, Dojimahama, Kita-ku, Osaka 530
   Tel: 06-348-3111
   Fax: 06-348-3192
   President: Saburo Takizawa
   U.S. Office: Not available

6. **Unitika**
   Sales: $2.6 billion
   4-1-3, Kita-Kyutaromachi, Chuo-ku, Osaka 541
   Tel: 06-281-5695
   Fax: 06-281-5697
   President: Keita Taguchi
   U.S. Office:
   Unitika America Corp.
   1180 Avenue of the Americas, New York, NY 10036
   Tel: 212-921-8883
   Fax: 212-921-9202

Other

1. **Japan Tobacco** (Tobacco)
   Sales: $7.8 billion
   Address not available
   U.S. Office: Not available

2. **Yamaha** (Musical Instruments)
   Sales: $3.7 billion
   10-1, Nakazawa-machi, Hamamatsu City, Shizuoka Pref. 430
   Tel: 053-460-2141
   Fax: 053-464-8554
   President: Hiroshi Kawakami
   U.S. Office:
   Yamaha Corporation of America
   6600 Orangethorpe Avenue, Buena Park, CA 90620
   Tel: 714-522-9011
   Fax: 714-527-0155

3. **Kawasaki Heavy Industries** (Transportation Equipment)
   Sales: $6.9 billion
   2-1-18, Nakamachidori, Chuo-ku, Kobe 650
   Tel: 078-371-9530
   Fax: 078-371-9568
   President: Hiroshi Ohba
   U.S. Office:
   Kawasaki Heavy Industries (USA), Inc.
   599 Lexington Avenue, Suite 2705, New York, NY 10022
   Tel: 212-759-4950
   Fax: 212-759-6421

Investment Banks

Investment banks can be crucial intermediaries in your dealings with Japanese companies. There are a number of "boutique" investment banks that specialize in transactions involving the Japanese. Most of the major New York investment banks also have merger and acquisition (M&A) departments with special expertise in Japan-related transactions. And all the large Japanese financial institutions are also represented in the United States.

The center of the investment banking community remains New York. Most of the major, and many of the boutique, institutions are located in Manhattan. However, many of these companies are also well represented on the West Coast, so it may not be necessary to cross the continent to seek assistance. Table 9-3 provides a listing of U.S. investment banks with Japanese practices.

Investment banks can offer a variety of services, some specifically related to Japanese M&A; others more in the nature of general financial and technical advice. Services may include

- *Strategic assistance.* Analyzing of the decision to sell, raise capital, and so on. How will each option fit with your strategic goals? What is the most appropriate option?
- *Contact network.* Using investment bank's contacts to find an appropriate Japanese partner for acquisition, joint venture, private placement, and so on.
- *Financial analysis/valuation.* Determining an appropriate price for assets, equity, or other securities to be issued.
- *Marketing the transaction.* Creating offering documents, approaching interested parties, providing information, and encouraging investors to buy/invest.
- *Negotiating the transaction.* Leading negotiating sessions, answering queries of buyers/investors, and advising client on details relating to the transaction.
- *Managing the transaction.* Managing the preparation of closing documents, hiring of attorneys, press releases, tender offers, and so on.
- *Fairness opinion.* Providing a professional opinion as to the fairness of an agreed purchase price.

In the case of Japanese acquisitions, perhaps what sets specialized players apart the most is the extensive contact networks they can bring to bear. It can be very hard indeed to scour the ranks of Japanese companies for potential buyers. Which companies are likely candidates? Who is the right person to contact? How do you convince them that your company is a worthwhile investment? An investment bank with the right contacts can smooth the way through all these issues.

Partnerships Between Japanese and U.S. Investment Banks

In recent years, a number of partnerships have been established between U.S. and Japanese investment banks. There have been good reasons on both sides for the formation of these partnerships. On the Japanese side, they provide access to the expertise of U.S. companies in a field in which Japanese firms have until recently had little experience. On the American side, Japanese firms provide instant access to a contact network in a society notorious for being somewhat impenetrable. In some cases, Japanese firms have also provided needed capital.

One such partnership is that between The Blackstone Group of New York and Nikko Securities of Tokyo. The Blackstone Group is a small investment banking "boutique," with a focus on cross-border mergers and acquisitions. Relying on a handful of high-profile partners, headed by former Commerce Secretary Peter D. Peterson, The Blackstone Group has pulled off some notable M&A coups, including representing Sony in its acquisition of Columbia Pictures. In 1988, Nikko Securities acquired a 20% stake in The Blackstone Group for a reported $100 million. Nikko now has a four-man M&A group operating out of Blackstone's headquarters. Nikko's group is headed by Masakatsu Sakamoto.

"In 1985, a boom began in Japanese cross-border transactions," says Sakamoto. "This was the result of high cash balances and low interest rates in the Japanese economy, as well as a sudden, dramatic increase in the value of the yen." At that time, few Japanese securities companies had any significant experience in mergers and acquisitions. "Our clients were looking to us to provide them with advice in these transactions. A rapid response was needed," says Sakamoto, adding: "Most of the brokerage houses had to accumulate know-how very quickly." The response of several brokerage companies and banks was to make investments in U.S. securities companies which had the needed expertise: Nikko in Blackstone, Nomura in Wasserstein-Perrella, Sumitomo in Salomon Brothers, Dai Ichi Kangyo in Dillon Read, Industrial Bank of Japan in Schroeders Bank, and Long-Term Credit Bank of Japan in Peers & Company.

Sakamoto points out that he and his colleagues at Nikko were able to cooperate with Blackstone in understanding the needs of Japanese companies and in finding Japanese clients and investors to match up with U.S. investment opportunities. "At the same time, Blackstone could help us acquire the expertise we need to provide advice to our clients."

"Blackstone is a boutique house, and so it must limit its targets in order to use its facilities most effectively," says Sakamoto. "Therefore, they tend to be interested mainly in larger transactions." Sakamoto points out that this focus is in keeping with the high-level personnel in Blackstone. "They have a 'top-to-top' approach," he says.

Sakamoto notes that there has been a marked slowdown in Japanese acquisitions in the Unites States, starting in the second half of 1990. He attributes this to political instability following Iraq's invasion of Kuwait as well as the declining Japanese stock market, higher Japanese interest rates, and a relatively strong dollar.

However, Sakamoto points to continuing Japanese interest in certain key strategic industries:

- *Finance.* Japanese companies are still interested in building market share in the asset management business.

- *Chemicals.* Japanese chemicals companies are still smaller than their U.S. or European counterparts. They are looking to overseas acquisitions in order to achieve global economies of scale.

- *Pharmaceuticals.* Japanese companies are looking for distribution channels in the United States. Japanese

companies are increasingly interested in marketing in the United States, in spite of the long FDA approval process, in order to help cover the enormous development costs for new drugs.
- *Computers and media.* U.S. companies are still leaders, especially in the software field. Japanese companies are ready to pay to catch up. "That includes media-related software," adds Sakamoto, pointing to the acquisitions by Sony and Matsushita of Record and movie companies.

Sakamoto comments that Japanese buyers (and their financial advisors) have become much more sophisticated, as they have worked their way up the experience curve. "In Japan, there used to be an allergy to the words M&A. Now, Japanese companies are better at understanding the strategic considerations that justify acquisitions." He points out that, although the number of acquisitions in the United States has declined recently, the number of domestic mergers in Japan continues to increase.

In the past, points out Sakamoto, Japanese companies have made acquisitions that in spite of restructuring of he acquired companies have not yet produced significant synergies. As examples, he points to Nippon Mining's acquisition of Gould and Bridgestone's acquisition of Firestone. But several factors are now combining to make Japanese buyers much more effective bargainers. "In the first place, Japanese companies have become more sophisticated as they familiarize themselves with the M&A process. In addition, the market has changed. In the 1980s it was a seller's market, and U.S. companies commanded high prices. Now it's a buyer's market, and multiples have come down substantially."

Sakamoto mentions some continuing weaknesses of Japanese buyers. "It's still difficult for Japanese companies to have the confidence to manage U.S. companies. Sony has done it, but Sony is really an exception." He notes that Japanese companies still prefer minority investments or joint venture agreements.

TABLE 9.3 INVESTMENT BANKS WITH JAPANESE PRACTICES

The Blackstone Group
345 Park Avenue, 30th Floor
New York, New York 10154
212-935-2626
Peter G. Peterson, Chairman
Note: Part owned by Nikko Securities

The Goldman Sachs Group, LP
85 Broad Street
New York, NY 10004
212-902-1000
Geoffrey T. Boisi, head, Investment Banking
Tel: 212-902-1000
Note: Part owned by Sumitomo Bank

First Boston Corporation
Park Avenue Plaza
New York, New York 10055
212-909-2000
Michael Koeneke, Mergers and Acquistions

IBJ Schroeder Bank & Trust Co.
One State Street
New York, NY 10004
Tel: 212-858-2395
Donald McCreg, CEO

Kidder Peabody & Co., Inc.
10 Hanover Square
New York, NY 10005
Tel: 212-510-3000
B.J. Megargel, Mergers and Acquisitions

Lazard Freres & Co
1 Rockefeller Plaza
New York, New York
212-489-6600
Felix G. Rohatyn, Mergers and Acquistions

Merrill Lynch Capital Markets
  1 Liberty Plaza
  New York, New York 10281
  212-449-1000
  Alain LeBec, Mergers and Acquisitions

Morgan Stanley & Co., Inc.
  1251 Avenue of the Americas
  New York, New York
  212-703-4000
  Stephen M. Waters, co-head, Mergers and Acquistions

Salomon Brothers, Inc.
  One New York Plaza
  New York, NY 10004
  Tel: 212-747-7000
  Charles M. Nathan, Mergers and Acquisitions

The Japanese Export Trade Organization (JETRO) is a Japanese government agency that assists U.S. businesses in locating Japanese trading partners. The majority of JETRO services are provided without charge. See Table 9-4 for a listing of JETRO offices by city in the U.S.

TABLE 9.4 JAPAN EXPORT TRADE ORGANIZATION OFFICES

New York
  McGraw Hill Building, 44th Floor
  1221 Avenue of the Americas
  New York, NY 10020
  Tel: 212-997-0400
  Fax: 212-997-0464

Chicago
  401 North Michigan Avenue, Suite 660
  Chicago, IL 60611
  Tel: 312-527-9000
  Fax: 312-670-4223

Los Angeles
  725 South Figueroa, Suite 1890
  Los Angeles, CA 90017

Tel: 213-624-8855
Fax: 213-629-8127

San Francisco
Quantas Building
360 Post Street, Suite 501
San Fransisco, CA 94108
Tel: 415-392-1333
Fax: 415-788-6927

Denver
1200 17th Street, Suite 1400
Denver, CO 80202
Tel: 303-629-0404
Fax: 303-8893-8522

Dallas
World Trade Center, 1st Floor
2100 Stemmons Freeway
Dallas, TX 75258
Tel: 214-651-1831
Fax: 214-651-1831

Houston
One Houston Center, Suite 1810
1221 McKinney
Houston, TX 77010
Tel: 713-759-9210
Fax: 713-759-9210

Atlanta
Marquis One Tower, Suite 2102
245 Peachtree Center Avenue
Atlanta, GA 30303
Tel: 404-681-0713
Fax: 404-681-0713

WHY TRADING COMPANIES ARE AMONG JAPAN'S BIGGEST BUYERS

At first glance, it might seem inconsistent that a 'trading company' should be active in acquiring other companies, either at home or overseas. After all, from its name one might assume that its only function was trading, that is, importing and exporting.

Importing and exporting were indeed the original functions of the trading companies, but for a variety of reasons, their roles have vastly expanded over the years. Trading companies nowadays are hybrid organizations—with some of the characteristics of merchant banks and some characteristics of conglomerate holding companies. They have also come to play a major role in acquisitions of companies and property overseas. The growth in their role has been due to

1. *Unique understanding of overseas markets.* Although many Japanese firms have become household names in the West, most have until recently remained exporters rather than true multinationals. Their manufacturing, sales, and marketing organizations have remained in Japan. In many cases, they relied on the trading companies to help them sell their products in overseas markets. Trading companies, by concentrating on building strong networks of expertise and contacts in overseas markets, could provide unparalleled efficiency in marketing Japanese products. Japanese trading companies have offices in virtually every country in the world, and they are renowned for their knowledge of local markets. Often they are better informed than many government intelligence networks. As a result of this unique expertise, trading companies are uniquely able to evaluate and act on overseas acquisition opportunities.

2. *Strong capital base.* Trading companies have always bought and sold on their own account. They are therefore accustomed to the idea of committing their capital to a business opportunity. As a result of decades of generally successful international activity, the Japanese trading companies have reached a position of commanding financial strength. They are currently among Japan's most profitable and best capitalized corporations. Acquisitions are one way to put this powerful capital position to productive use.

3. *Interlinked corporate structures.* Several of the major trading companies are at the center of vast systems of interlinked companies (known in Japan as *Keiretsu*). As such, they operate for the benefit of their group as well as on their own account. These groups have interests in most major industries and are therefore interested in expansion opportunities overseas in virtually any field. The trading company can act as a scout to identify and make an initial investment in promising business opportunities, including overseas acquisitions, that will ultimately benefit other members of the *keiretsu*.

Trading Companies

The general trading companies of Japan (*sogo shosha*) have grown to join the ranks of the world's most powerful corporations through their role as intermediaries in Japan's export-oriented growth. Their offices span virtually every country in the globe, and their employees are among the elite of Japan's business community. As recently as 1980, as much as 60% of Japan's imports and exports were channeled through a dozen trading companies.

But the 1990s represent new challenges for these companies and will require innovative strategies to respond to the opportunities and threats of the current business environment. At the root of these challenges is the increasing globalization of the world's business.

The Challenge of Globalization

The traditional role of the trading companies has been trade—acting as intermediaries between Japanese manufacturers and buyers around the world. But the powerful growth of Japanese industry has catapulted Japanese manufacturers into the top league of companies worldwide. Many are now pursuing their own strategies of globalization, and increasingly they are investing in direct marketing facilities overseas. "The trading companies can no longer stay in the middle," says Mike Furuhata, former president of C. Itoh & Co. (America), Inc. "Time and again, we've worked to improve ties between manufacturers and customers, only to find ourselves eventually being cut out of the loop. We've learned many bitter lessons from that."

Another challenge arises from a paradoxical development: The rise of the global business has brought with it a need for corporations to create deeper local roots. The concept of globalization implies fuller integration with the economies and societies in which the corporation does business and decreasing dependence on the home base.

"Global" Means Local

Most of the trading companies have long-established overseas subsidiaries. But until recently these have been characterized by expatriate staffs and a strong degree of control from Japan. Now the changing dynamics of global business are dictating a new emphasis on local self-sufficiency. "C. Itoh America would like to be more and more independent from C. Itoh Japan," says Furuhata. "We are trying to localize our operations more and more."

Ironically, the trend toward greater independence of overseas subsidiaries has in many cases come about as much by accident as by design. Furuhata describes an example: "Some years ago we invested in a California fence manufacturer and distributor, Master-Halco, Inc. At the time, our strategy was to supply this company with Japanese steel and to take advantage of its finishing and distribution capabilities to increase penetration of the American market. But when the yen appreciated, Japanese steel became uncompetitive, and we started importing from Korea. Now we use American steel. Master-Halco is now a totally American company, with virtually no direct links with Japan. Eventually, we would like to start exporting its products to Japan and other countries."

Although the localization of Master-Halco came about almost by accident, the development is consistent with the evolving goals of the trading companies. Profits are no longer dependent on currency fluctuations. By deepening local roots overseas, the company is actually able to expand its global reach—and in the process to lessen its dependence on the fortunes of its home base. Its local identity brings it closer to its American customers. And political pressures are eased as the company becomes accepted as a domestic presence.

Getting Closer to the End User

Responding to the challenge of the declining role for intermediaries, the trading companies have moved to expand their capabilities at both ends of the distribution chain. "Downstream, C. Itoh and other trading companies are investing to strengthen capabilities in sales," says Furuhata. "We don't expect to become retailers, but we are getting closer to the end user by acquiring leasing operations, distributors, and companies that convert semifinished materials into finished products."

At the other extreme, trading companies are increasing their involvement in primary manufacturing processes through joint ventures and minority stakes in established manufacturers. "We can add our expertise in marketing, sales, and international business. And we might well participate as a minority investor with a Japanese manufacturer in overseas acquisitions." Often, the stake in the acquisition might be no more than a token 5%, as a witness of the trading company's commitment to the success of the venture over the long run. However, in cases where C. Itoh previously represented the manufacturer overseas, Furuhata envisions a greater commitment (up to 40%) in order to protect that relationship.

Adding Value

The global strategies of C. Itoh and other trading companies are being implemented in large measure through substantial investments in overseas assets, including equity stakes, joint ventures, and outright acquisitions. However, unlike some of the more flamboyant recent Japanese investments, those of the trading companies have tended to be in nuts-and-bolts industries and generally pass unnoticed by the media.

The concept of value added is crucial to Furuhata's assessment of viable investment opportunities. "It's my firm belief that if a cross border investment (whether joint venture or acquisition) brings benefits to the parties involved as well as to the end users, then in the context of globalization, that's the way we have to go. We're more and more integrated in a host of ways." The benefits that trading companies are able to provide include technological know-how as well as marketing and financing capabilities.

For example, one 50%-owned subsidiary of C. Itoh (America), an Illinois auto parts distributor, has become a major supplier to Japanese "transplant" automobile factories in the United States. In addition to its marketing clout, C. Itoh supplied expertise in the design and implementation of "just-in-time" delivery systems to enhance the capabilities of the American subsidiary. "The know-how we provided enabled our subsidiary to offer state-of-the-art services to win major new customers. And improvement of the delivery system has actually enabled these automakers to purchase parts from American companies that they would otherwise have bought from their Japanese counterparts. Our goal now is to offer the same efficient service to GM and other U.S. manufacturers."

Furuhata emphasizes that "beneficial" investments should work both ways. In Japan, he initiated joint ventures with U.S. and European companies, despite political opposition, to provide telecommunications services to the Japanese market. At the same time, Furuhata is critical of Japanese investments that do not add value. "There's a tendency on the part of real estate investors in particular to rush in to invest in big-name properties. I think that should change."

Increased Overseas Investment

Furuhata sees a continuing investment by the trading companies in overseas acquisitions in the coming years. "For the next year or two there will be many opportunities to invest in the United States because of the difficulties of companies purchased through LBO's [leveraged buyouts]. Many of these companies are really victims—they're sound from an operational point of view, but because of the loans, they're in the red. If a company that approaches us fits with our strategy, if it will be profitable in the long run (not necessarily this year or next), if we can add some value, then we're interested." Furuhata adds: "In America, there are always sellers!"

Table 9.5 provides a list of U.S. subsidiaries of major Japanese trading companies.

TABLE 9.5 U.S. SUBSIDIARIES OF MAJOR TRADING COMPANIES

C. Itoh & Co. (America), Inc.
335 Madison Avenue
New York, NY 10017
Tel: 212-818-8000
Fax: 212-818-8361

Itoman (USA), Inc.
1211 Avenue of the Americas
New York, NY 10038
Tel: 212-869-1700
Fax: 212-869-2647

Marubeni America Corp.
200 Park Avenue
New York, NY 10166
Tel: 212-599-3700
Fax: 212-953-0388

Mitsubishi International Corp.
520 Madison Avenue
New York, NY 10022
Tel: 212-605-2000
Fax: 212-605-2597

Mitsui & Co (USA), Inc.
200 Park Avenue
New York, NY 10166
Tel: 212-878-4000
Fax: 212-878-6748

Nissho Iwai American Corp.
1211 Avenue of the Americas
New York, NY 10036
Tel: 212-704-6500
Fax: 212-704-6543

Sumitomo Corp. of America
345 Park Avenue
New York, NY 10154
Tel: 212-207-0700
Fax: 212-207-0456

Toyomenka (America), Inc.
104 West 40th Street
New York, NY 10018
Tel: 212-397-4600
Fax: 212-582-2007

INDEX

A

Abegglen, James, 97
Accountants, need for, 193-94
Acquisitions, 9-14, 20-21
  in aviation, 10
  buyer, selecting, 65-66
  in chemicals, 12
  in computers, 12
  in electronics, 11
  in engineering, 10
  in financial services, 10
  in foods, 12
  in hotels/resorts, 9-10
  in music/entertainment, 13
  in optics, 13
  in pharmaceuticals, 13
  in printing, 11
  in publishing, 12
  in real estate, 13-14
  as threat to U.S. defense capabilities, 63-64, 65
  U.S. acquisitions in Japan, 31, 36-37
Agricultural equipment, Japanese investors, 233-35
Agricultural products market, Japan's protection of, 34
Aisin Seiki, 240-41
Ajinomoto, 230-31
Alps Electric, 229
American know-how, Japanese thirst for, 101-3
Andrew Jergens Company, Kao Corporation acquisition of, 67
Anritsu, 217
Ansutech, 10
Antitrust rules, implementation of, 64
Aoki Corporation, 215
Arai, Ryoichiro, 53
Art galleries, Japanese interest in, 194-95
Asahi Breweries, 221-22
Asahi Chemical Industry, 247
Asahi Glass, 223
Asahi Weekly, 206
Asian markets:
  expanding in, 144, 149
  Japan's access to, 129
Assets, list of, providing, 161
Association of South East Asian Nations (ASEAN), 129
Aviation, acquisitions in, 10

B

Bakers, Japanese interest in, 195
Bank of Tokyo Ltd., 5-6, 103, 115, 150, 216, 219
Banks:
  debt financing from, 150-51
  Japanese investors and, 99-100, 108, 217-21
Beauty salons, Japanese interest in, 195
Beikoku Mainichi, 206

Beverages, Japanese investors, 222
Blackstone Group, 147, 158, 251-52, 254
Boeing Corporation, 23-24, 101
Bond issues, Japanese, 152-53
Borderless World (Ohmae), 48
Brand names, investments in, 115, 210
Bridgestone, acquisition of Firestone, 70-75, 145, 215, 245, 252
Brierley, Sir Ron, 145
Brochure, preparing, 212-13
Brokers, Japanese, 212
Building materials, Japanese investors, 222
Business consultants, need for, 198
Buyer's strategies:
   detailed information:
      requests for, 122-23
      speed of negotiations, 123-25
   understanding, 121-25

C

California, Japanese bank investments in, 103-4
Canon Corporation, 227
Capital issue, Japan, 163-65
Capital Japanese investors, 126-27
Career development, in Japanese companies, 183
Chateau St. Jean, acquisition of, 107
Cheap money, 88
Chemicals:
   acquisitions in, 12
   Japanese investors, 222-25
Childbirth education, Japanese interest in, 196
Chinese Exclusion Act, 52
C. Itoh & Co., 111, 114, 259-62
Clarion Company Ltd., McIntosh Laboratory acquisition, 13
Clothing, Japanese interest in, 196
Coming War with Japan (Friedman/LeBard), 43
Commercial Alliance Corporation, ORIX Corporation acquisition of, 10
Committee on Foreign Investment in the United States (CFIUS), 41, 65
Computer equipment/services, Japanese interest in, 196-97
Computers:
   acquisitions in, 12
   Japanese investors, 225-29
Confidential Memorandum, items included in, 163
Consensus building, Japanese process of, 123-24
Coopers & Lybrand, 194
Cosmo Oil, 243
Curtains/draperies, Japanese need for, 197

D

Daido Steel, 237
Daihatsu Motor, 240
Dai-Ichi Kangyo Bank, 215, 216, 217, 252
Dainippon Ink & Chemicals, 215, 223
Dai Nippon Printing, 244-45
Daishowa Paper Manufacturing, 233
Daiwa Bank, 216, 220
Debt financing:
   corporate, 151-52
   from Japanese bank, 150-51
Decision-making process, 123-24
Defense, acquisitions as threat to, 63-64, 65

INDEX

Dentists, need for, 197
Depository receipt listing, 164-65
Descriptive Memorandum:
 preparing, 159, 160-62
  items included in, 161
Devaluation of dollar, 32-34
Differentiated products, creating, 209
Dillon Read, 252
Direct equity investments:
 minority position, 146-48
 100% acquisition, 148-50
Dollar value, maximizing to shareholders, 142, 148-49

E

Electronics, 38-39
 acquisitions in, 11
 Japanese investors and, 108, 225-29
Employees, protecting, 67-68
Employment, 3, 45-46
Employment agencies, need for, 197-98
Engineering, acquisitions in, 10
Enprotech, 112-13
Epitaxx Inc., acquisition of, 13
Equity issues, Japanese, 153-55
Exclusion Act (1924), 56
Exon-Florio Amendment, 41, 65, 162

F

Financial advisor, hiring, 165
Financial forecasts, Confidential Memorandum, 163
Financial information, providing, 122-23, 136, 161, 163
Financial motives, Japanese, 85-89
Financial projections, Descriptive Memorandum, 161
Financial returns, on Japanese investments, 89-90, 103

Financial services, acquisition of, 10
Firestone Tire and Rubber Company:
 acquisition of, 5, 145, 215, 245, 252
 case study, 70-75
First Boston Corporation, 254
Food markets, need for, 198-99
Foods:
 acquisitions in, 12
 Japanese investors, 230-32
Ford Motor Company, globalization of, 94-95
Foreign Direct Investment in the United States (Graham/Krugman), 51
Foreign investment, U.S. gains from, 63
Forest products, Japanese investors, 232-33
Friedman, George, 43
Fuji Bank, 217-18
Fuji Electric, 228
Fuji Heavy Industries, 217, 240
Fuji Photo Film, 155, 170, 246
Fujisawa Pharmaceutical, 216
Fujitsu Corporation, 226
 Pocket Computer Corp. acquisition, 12
Fuji-Xerox, 155, 168, 170-72
Furniture/furnishings, Japanese interest in, 197
Furuhata, Mike, 259-62
Furukawa Electric, 236

G

General Coast Enterprises, Pebble Beach Company acquisition, 7-8, 107, 119
Global industries, as acquisition targets, 105-6
Globalization:

and Japanese equity issues, 154
as strategic motive, 91-97
trading companies and, 259
Goldman Sachs & Co., 4-5, 142, 254
Golf courses, purchases in, 7-8, 107
Good citizenship, of Japanese, 50
Gould Inc., acquisition of, 6, 252
Graham, Edward, 51

H

Health and exercise, 199
Herd instinct, 103-4
Hino Motors, 241
Historical financial data, Confidential Memorandum, 163
Hitachi Corporation, 216, 225
    Fairchild Semiconductor acquisition by, 18-19
Honda Motor Corporation, 104, 238
Honshu Paper, 233
Hori and Bunker real estate company, 212
Hotels/resorts, 199-200
    purchases of, 9-10, 107
House:
    finding buyer for, 212-13
        advertising in Japanese media, 212
        preparing Japanese brochure, 212-13
        using Japanese brokers, 212
    selling to Japanese, 209-12
        commuting distance, 211-12
        maintenance requirements, 211
        neighbors, 210-11
Hoya Corporation, acquisition of Micro Mask, Inc., 11

I

IBJ Schroeder Bank & Trust Co., 252, 254
Idemitsu Kosan, 242-43
Industrial Bank of Japan, 216, 218, 252
Industrial equipment, Japanese investors, 233-35
Industries:
    attractive to Japanese, 107-8
    Japan's destruction of American industry, 38-39
Industry analysis, Descriptive Memorandum, 161
Initial public offerings, 166
Innovation, U.S., 98
Insurance, 200
Intercontinental Hotel Corporation, acquisition of, 6, 107
Interest rates, returns, 89
Intermediaries:
    and Japanese equity capital, 157-60
    selecting, 158-60
Internment, 57-59
Investment banks, 249-55
    with Japanese practices, 254-55
    partnership between U.S. and Japanese, 251-54
Investments, 2-3, 9
    Japanese perspective, 111-15
Ishihara Sangyo Kaisha Ltd., SDS Enterprises, Inc. acquisition, 12
Ishihara, Shintaro, 40, 49
Ishikawajima-Harima Heavy Industries, 234
Isuzu Motors, 239
Itoham Foods, 231, 262
Ito-Yokado, 216

J

Japan-basher syndrome, 31, 49-50

INDEX

Japan Companies Handbook, 160
Japanese:
    acquisitions, 4-14
    as employers, 3, 173-91
    financial motives, 85-89
    herd instinct, 103-4
    hiring, 208
    investments, 2-3
    as managers, 30-31, 210
    Ministry of International Trade and Industry (MITI), 23, 24, 35-36, 120
    prestige, 104-5
    selling to, 193-213
    strategic motives, 90-103, 116
    trade, 1-2
    See also Japanese investor
Japanese-Americans:
    integration, 61
    internment of, 57-59
Japanese-American Yellow Pages, 193, 194, 206
Japanese areas, locating in, 207
Japanese business, winning, 206-9
Japanese debt capital, gaining access to, 163
Japanese employers:
    racism/sexism of, 42
    selling yourself to, 185-86
Japanese equity capital:
    Descriptive Memorandum, preparing, 160-62
    Exon-Florio Act, 162
    gaining access to, 157-62
    intermediary:
        selecting, 158-60
        using, 157-58
    Letter of Intent, 162
    target list, selecting, 160
Japanese Export Trade Organization (JETRO):
    function of, 255
    offices, 255-56
Japanese Independent Communication Co. Ltd., New American Magazine Co. acquisition, 12
Japanese investment:
    alternative vehicles for accessing, 146-56
        debt financing (bank), 150-51
        debt financing (corporate), 151-52
        direct equity investment (100% acquisition), 148-50
        direct equity investment (minority position), 146-48
        Japanese bond issue, 152-53
        Japanese equity issue, 153-55
        joint venture/strategic alliance, 155-56
    case studies, 70-84
        Firestone Tire and Rubber Company, 70-75
        Materials Research Corporation, 75-82
        NUMMI, 82-84
    convincing buyers to pay top dollar, 119-21
    encouragement of, 48
    in overseas assets, 99, 115-19
    technological consequences of, 21-25
Japanese investor:
    motives for seeking, 142-46
        avoiding closure, 143
        expanding in Asian markets, 144
        gaining access to technologies, 145-46
        maximizing value to shareholders, 142, 148-49
        seeking additional capital, 142
        seeking financial restructuring, 143
        seeking White Squire, 144-45

negotiation pitfalls, 138-39
    aggression, 138
    arguing, 139
    hiding unpleasant facts, 139
  negotiation tips, 135-39
    be courteous, 137
    be patient, 136
    explain your position, 136
    provide detailed information, 136
    respond in detail to inquiries, 136-37
    treat Japanese as honored guests, 137-38
  strengths of, 125-31
    access to Asian markets, 129
    capital, 126-27
    choice of targets, 129-30
    lack of shareholder accountability, 131
    long-term outlook, 130-31
    low cost of funds, 127-28
    strong domestic base, 128
    technology, 128-29
  weaknesses of, 131-35
    lack of M&A experience, 134-35
    lack of U.S. management skills, 132-33
    language, 133
    long-term outlook, 134
    unfamiliarity with financial analysis techniques, 134
    unfamiliarity with local markets, 131-32
Japanese language media, advertising in, 206
Japanese market, raising capital in, 163-66
"Japanese premium," 48, 117
Japanese presence in America, 15-17
Japanese social groups, joining/supporting, 207
Japanese "threat," extent of, 18-25
Japanese workers, attitudes of, 46-47
Japan That Can Say NO, The (Ishihara), ix, 40, 49-50
Japan Tobacco, 248-49
JETRO, *See* Japanese Export Trade Organization (JETRO)
Jewelry properties, purchases of, 107
Joint ventures, 10, 23, 101, 116, 155-56, 166-72
  advantages/disadvantages of, 167
  approvals/licenses, 169
  employment practices, 169
  facilities, construction of, 169
  financing, 169
  Fuji-Xerox joint venture, 155, 170-72
  management structure, 169
  negotiating issues, 168
  negotiating timetable, 168
  profits, distribution of, 169
  recommendations for, 167-68
Jujo Paper, 232
Jusco, 216
Just-in-time production, 46

K

Kaisha (Abegglen), 97
Kanban, 46
Kanebo Corporation, 247-48
Kanto Auto Works, 241-42
Kao Corporation, 67, 216, 246-47
Kawasaki Heavy Industries, 249
Kawasaki Steel, 216, 236
Keiretsu, 37
Kelly, Paul, 115-19
Kidder Peabody & Co., Inc., 254
Kirin Brewery, 221

INDEX

Kitamura, Ryuji, 111-15
Knox & Co., 115
Kobe Steel, 235
Koito Company, 37
Komatsu, 234
Konica Corporation, 246
Krugman, Paul, 51
Kubota, 216, 234
Kyocera Corporation, 216, 229
  Elco Group of Companies acquisition, 11
Kyotaru Company Ltd., Best Western Foods acquisition, 12
Kyowa Saitama Bank, 221
Kyo-ya Company Ltd., Grand Cypress Resort acquisition, 10

L

Language factor, negotiations and, 124
Language schools, 204-5
Language support, providing, 209
Lawyers, need for, 200-202
Lazard Freres & Co., 254
LeBard, Meredith, 43
Letter of Intent, 162
Levien, Roger, 170-72
Licensing agreements, purchase of, 97-98
Limousines, 202
Long-Term Credit Bank of Japan, 115, 217, 220, 252
Long-term outlook, Japanese investors, 130-31, 134

M

McCloy, John J., 58
Made in Japan (Morita), 92
Major U.S. investors, 215-17
Maki, Akira, 196
Market research, 207
Marubeni America Corp., 263
Master-Halco, Inc., 260

Materials Research Corporation (MRC), case study, 75-82, 123, 125, 143
Matsuo Pacific, 25-26
Matsushita Electric Industrial, 104, 215, 225
  MCA acquisition, 8
Matsushita Electric Works, 233-34
Mazda Motor Corporation, 239
Meiji Milk Products, 231
Mergers and acquisitions (M&A), Japanese companies' inexperience with, 124, 134
Merrill Lynch Capital Markets, 255
Metals, Japanese investors, 235-37
Military, rebuilding of, 44-45
Ministry of International Trade and Industry (MITI), 23, 24, 35-36, 120
Mitsubishi Bank, 150, 218
Mitsubishi Corporation, 131, 216
Mitsubishi Electric, 226
Mitsubishi Estate Corporation, 48, 216
  stake in Rockefeller Group, 7, 18, 50
Mitsubishi Heavy Industries, 233
Mitsubishi International Corp., 263
Mitsubishi Kasei, 217, 222-23
Mitsubishi Materials, 236
Mitsubishi Mining and Cement, 216
Mitsubishi Motors, 238-39
Mitsubishi Oil, 244
Mitsubishi Petrochemical, 224
Mitsubishi Trust & Banking, 219
Mitsui & Co., Inc., 216, 263
Mitsui Taiyo Kobe Bank, 219
Mitsui Toatsu Chemicals, 224
Mitsui Trust & Banking, 220

Mitsukoshi, Tiffany & Co. acquisition, 107, 115, 119, 142
Morgan Stanley & Co., Inc., 255
Morinaga Milk Industry, 231-32
Morita, Akio, 92
Motor vehicles/parts, Japanese investors, 238-42
Moving companies, 202
Music/entertainment:
  acquisitions in, 13
  Japanese investors and, 108, 249

N

Nakasone, Yasuhiro, 33, 42
Name card, presenting, 189-91
National boundaries, global economy and, 48-49
NEC, 226
Negotiating timetable, joint ventures, 168
Negotiator/negotiation tactics, 120-21
Neocolonialism, 25-31
New American Magazine Co., acquisition of, 12
Nikko Securities, 147, 216, 251
Nippon Credit Bank, 221
Nippondenso, 239
Nippon Life Insurance, 216
Nippon Light Metal, 237
Nippon Meat Packers, 230
Nippon Mining Co. Ltd., 6, 216, 243, 252
Nippon Oil, 242
Nippon Sanso, 10, 217
Nippon Seiko, 242
Nippon Sheet Glass Co. Ltd., 216
  Epitaxx Inc. acquisition, 13
Nippon Steel, 217, 235
Nippon Suisan Kaisha, 230
Nissan Deisel Motor, 242
Nissan Motor Corporation, 45, 104, 238
Nissan Shatai, 241
Nisshin Flour Milling, 231
Nisshin Steel, 237
Nissho Iwai American Corp., 263
NKK, 216, 235
NUMMI, case study, 82-84

O

Ohmae, Kenichi, 48-49, 94
Oji Paper, 232
Oki Electric Industry, 228
Omron, 229
Onoda Cement, 145, 216, 222
Ono Pharmaceutical Co., Telios Pharmaceuticals acquisition, 13
Optics, acquisitions in, 13
ORIX Corporation, 216
  Commercial Alliance Corporation acquisition, 10
Overseas investments, 99, 115-19
  trading companies, 262

P

Paintings, purchases of, 107
Paloma Industries, 216
Pearl Harbor, 57-58
Pebble Beach Company, acquisition of, 7-8, 107, 119
Peers & Co., 115-18, 252
Pensions, Japanese, 87
Peterson, Peter D., 251
Petroleum refining, Japanese investors, 242-44
Pharmaceuticals:
  acquisitions in, 13
  Japanese investors, 244
Photographic industries, Japanese investors, 246
Physicians, 202-3
Pickens, T. Boone, 37-38
Pioneer Electric, 216, 228
Prejudices, of Japanese employers, 42

Prestige, as buying motive, 104-7
Prestowitz, Clyde V. Jr., 34-36, 103
Printing:
 acquisitions in, 11
 Japanese investors, 244-45
Private debt offerings, 164
Private stock placement, 164
Protectionism, 20
Public debt offerings, 164
Public stock offerings, 164
 initial public offerings (IPOs), 166
 process of, 165-66
Publishing, acquisitions in, 12

Q

Quality, 46-47, 115
 research quality, 101

R

Racial consciousness, and colonialism, 28-9
Racism:
 toward Japanese, 49-50, 54-55
 of Japanese employers, 42
Rank Xerox, See Fuji-Xerox
Real estate, 203
 purchases in, 13-14, 107
 returns on, 89-90
Recruitment of American workers, 177
 information sources, 191
Reischauer, Haru, 53
Remilitarization, 44-45
Research quality, 101
Responsible buyers, buyer, 65-66
Restaurants, 204
Ricoh Corporation, 227-28
Rockefeller Center, 7, 18, 48, 50, 90, 115
Rohto Pharmaceutical Co., Mentholatum Co. acquisition, 144

Rubber/plastics, Japanese investors, 245-46
Ryobi, 216

S

Saison Group, 215
Sakamoto, Masakatsu, 158, 251-53
Sakata Inx Corporation, Knight Color and Chemical Company acquisition, 11
Sales, alternatives to, 69
Salomon Brothers, Inc., 252, 255
Sanken Electric Co., Sprague Technologies acquisition, 12
Sankyo, 244
Sanwa Bank, 103, 216, 218
Sanyo Electric, 227
Sanyo-Kokusaku Pulp, 232
Savings, Japanese, 87
Schools, 204-5
Schwartz, Daniel, 163-66
Secom, 216
Sekisui Chemical, 223-24
Separateness, 28-29
Service, emphasizing, 208-9
Service categories:
 accountants, 193-94
 art galleries, 194-95
 bakers, 195
 beauty salons, 195
 business consultants, 198
 childbirth education, 196
 clothing, 196
 computer equipment/services, 196-97
 curtains/draperies, 197
 dentists, 197
 employment agencies, 197-98
 food markets, 198-99
 health and exercise, 199
 hotels, 199-200
 insurance, 200
 lawyers, 200-202

limousines, 202
moving companies, 202
physicians, 202-3
real estate, 203
restaurants, 204
schools, 204-5
sporting areas/goods, 205
travel agencies, 205-6
Settsu, 216
Sexism, of Japanese employers, 42
Shareholder accountability, lack of, 131
Sharp Electronics Corporation, 227
Shin-Etsu Chemical, 224-25
Shiseido Corporation, 216, 247
Showa Chemical, 224
Showa Shell Sekiyu, 243
Snow Brand Milk Products, 230
Soaps/cosmetics, Japanese investors, 246-47
Sony Corporation, 92-93, 96-97, 123, 215, 226-27
    CBS Records Group acquisition, 5, 97
    Columbia Pictures Entertainment Inc. acquisition, 6-7, 97, 104
    Materials Research Corporation (MRC) acquisition, 75-82, 123, 125, 143
Speaking support, providing, 209
Special products, creating, 209
Sporting areas/goods, 205
Steel, Japanese investors and, 108
Stocks, returns on, 89-90
Strategic alliances, See Joint ventures
Strategic analysis, Descriptive Memorandum, 161
Strategic motives, Japanese, 90-103, 116
    globalization, 91-97
    technology, 97-103

Strategic summary, Confidential Memorandum, 163
Strategies, understanding, 121-25
"Structural Impediments Initiative," 34
Sumitomo Bank, 4-5, 42, 142, 216, 217, 252
Sumitomo Chemical, 223
Sumitomo Corp. of America, 263
Sumitomo Heavy Industries, 234-35
Sumitomo Metal Industries, 235-36
Sumitomo Rubber Industries, 216, 245
Sumitomo Trust & Banking, 219
Suzuki Motor, 239-40
Synergies, looking for, 66-67

T

Taiyo Fishery, 230
Takeda Chemical Industries, 244
Target list, selecting, 160
TDK, 217, 229
Technology:
    effect of Japanese investment on, 21-25, 39-42
    Japan's interest in, 145
    and joint ventures, 156
    selling price, 68-69, 97-98
    as strategic motive, 97-103
    technologies attractive to Japanese buyers, 108
Teijin Corporation, 248
Term sheet, Confidential Memorandum, 163
Textiles, Japanese investors, 247-48
Thermos Company, acquisition by Nippon Sanso, 10
Tiffany & Co., acquisition of, 107, 115, 119, 142
Tobacco, Japanese investors, 248
Tokai Bank, 218-19

Tokio Marine and Fire Insurance, 216
Tokuyama Soda Co., General Ceramics, Inc. acquisition, 11
Tokyo Stock Exchange, 154, 164
Tonen, 243-44
Toppan Printing, 245
Toray Industries, 247
Toshiba Corporation, 217, 225
Toyobo Corporation, 248
Toyoda Automatic Loom Works, 241
Toyomenka, Inc., 263
Toyo Sash, 237
Toyo Seikan, 237
Toyota Motor Corporation, 104, 238
  acquisition of Airflite, 10
  globalization of, 95-96
Toyo Trust & Banking, 220-21
Trade, 1-2
Trade barriers, 32-33
Trade practices, 31-38
Trading companies, 257-63
  capabilities, improvements in, 260-61
  globalization, 259
  localization, 259-60
  overseas investment, increases in, 262
  U.S. subsidiaries of, 262-63
  value added concept, 261-62
Trading Places (Prestowitz), 34
Training quality, 101
Transportation equipment, Japanese investor, 249
Travel agencies, 205-6

U

Ube Industries, 222
UGI Corp, joint venture, 10
Ulmer Brothers, Inc., 157, 164
U.S.:
  economy, Japanese investment and, 50-51
  foreign investments, benefits of, 63
  innovation, 98
  laws, ensuring Japanese firms' compliance with, 64-65
  returns offered by, 89-90
U.S.-Japan relations:
  arguments/counterarguments:
    doves, 45-51
    hawks, 31-45
  historical perspective, 51-61
Unitika Corporation, 248

V

Van Gogh's *Irises*, purchase of, 195
Victoria Company, Stratton Corporation acquisition, 10

W

Weinig, Sheldon, 75-82, 125
White squire, 144-45, 147
Wineries, acquisition of, 107
Women employees, sexism felt by, 42
Working for the Japanese, 173-91
  interviewing guidelines, 186-89
    avoid arguments, 187-88
    avoid over-ambitious attitude, 188-89
    be modest, 186-87
    emphasize technical qualifications, 189
  Japanese employers, selling yourself to, 185-86
  name card, presenting, 189-91
  pluses/minuses of, 185
Workingman's Party of California, 52

X

Xerox Corporation, Fuji-Xerox joint venture, 155, 168, 170-72

Y

Yamaha Corporation (musical instruments), 249
Yamaha Motor, 241
Yamanouchi Pharmaceutical, 216
Yamazaki Baking, 231
Yaohan Mall, 198-99
Yasuda Fire and Marine Insurance Company, 119
Yasuda Mutual Life Insurance, 216
Yasuda Trust & Banking, 220
Yen bonds, 152-53
Yokohama Rubber, 246